TRANSGENDER HISTORY

SECOND EDITION

TRANSGENDER HISTORY

THE ROOTS OF TODAY'S REVOLUTION

SUSAN STRYKER

SEAL PRESS

Seal Press
Hachette Book Group
1290 Avenue of the Americas, New York, NY 10104
sealpress.com

Printed in Canada

Second Edition: November 2017

Published by Seal Press, an imprint of Perseus Books, LLC, a subsidiary of Hachette Book Group, Inc.

Print book interior design by Trish Wilkinson

Library of Congress Cataloging-in-Publication Data

Names: Stryker, Susan, author.
Title: Transgender history : the roots of today's revolution / Susan Stryker.
Description: Second edition. | Berkeley : Seal Press, 2017. | Revised edition of the author's Transgender history, c2008.
Identifiers: LCCN 2017025964| ISBN 9781580056892 (paperback) | ISBN 9781580056908 (ebook)
Subjects: LCSH: Transgenderism—History. | Gender identity—History. | Transgender people—History.
Classification: LCC HQ77.9 .S77 2017 | DDC 306.76/8—dc23
LC record available at https://lccn.loc.gov/2017025964

MRQ

10 2023

This book is dedicated to the trans people who lived the lives that made the history I've outlined here, and to the trans people, and our friends and allies living today, who continue to make history by advancing the cause of social justice.

CONTENTS

PROLOGUE

ALTHOUGH THE TITLE of this book is simply *Transgender History,* the subject is both narrower and broader—narrower in that it is primarily a history of the transgender movement in the United States, concentrating mostly on the years after World War II, and broader in that *transgender,* once a very expansive term, now fails to fully capture the complexity of contemporary gender. And although this book bears the same title as the previous edition first published in 2008, the revisions needed for this second edition to adequately address the remarkable changes of the past decade are extensive enough that the second edition is a substantially new book. The text of the first edition has therefore been updated throughout—particularly in the first chapter—and a new chapter has been added at the end.

Piecing together this story of trans history in the United States was a big focus of my professional life as a historian for nearly twenty years. As a transsexual woman I've also been a participant in making that history, along with multitudes of other people. Although I try to tell that story in an expansive and inclusive way, what I have to say is unavoidably informed by my own involvement in transgender social movements, by my other life experiences, and by the particular ways that I consider myself to be transgender.

I'm one of those people who, from earliest memory, always felt feminine-identified even though I was assigned male at birth, even though everybody considered me to be a boy and raised me as such, and even though my body was apparently a typical male body. I didn't have any good explanation for those feelings when I was younger, and after a lifetime of reflection and study I'm still open-minded about how best to explain them. Not that I feel the need to explain them in order to justify my existence. I know only that those feelings persist no matter what. I know that they make me who I am to myself, whatever other people may feel about me or do toward me for having them.

The fear of being ridiculed, stigmatized, or discriminated against, as well as my own early uncertainty about how I would act on my transgender feelings, led me to hide them from absolutely everybody until I was in my late teens, in the early 1980s. That's when I first started opening up privately to my romantic partners about my sense of self. A few years later, in the second half of the 1980s, I found an underground queer community; until then, I'd never knowingly met another trans person. I didn't come out publicly as trans or start my medical and social transition until 1991, when I was thirty years old.

When I started living full-time as an openly transsexual lesbian woman in San Francisco in the early 1990s, I was finishing my PhD in United States history at the University of California, Berkeley. Transitioning was something I needed to do for my personal sense of well-being, but it wasn't a great career move. However wonderful it was for me to finally feel right about how I presented myself to others and how others perceived me, making the transition from living as a man to living as a woman had negative effects on my life. Like many other transgender women, I spent years being marginally employed because of other people's discomfort, ignorance, and prejudice about me. Transitioning made relationships with many friends and relatives more difficult. It made me more vulnerable to certain kinds of legal discrimination, and it often made me feel unsafe in public.

Because for many years I had lived in the world being perceived as a well-educated, able-bodied, cisgender, heterosexual white man before coming out as the woman I felt myself to be, I have a very clear measuring stick for gauging various kinds of oppression related to embodiment, gender, and sexuality. Transitioning put my skin in the game of resisting those oppressions in a new way. Because I have experienced misogyny and sexism, my transgender experience informs the strong commitment I feel to feminist activism that aims to make the world a better place for all women and girls. Because I now live in the world as a woman who loves women, and because there are times (more common in the past than now) when I've been perceived as an effeminate gay man, I also have a direct experience of homophobia. My transgender experience is thus also part of why I feel a strong commitment to lesbian, gay, and bi rights. Although I have a stable sense of being a woman rather than a man, and have taken a lot of steps to get my body, my state-issued IDs, and other paperwork aligned with my sense of self, I know that I can never align everything the way cisgender people do and that there will always be some discordance and incongruence. For me, that means that, even though I identify as a transsexual woman, I am also, in practice, unavoidably gender nonconforming, genderqueer, and nonbinary.

Being perceived or "passed" as a gender-normative cisgender person grants you a kind of access to the world that is often blocked by being perceived as trans or labeled as such. This lack of access, created by the way the world is organized to benefit people whose embodiments are different from my own, limits the scope of my life activities and can therefore be understood as producing a disability. And just as my transness creates an overlap for me with disability politics whether or not I am otherwise disabled, it intersects as well with other movements, communities, and identities that also contest the negative effects of living in a society that governs us all by norming our bodies. I feel that being trans makes me kin with intersex people, fat people, people who don't embody beauty norms, people on the neurocognitive diversity spectrum, people who are "enfreaked" for whatever reason—whether or not I am any of those other things apart from the ways they intersect with being trans.

Although I can't claim that being a white transgender person gives me any special insight into the experience of minoritized communities of color, I do as a transsexual experience the injustice of being targeted for structural violence through being labeled a kind or type of person who is not as deserving of life as other people, within a social order that tries to cement me into that often death-dealing hierarchy based on some of my body characteristics. Because transness sticks to my cut flesh even though I am white, it provides me with a basis not just for antiracist white allyship with the struggles of people of color but also with a real commonality of interest in dismantling a system that relentlessly sorts all of us into biologically based categories of embodied personhood deemed more or less worthy of life. I am determined to bring what I know from living my trans life to that larger and deeper struggle. Still, as a white transgender person who has come to this insight only over the past few decades, as one who can still stumble and fumble in my coalitional work in spite of my best intentions, I know I have a lot to learn from the accumulated centuries of experience-based wisdom, social critique, life skills, and freedom dreams that millions of people of color have developed for themselves to survive within colonialism and racism.

Starting in the early 1990s, I've had the privilege of using my education as part of a transgender movement for social change. I became a community-based historian, activist, cultural theorist, media-maker, and eventually an academic who has tried to chronicle various dimensions of transgender experience. The ideas and opinions I share in this book first crystallized more than a quarter century ago when I was part of a very politically and artistically engaged queer community in San Francisco, now sadly somewhat dispersed and depleted by the city's increasing income disparities, its relentless gentrification, and the displacement of many nonwealthy people. All of this is to say that my point of view is both generationally and geographically specific. I worked for many years at the GLBT Historical Society, one of the world's great repositories of queer and trans archival materials, and as a consequence the parts of transgender history I know the best are the ones closest to lesbian and gay life. I've worked and taught and been a visiting scholar at universities in cities from one end of North America to the other as well as places in between—the Bay Area, Boston, Vancouver, Indiana, Tucson—and have had the very great privilege of being able to travel frequently, for work and for play, to countries in Eastern and Western Europe, the Near East, Southeast Asia, Latin America, Australia, and New Zealand. All of these experiences—as well as my incessant snooping around online and participating in social media networks—hopefully help broaden some of the limiting provincialisms undoubtedly embedded in the stories I tell about the things that are most familiar to me.

Writing and revising this book have been ways for me to summarize some of what I've gleaned from the life I've lived over the past few decades and to pass it along to others who might find it somehow life-sustaining, or at least useful, and, if nothing else, interesting. I hope it gives you something you need.

CHAPTER 1

CONTEXTS, CONCEPTS, AND TERMS

Foundations of a Movement

Transgender is a word that has come into widespread use only in the past couple of decades, and its meanings are still under construction. I use it in this book to refer to people who move away from the gender they were assigned at birth, people who cross over (*trans-*) the boundaries constructed by their culture to define and contain that gender. Some people move away from their birth-assigned gender because they feel strongly that they properly belong to another gender through which it would be better for them to live; others want to strike out toward some new location, some space not yet clearly described or concretely occupied; still others simply feel the need to challenge the conventional expectations bound up with the gender that was initially put upon them. In any case, it is the movement across a socially imposed boundary away from an unchosen starting place, rather than any particular destination or mode of transition, that best characterizes the concept of transgender that I develop here. I use *transgender* in its broadest possible sense.

Until fairly recently, transgender issues have been presented as personal issues—that is, as something that an individual experienced inwardly, often in isolation—rather than being seen in a wider social context. Thankfully, that's changing. Most of the literature on transgender topics used to come from medical or psychological perspectives, almost always written by people who were not themselves transgender. Such works framed being trans as an individual psychopathological deviation from social norms of healthy gender expression and tended to reduce the complexity and significance of a transgender life to its medical or psychotherapeutic needs. There have been many autobiographies written by people who have "changed sex," and an increasing number of self-help guidebooks for people contemplating such a change, or for people seeking a better understanding of what a loved one is going through, or for parents of children who express their gender in ways that run counter to the dominant culture's expectations. But both the medical and self-help literatures, even when written from a transgender or trans-affirming perspective, still tend to individualize rather than collectivize trans experience.

This book takes a different approach. It is part of a rapidly growing body of fiction and nonfiction literature, academic writing, documentary films, television shows, movies, blogs, YouTube channels, and other forms of DIY cultural production by and about trans people that places us in cultural and historical context and imagines us as part of communities and social movements. It focuses specifically on the history of trans and gender-nonconforming social change activism in the United States—that is, on efforts to make it easier and safer and more acceptable for the people who need to cross gender boundaries to be able to do so. It's not designed, however, to be a comprehensive account of US transgender history, let alone a more global history of being trans. My goal is to provide a basic framework that focuses on a handful of key events and personalities that help link transgender history to the history of minority movements for social change, to the history of sexuality and gender, and to feminist thought and politics.

Back in the 1970s, the liberal feminist movement popularized the slogan "The personal is political." Some feminists back then were critical of transgender practices such as cross-dressing, taking hormones to change the gendered appearance of the body, having genital or chest surgery, and living as a member of a gender other than one's birth-assigned gender. They often considered such practices to be "personal solutions" to the inner experience of distress about experiencing gender-based oppression—that is, they thought that a person assigned female at birth and passing as a man was just trying to escape the poor pay (or no pay) of "women's work" or to move about more safely in a world that was hostile to women; a feminine person assigned male at birth, they thought, should work for the social acceptability of "sissies" or "queens" and be proudly effeminate instead of pretending to be a "normal" woman or a "real" one. Feminism, on the other hand, aimed to systematically dismantle the social structures that created gender-based oppression in the first place and that made women the "second sex." Mainstream liberal feminism wanted to raise women's consciousnesses about their own private suffering by grounding that experience in a political analysis of the categorical oppression of all women. It wanted to offer men an education in feminist values in order to eradicate the sexism and misogyny they (knowingly or unknowingly) directed at women. This sort of feminism was, and still is, a necessary movement to change the world for the better, but it needs to have a better grasp on trans issues.

One of the goals of this book is to situate transgender social change activism within an expansive feminist framework. Doing so requires us to think in different ways about *how* the personal is political, and about what constitutes gender-based oppression, and about how we understand the historical development of feminist movements. Generally speaking, "first wave" feminism in the nineteenth and early twentieth centuries focused on dress reform, access to education, political equality, and, above all, suffrage—the right to vote. "Second wave" feminism, also known as the "women's movement," took off in the 1960s and addressed a wide range of issues that included equal pay, sexual liberation, lesbianism, reproductive freedom, recognition of women's unpaid work in the household, better media representations of women, self-defense, and the prevention of rape and domestic violence. A feminist "third wave" emerged in the 1990s, partly in response to the perceived shortcomings of earlier generational inflections of feminism, and partly to focus on emerging issues. Third wave feminists considered themselves more sex-positive than their mothers and grandmothers—staging SlutWalks rather than Take Back the Night marches, making feminist porn instead of denouncing all pornography as inherently degrading to women, supporting sex-worker activism and self-empowerment instead of imagining themselves as rescuing disempowered women from prostitution. They were more interested in contesting body-shaming politics, in having a subversive or ironic relationship to consumer culture, and in engaging in online activism through social media. There's even talk of a fourth wave, taking shape in the aftermath of the 2008 financial crisis, that is more attuned than its predecessors to the politics of Occupy, Black Lives Matter, environmental justice, techno-literacy, and spirituality.

More important than parsing the various generational "waves" of feminism, however, is the emergence of what has come to be called "intersectional" feminism. Rooted in black and Chicana feminist thought, intersectional feminism calls into question the idea that the social oppression of women can be adequately analyzed and contested solely by concentrating on the category "woman."

Intersectional feminism insists that there is no essential "Woman" who is universally oppressed. To understand the oppression of any particular woman or group of women means taking into account all of the things that intersect with their being women, such as race, class, nationality, religion, disability, sexuality, citizenship status, and myriad other circumstances that marginalize or privilege them—including having transgender or gender-nonconforming feelings or identities. Intersectional perspectives emerged in the second wave but divided it into different camps and continue to cut across all subsequent feminist formations. One powerful strain within contemporary trans movements for social change is rooted in intersectional feminist perspectives that first emerged in the second wave but more often than not finds far more congenial and supportive alliances in third (or fourth) wave movements that are explicitly trans-affirming. Feminisms inclusive of trans people still fight to dismantle the structures that prop up gender hierarchy as a system of oppression, but they do so while recognizing that oppression can happen because of the consequences of changing gender or contesting gender categories as well as being categorized as a member of the "second sex."

To reconcile the relationship between transgender and feminist politics—to create a transfeminism—it is essential simply to acknowledge that how each of us experiences and understands our gendered sense of self, our sense of being a man or a woman or something that resists or mixes those terms, is a very idiosyncratic personal matter, related to many other attributes of our lives. It is something prior to, or underlying, our political actions in the world and not necessarily in itself a reflection of our political beliefs. It is neither radical nor reactionary to embrace a trans identity. Non-transgender people, after all, think of themselves as being women or men, and nobody asks them to defend the political correctness of their "choice" or thinks that their having a sense of being gendered

A BIOLOGICAL BASIS?

Many people believe that gender identity—the subjective sense of being a man or a woman or both or neither—is rooted in biology, although what the biological "cause" of gender identity might be has never been proven (in spite of numerous conflicting assertions to the contrary). Many other people understand gender to be more like language than like biology; that is, although they understand us humans to have a biological capacity to use language, they point out we are not born with a hard-wired language "preinstalled" in our brains. Likewise, whereas we have a biological capacity to identify with and to learn to "speak" from a particular position in a cultural gender system, we don't come into the world with a predetermined gender identity.

Evolutionary biologist Joan Roughgarden suggests a way to blend learned versus innate models of gender identity development. In *Evolution's Rainbow: Diversity, Gender, and Sexuality in Nature and People,* she writes:

> *When does gender identity form during development? Gender identity, like other aspects of temperament, presumably awaits the third trimester, when the brain as a whole is growing. . . . The time around birth may be when the brain's gender identity is being organized. . . . I envision gender identity as a cognitive lens. When a baby opens his or her eyes after birth and looks around, whom will the baby emulate and whom will he or she merely notice? Perhaps a male baby will emulate his father or other men, perhaps not, and a female baby her mother or other women, perhaps not. I imagine that a lens in the brain controls who to focus on as a "tutor." Transgender identity is then the acceptance of a tutor from the opposite sex. Degrees of transgender identity, and of gender variance generally, reflect different degrees of single-mindedness in the selection of the tutor's gender. The development of gender identity thus depends on both brain state and early postnatal experience, because brain state indicates what the lens is, and environmental experience supplies the image to be photographed through that lens and*

continues

ultimately developed immutably into brain circuitry. Once gender identity is set, like other basic aspects of temperament, life proceeds from there.

While researching her book *The Riddle of Gender: Science, Activism, and Transgender Rights,* science writer Deborah Rudacille became convinced that environmental factors helped explain the seeming increase in the prevalence of reported transgender phenomena. Rudacille draws on the 2001 paper "Endocrine Disrupting Chemicals and Transsexualism," in which author Christine Johnson posits a causal link between the "reproductive, behavioral, and anatomical effects" of exposure to chemicals commonly found in pesticides and food additives and "the expression of gender identity and other disorders such as reproductive failure." Rudacille links transgenderism to falling sperm counts among human males; to rising numbers of alligators with micropenises and hermaphroditic birds, fish, and amphibians; and to other anomalies purportedly associated with endocrine-disrupting chemicals in the environment.

somehow compromises or invalidates their other values and commitments. Being trans is like being gay: some people are just "that way," though most people aren't. We can be curious about *why* some people are gay or trans, and we can propose all kinds of theories or tell interesting stories about how it's possible to be trans or gay, but ultimately we simply need to accept that some minor fraction of the population (perhaps including ourselves) simply *is* "that way."

Because members of minority groups are, by definition, less common than members of majority groups, minorities often experience misunderstanding, prejudice, and discrimination. Society tends to be organized in ways that either deliberately or unintentionally favor the majority, and ignorance or misinformation about a less common way of being in the world can perpetuate harmful stereotypes and mischaracterizations. On top of that, society can actually privilege some kinds of people over other kinds of people, with the former benefiting from the exploitation of the latter: settlers benefited from the appropriation of indigenous lands, slaveholders benefited from the labor of the enslaved, men have benefited from the inequality of women. Violence, law, and custom hold these social hierarchies in place.

People who feel the need to resist their birth-assigned gender or to live as a member of another gender have encountered significant forms of discrimination and prejudice, including religious condemnation. Because most people have great difficulty recognizing the humanity of another person if they cannot recognize that person's gender, encounters with gender-changing or gender-challenging people can sometimes feel for others like an encounter with a monstrous and frightening unhumanness. That gut-level reaction can manifest as panic, disgust, contempt, hatred, or outrage, which may then translate into physical or emotional violence—up to and including murder—being directed against the person who is perceived as not-quite-human. One has to ask why the typical reaction to an encounter with nonprivileged forms of gender or embodiment is not more often experienced with wonder, delight, attraction, or curiosity.

People who are perceived as not-quite-human because of their gender expression are often socially shunned and may be denied such basic needs as housing and employment. They may lose the support of their families. Within modern bureaucratic society, many kinds of routine administrative procedures make life very difficult for people who cross the social boundaries of their birth-assigned genders. Birth certificates, school and medical records, professional credentials, passports, driver's licenses, and other such documents provide a composite portrait of each of us as a person with a particular gender, and when these records have noticeable discrepancies or omissions, all kinds of problems can result: inability to cross national borders, qualify for jobs, gain access to needed social services, and secure legal custody of one's children. Because transgender people typically lack the same kind of support that fully accepted members of society automatically expect, they may be more vulnerable to risky or self-harming behaviors and consequently may wind up having more health problems or trouble with the law—which only compounds their already considerable difficulties.

In the United States, members of minority groups often try to oppose or change discriminatory practices and prejudicial attitudes by banding together to offer one another mutual support, to voice their issues in public, to raise money to improve their collective lot in life, to form organizations that address their specific unmet needs, or to participate in electoral politics or lobby for the passage of protective legislation. Some members engage in more radical or militant kinds of activism aimed at overturning the social order or abolishing unjust institutions rather than reforming them, and others craft survival tools for living within conditions that can't at that moment be changed. Some make art or write literature that feeds the souls of community members or shifts the way others think of them and the problems they face. Some do the intellectual and theoretical work of analyzing the roots of their particular forms of social oppression and devising strategies and policies that will bring about a better future. Others direct their attention toward promoting self-acceptance and a sense of self-worth among members of the minority community who may have internalized disempowering attitudes or beliefs about their difference from the dominant majority. In short, a multidimensional activist movement for social change often begins to take shape. Just such a movement to address trans social justice issues developed in the United States over the second half of the twentieth century.

Terms and Concepts

Trans issues touch on existential questions about what it means to be alive and take us into areas that we rarely consciously consider with any degree of care—similar to our attitudes about gravity, for example, or breathing. Usually, we simply experience these things without thinking about them too much. In the everyday course of events, most people have no reason to ask questions such as "What makes a man a man, or a woman a woman?" or "How is my body related to my social role?" or even "How do I know what my gender is?" Rather, we just go about our everyday business without questioning the unexamined perceptions and assumptions that form part of our working reality. But gender and identity, like gravity and breathing, are really complicated phenomena when you start taking them apart and breaking them down.

Because of this complexity, it can be helpful to set out some more technical definitions of words that we use in everyday speech, as well as to define some words that we don't usually need to use at all, before getting into the historical story. Spending a little time discussing terms and concepts can help bring into view some of the hidden assumptions we usually make about sex and gender and helps introduce some of the arguments that will play themselves out in the chapters ahead.

Please keep in mind that new terms and concepts come into existence all the time, and that words being used when this book was written may well have fallen out of currency, or out of favor, by the time this book is being read. To keep really current on the conversation, make the Internet your friend.

(asterisk): The asterisk is popping up more and more frequently in discussion about transgender issues. Its use originated in database and Internet searches, where the symbol functioned as a wildcard operator. That is, a query with an asterisk in it would find the specific string of characters being searched for, plus any others. For example, searching for *over** would retrieve *overkill, overdrive, overtime,* or any other words the start with the character string *over*. Using *trans** rather than *transgender* became a shorthand way of signaling that you were trying to be inclusive of many different experiences and identities rooted in acts of crossing, and not get hung up on fighting over labels or conflicts rooted in different ways of being different from gender norms. The asterisk can also represent a provocation to think about the interconnections between transgender and other kinds of categorical crossings. How does the *trans-* in *transgender* relate to the *trans-* in *transgenic* or *transspecies* or *transracial*? You could image the asterisk as the visual representation of an intersection of innumerable hyphens pointing in different directions, each connecting the idea of crossing with a particular thing to be crossed.

Acronyms: Members of the T section of the LGBTIQQA A (lesbian, gay, bisexual, transgender, intersex, queer, questioning, asexuals, and allies) community use a lot of acronyms. MTF and FTM refer, respectively, to "male-to-female" and "female-to-male," indicating the direction of gender crossing; it would be more accurate to talk about "male-to-woman" or "female-to-man," but the fact of the matter is that in practice nobody actually says those things. Some transgender people resent and resist these "directional" labels, claiming they make about as much sense as calling someone a "heterosexual-to-gay" man or "heterosexual-to-lesbian" woman, and that they serve only to marginalize transmen and transwomen within the larger populations of other men and women. The two acronyms themselves are much less common than they used to be. CD (or sometimes XD) means "cross-dressing." TS refers to a transsexual, who might be pre-op or post-op or even no-ho/no-op (electing neither hormones nor surgery but still identifying as a member of the gender he or she was not assigned to at birth), while a TG is "a transgender," used as a noun for a particular kind of person rather than "transgender" as an adjective describing how a person is gendered. The right term to use in reference to any particular person really isn't in the eye of the beholder—it should be determined by the person who applies it to him-, her-, or themselves.

Agender: Feeling that one has no gender identity rather than a gender identity at odds with the gender one was assigned at birth; it can be considered part of the trans rubric to the extent that an agender person has moved away from a gender compulsorily assigned at birth.

AMAB and AFAB: Acronyms for "assigned male at birth" and "assigned female at birth." These terms point out that when we come into the world, somebody else tells us who they think we are. Midwives, ultrasound technicians, obstetricians, parents, family members, and innumerable others look at our bodies and say what they think our bodies mean to them. They determine our sex and assign us a gender. We come into self-awareness and grow up in the context created for us by these meanings and decisions, which predate our individual existence. Bodily differences are real, and they set us on different trajectories in life, but what people who use these "assigning" terms are trying to point out is that our bodies and the paths they put us on, however unchosen they were initially, need not determine everything about us. Our assigned categories remain situations within which we can make decisions about ourselves and take meaningful actions to change our paths, including reassigning ourselves.

Binary gender: The idea that there are only two social genders—man and woman—based on two and only two sexes—male and female. The history of trans* people teaches us that both gender and sex can be understood in nonbinary ways.

Cisgender: A word that gained traction only in the twenty-first century but quickly came to enjoy widespread use as a synonym for "nontransgender." The prefix *cis-* means "on the same side as" (that is, the opposite of *trans-*, which means "across"). It is meant to mark the typically unstated or assumed privilege of being nontransgender. The idea behind the term is to resist the way that "woman" or "man" can mean "nontransgender woman" or "nontransgender man" by default, unless the person's transgender or nonbinary status is explicitly named. It's the same logic that would lead somebody to prefer saying "white woman" and "black woman" rather than simply using "woman" to describe a white woman (thus presenting white as the unmarked norm) and "black woman" to indicate a departure from the norm.

Use of *cis-* terminology has become prevalent among people, particularly those at colleges and universities or who do community-based activist work, who think of themselves as allies to trans or nonbinary people and who seek to signal their awareness of the privileges they enjoy because they are binary or not trans. But *cisgender* is not without conceptual contradictions or weaknesses of its own. Using the term too rigidly can foster another kind of gender binary, cis- versus trans-. It aligns binary and cis- with the cultural politics of normativity and nonbinary and trans- with notions of transgression or radicalness, when in fact the politics of normativity and transgression cut across both cis and trans categories. Rather than using *cis* and *trans* to identify two entirely distinct kinds of people, it's more productive to ask *how* somebody is cis (that is, how different aspects of their bodies and minds line up on the side of gender divisions in privileged ways) and *how* they are trans (that is, how they cross the boundaries of their birth-assigned gender in ways that can have adverse social consequences) and to recognize that all people, however they are cis or trans, are subjected to nonconsensual social gendering practices that privilege some and discriminate against others.

Cross-dresser: A term intended as a nonjudgmental replacement for *transvestite,* it is usually considered to be neutrally descriptive of the practice of wearing gender-atypical clothing. The practice of cross-dressing can have many meanings and motivations. Besides being a way to resist or move away from a birth-assigned social gender, it could be a theatrical practice (either comic or dramatic), part of fashion or politics (such as the practice of women wearing pants once was), part of religious ceremonies, or part of celebrating public festivals and holidays (such as Mardi Gras, Carnival, or Halloween). Transgender or transsexual people who are dressing in the fashion of the gender they consider themselves to be do not consider themselves to be cross-dressing—they are simply dressing.

Gender: *Gender* is not the same as *sex,* though the two terms are often used interchangeably, even in technical or scholarly literature, which can lead to a great deal of confusion when you are trying to be analytically precise. Generally speaking, gender is considered to be cultural, and sex, biological. It's usually a safe bet to use the words *man* and *woman* to refer to gender just as *male* and *female* are used to refer to sex. Though we are all born with a certain kind of body that the dominant culture calls our "sex," no one is born as a boy or girl, a woman or a man; rather, we are all assigned to a gender and come to identify (or not) with that gender through a complex process of socialization.

Gender is derived from the Latin word *genus,* meaning "kind" or "type." Gender is the social organization of bodies into different categories of people. In the contemporary United States, this sorting into categories is based on sex, but historically and cross-culturally there have been many different social systems of organizing people into genders. Some cultures, including many Native American cultures, have had three or more social genders. Some attribute social gender to the work people do rather than to the bodies that do that work. In some cultures, people can change their social gender based on dreams or visions. In some they change it with a scalpel or a syringe. The important things to bear in mind are that gender is historical (it changes over time), that it varies from place to place and culture to culture, and that it is contingent—that is, it depends on many different and seemingly unrelated things coming together in a unique and particular way.

One complication in drawing a hard and fast distinction between *sex* and *gender,* however analytically and conceptually different these terms are, has to do with our cultural beliefs. Although it's true that sex typically is used to determine gender categorization, it's also true that what *counts as sex* is a cultural belief. We believe that sex is chromosomal or genetic, that it's related to being able to produce sperm or eggs, that it refers to genital shape and function, that it involves secondary characteristics like beards and breasts. But as described below, chromosomes, reproductive capacity, genital type, body shape, and secondary sex characteristics don't always go together in a biologically predetermined pattern. Some of these characteristics are unchangeable, whereas some are transformable. This leaves us with the collective social task of deciding which aspects of physical embodiment count the most for determining social gender categorization. The criteria used to make that decision are as historical, cultural, and contingent as they are biological—after all, nobody talked about using "chromosomal sex" to determine social gender before the development of genetics, or using birth certificates as proof of identity before issuing birth certificates became commonplace in the early twentieth century. Moreover, the perceived need to make a decision about someone's sex and to determine their gender is based as much on aesthetics as on biology; no one would question the sex of an elite woman athlete like the South African runner Caster Semenya if she looked stereotypically feminine.

It's therefore possible to understand sex being just as much of a social construct as gender. What this boils down to is saying that we believe sex is a stable basis for determining a fixed social gender, but the reality of the situation is that physical bodies are complex and often nonbinary, and social categories, which are themselves highly changeable, can't be unproblematically grounded in the flesh. It's another way of saying that trying to relate sex to gender in some deterministic way always fails at some level and that any correlation we do establish has a cultural, historical, and political dimension that must be established, asserted, and reasserted over and over again for it to remain "true."

This takes us into one of the central issues of transgender social movements—the assertion that the sex of the body (however we understand *body* and *sex*) does not bear any *necessary* or *predetermined* relationship to the social category in which that body lives or to the identity and subjective sense of self of the person who lives in the world through that body. This assertion, drawn from the observation of human social, psychological, and biological variability, is political precisely because it contradicts the common belief that whether a person is a man or a woman in the social sense is fundamentally determined by bodily sex, which is self-apparent and can be clearly and unambiguously perceived. It's political in the additional sense that how a society organizes its members into categories based on their unchosen physical differences has never been a politically neutral act.

One of the main points of feminism is that societies tend to be organized in ways that are more exploitative of women's bodies than of men's bodies. Without disagreeing with that basic premise, a transgender perspective would also be sensitive to an additional dimension of gender oppression: that our culture today tries to reduce the wide range of livable body types to two and *only* two genders, one of which is subject to greater social control than the other, with both genders being based on our beliefs about the meaning of biological sex. Lives that do not conform to this dominant pattern are generally treated as lives that are not worth living and that have little or no value. Breaking apart the forced unity of sex and gender, while increasing the scope of livable lives, needs to be a central goal of feminism and other forms of social justice activism. This is important for everybody, especially, but not exclusively, for trans people.

Gender Dysphoria: Literally, a sense of unhappiness (the opposite of *euphoria,* a sense of joy or pleasure) over the incongruence between how one subjectively understands one's experience of gender and how one's gender is perceived by others. *Gender dysphoria* was a common term among medical and psychotherapeutic professionals who worked with transgender populations in the 1960s through the 1980s, but it was gradually supplanted by the now-discredited diagnostic category Gender Identity Disorder, which was first adopted by the American Psychiatric Association in 1980 in the third edition of its *Diagnostic and Statistical Manual of Mental Disorders* (*DSM-III*) and retained in the fourth edition of 1994 (*DSM-IV*). Partly in response to transgender activism that contested the pathologization of trans identities, *gender dysphoria* came back into fashion in the twenty-first century as part of an argument for why transgender health care needs should be covered by medical insurance. It suggests that it is the sense of unhappiness that is not healthful and that is susceptible to therapeutic treatment rather than that a transgender person is inherently disordered; similarly, it suggests that the feeling of unhappiness about gender could be transient rather than a defining characteristic of a kind of self. *Gender Dysphoria* replaced GID in the 2013 fifth edition of the *Diagnostic and Statistical Manual* (*DSM-V*). The tenth edition of the World Health Organization's International Classification of Diseases (ICD-10), which has been in place since 1992, still uses the GID terminology; the ICD-11, scheduled for release in 2018, is currently expected to revise its nomenclature as well.

GENDER DYSPHORIA

As stated in the fifth edition of the *Diagnostic and Statistical Manual of Mental Disorders* of the American Psychiatric Association, "*Gender dysphoria* as a general descriptive term refers to an individual's affective/cognitive discontent with the assigned gender," and when used as a diagnostic category "refers to the distress that may accompany the incongruence between one's experienced or expressed gender and one's assigned gender." The clinical focus is on dysphoria as the problem, not—as was the case in the older diagnostic category of Gender Identity Disorder—the psychopathologization of identity, per se. The *DSM-V* also notes that many individuals who experience gender incongruence are not distressed by it, but that considerable distress for gender-incongruent people can occur "if the desired physical interventions by means of hormones and/or surgery are not available."

Gender Dysphoria in Children 302.6

A. least 6 months' duration, as manifested by at least six of the following (one of which must be Criterion A1):

continues

1. A strong desire to be of the other gender or an insistence that one is the other gender (or some alternative gender different from one's assigned gender).
2. In boys (assigned gender), a strong preference for cross-dressing or simulating female attire; or in girls (assigned gender), a strong preference for wearing only typical masculine clothing and a strong resistance to the wearing of typical feminine clothing.
3. A strong preference for cross-gender roles in make-believe play or fantasy play. A strong preference for the toys, games, or activities stereotypically used or engaged in by the other gender.
4. A strong preference for playmates of the other gender.
5. In boys (assigned gender), a strong rejection of typically masculine toys, games, and activities and a strong avoidance of rough-and-tumble play; or in girls (assigned gender), a strong rejection of typically feminine toys, games, and activities.
6. A strong dislike of one's sexual anatomy.
7. A strong desire for the primary and/or secondary sex characteristics that match one's experienced gender.

B. The condition is associated with clinically significant distress or impairment in social, school, or other important areas of functioning.

Gender Dysphoria in Adolescents and Adults 302.85

A. A marked incongruence between one's experienced/expressed gender and assigned gender, of at least 6 months' duration, as manifested by at least two of the following:

1. A marked incongruence between one's experienced/expressed gender and primary and/or secondary sex characteristics (or in young adolescents, the anticipated secondary sex characteristics).
2. A strong desire to be rid of one's primary and/or secondary sex characteristics because of a marked incongruence

continues

GENDER DYSPHORIA *continued*

with one's experienced/expressed gender (or in young adolescents, a desire to prevent the development of the anticipated secondary sex characteristics).

3. A strong desire for the primary and/or secondary sex characteristics of the other gender.
4. A strong desire to be of the other gender (or some alternative gender different from one's assigned gender).
5. A strong desire to be treated as the other gender (or some alternative gender different from one's assigned gender).
6. A strong conviction that one has the typical feelings and reactions of the other gender (or some alternative gender different from one's assigned gender).

B. The condition is associated with clinically significant distress or impairment in social, occupational, or other important areas of functioning.

Gender expression: We all perform our sense of self through how we comport our bodies to express our gender. In recent years, as transgender issues have become the subject of more and more legal attention and bureaucratic regulation, *gender expression* is often listed as a protected status along with *gender identity*. The intention here is to protect people who express their gender in nonbinary or nonconformist ways, such as a tech-industry woman who doesn't wear makeup and who feels more comfortable in a T-shirt than a strapless floor-length gown, or a young man at art school who has a fondness for glitter nail polish. The idea is that such expressions of self should not be illegal, stigmatized, discriminated against or result in harm to the persons who express themselves in those ways. *Gender expression* is also a useful term in situations where some members of the public, or some business owners, might not accept or recognize transgender people as actually belonging to the gender they identify with and persist in thinking of a trans woman as a "man in a dress" or a trans man as a woman with facial hair. It doesn't matter as much what somebody else thinks you are if you can express yourself without fear in whatever manner feels right to you. Some trans people, particularly those who feel that their transness has a biological basis and requires medical treatment, draw a distinction between gender expression and gender identity to argue that gender identity is more serious, less chosen, and in greater need of protection than gender expression, which is considered more voluntary and less important.

Gender identity: Each person has a subjective sense of fit (or lack of fit) with a particular gender category; this is one's gender identity. For most people, there is a sense of congruence between the category one has been assigned to at birth and socialized into and what one considers oneself to be. Transgender people demonstrate that this is not always the case, that it is possible to form a sense of oneself as *not like* other members of the gender one has been assigned to at birth or to feel oneself to properly belong to another gender category or to resist categorization at all. Many people who have never felt a sense of gender incongruence themselves can't really understand what it feels like for others, and they may even doubt that transgender people actually experience this or that it can be persistent and intractable and emotionally painful, whereas transgender people who do experience this incongruence often have a hard time explaining to others what this feels like or why it's so important to address. How gender identity develops in the first place and how gender identities can be so diverse are hotly debated topics that go straight into the controversies about nature versus nurture and biological determinism versus social construction. Some people think that gender identity and transgender feelings are caused by inborn physical characteristics; others think that they are caused by how children are raised or by the emotional dynamics in their families; still others consider identity, and the desire to express it differently, to be rooted in spiritual beliefs, aesthetic preferences, or erotic desires. As noted above, it's more important to acknowledge *that* some people experience gender differently from how most do than to say *why* some people experience gender differently from how most do.

Gender-neutral pronouns: English, the most common language in the United States, doesn't easily allow us to refer indirectly to other individuals without gendering them. We have to choose between *he, she,* or *it,* with the latter not considered appropriate for reference to humans precisely because it doesn't indicate a gender. There is, however, a long history of gender-neutral third-person pronouns in various English dialects (like the Anglo-Saxon relic *a* still being used around Yorkshire in the United Kingdom to mean he/she/it, or *yo,* an African American vernacular term popularized by hip-hop, being used the same way around Baltimore today). There is also a long history of attempting to deliberately introduce newly invented pronouns (like the word *thon,* which was proposed in 1858 as a contraction of "that one" and which was seen as similar to the archaic *thine* for "your") and of using gender-neutral plurals (*they/them*) as a substitute for the binary-gendered singular. The first such uses of plural-for-singular were recorded in the fourteenth century and remain common even now in regional variations like *y'all* (you all) and *y'uns* or *yinz* (you ones), which are sometimes used in reference to an individual. It is increasingly common to use the plural *they/them/their* in place of a gendered singular pronoun when the sex or gender of the person being referred to is unknown or irrelevant—even to the point of saying something clunky like "the person themself." Some people who favor gender-neutral English pronouns might use *ze* or *sie* in place of *he* and *she,* or the word *hir* instead of *his* and *her*. Sometimes, in writing, people use the unpronounceable *s/he*. None of the solutions to linguistic gendering in English is entirely satisfactory; the newly coined words can sound fake or jarring, and the use of the plural in place of the singular can sound ungrammatical. But language evolves, often in response to historical events (like the Roman and Norman conquests of England, which introduced a lot of Latin vocabulary into English)—if it didn't, contemporary English speakers would still talk like Chaucer or Shakespeare. Transgender and nonbinary people are pushing language to evolve today to take into account the new social reality that such people are creating.

Spanish, the second-most common language in the United States, presents even greater difficulties than English when trying to communicate in a nongendering way, given that grammatical gendering in Spanish, along with most other Indo-European languages, is reflected in other parts of speech than the pronouns. One recent development, which works better in writing than in speaking, is to replace the gendered *-o* (masculine) or *-a* (feminine) word endings with the gender-neutral *-x*; for example, *Latinx* rather than *Latino* and *Latina*. Conversely, in the third most common language in the United States, Mandarin Chinese, the third-person pronouns

Anonymous cross-dresser at Casa Susanna, a private resort for cross-dressers in New York's Catskill Mountains in the 1950s and 1960s. (Photo credit: powerHouse Books.)

are not gendered when spoken, as all are pronounced the same way: *tā*. Interestingly, the written characters for the personal pronouns are based on the shape that represents the generic concept "human." Non-gender-specific third-person pronouns are actually the rule rather than the exception in most non-Indo-European languages.

Appropriate use of gender-neutral pronouns can be tricky. On the one hand, gender-neutral language can be a way to avoid sexism (as in not using *he* or *man* to refer to people in general) or to avoid making assumptions about a person's gender identity. On the other hand, some transgender people—often those who have worked very hard to attain a gender status other than the one assigned to them at birth—can take offense when referred to by gender-neutral pronouns, rather than the appropriately gendered ones, because they perceive this as a way that others fail to acknowledge how they are obviously and deliberately presenting their gender. A good rule of thumb is to treat gender-neutral terms as more polite and formal, for use when you don't know the person being referred to very well, and to treat gendered terms as more familiar, for use in situations where you know the person and what they prefer.

Gender-nonconforming, genderqueer, and nonbinary: The terms all refer to people who do not conform to binary notions of the alignment of sex, gender, gender identity, gender role, gender expression, or gender presentation. If there are subtle distinctions to make, they are that *gender nonconforming* (or *gender variant*) is more neutrally descriptive of behavior; *genderqueer* (or *gender queer*) is associated more with particular subcultural forms of gender expression that have emerged in LGBT communities or in punk-, goth-, or fetish-inspired countercultural fashion that emphasizes piercings, tattoos, and dramatic styles of makeup and hair; and *nonbinary* is an emerging terminological preference among younger generations who consider binary gender identity to be something more relevant to their grandparents than to themselves. Because transsexual and transgender people do not conform to the social expectation that people who are assigned male at birth will be men or that people assigned female at birth will be women, they can be considered gender-nonconforming and might be as genderqueer or nonbinary as anybody else. In practice, however, these terms usually refer to people who reject the terms *transgender* and *transsexual* for themselves, because they think the terms are either old-fashioned or too conceptually enmeshed in the gender binary.

Gender presentation: Very similar to gender expression, the term refers to looking and acting like what your culture expects a man or a woman to look or act like (or, alternatively, to present yourself in such a way that you make your gender nonconformity visible). Everybody presents their gender.

Gender role: *Gender role* refers to expectations of proper behavior and activities for a member of a particular gender. It is an increasingly inconsequential term in contemporary secular society because of lessened sex stereotyping, more participation by men in child rearing and domestic responsibilities, and a greater range of employment opportunities for women. But to the extent that the concept still has meaning, it often expresses cultural customs, religious beliefs, or assumptions rooted in social-scientific theories. It is the social script that says a man should wear a *yarmulke* or a woman a *hijab,* as well as one that says men are aggressive and women passive, or that a man should be a doctor but a woman should be a nurse, or that mothers should stay at home with their children and fathers should have steady jobs outside the home. Although it is certainly possible to live a happy and fulfilled life by choosing to do things that are (or once were) socially conventional such as being a stay-at-home mom, or that express one's sense of religious duty or ethnic belonging, gender roles tell us that if we don't perform according to prescribed expectations, we are failing to be proper women or men. Transgender people sometimes experience great social and psychological difficulties when they don't embody the gender roles other people might expect of them, particularly when these expectations are grounded in either scientific, cultural, or religious beliefs about what is natural, normal, or divinely given.

Habitus: Habitus just means our habitual or customary way of carrying ourselves and styling our bodies. A lot of our habitus involves manipulating our secondary sex characteristics to communicate to others our own sense of who we feel we are—whether we sway our hips, talk with our hands, bulk up at the gym, grow out our hair, wear clothing with a neckline that emphasizes our cleavage, shave our armpits, allow stubble to be visible on our faces, or speak with a rising or falling inflection at the end of sentences. Often these ways of moving and styling have become so internalized that we think of them as natural even though—given that they are all things we've learned through observation and practice—they can be better understood as a culturally acquired "second nature."

Paying attention to habitus calls our attention to the fact that, although bodies are certainly different from one another, it's what we do with those bodies, how we use and transform those bodies, that is often even more important in making us who we are than what we're born with. All human bodies are modified bodies: they are bodies that diet and exercise, that get pierced and tattooed, whose feet get shaped by the kind of shoes they wear. Shaping, styling, and moving the body to present oneself to others in a particular way is a fundamental part of human cultures—such an important part that it's virtually impossible to practice any kind of body modification without other members of society having an opinion about whether the practice is good or bad, or right or wrong, depending on how or why one does it. Everything from cutting one's nails to cutting off one's leg falls somewhere on a spectrum of moral or ethical judgment. Consequently, many members of society have strong feelings and opinions about practices deemed to be "transgender" body modifications, often disparaging them as "unnatural," even though cultivating a particular style of embodiment to express identity is something we all do in some fashion.

Identity: Identity is who you are. It's a word with a paradox at its core. It means that two things that are not exactly the same can be substituted for one another as if they are the same. In math, to say that (1 + 4) = (2 + 3) is to say that even though the two sets are made up of different numbers, they are mathematically identical because they add up to the same thing. In society and culture, the concept of identity works similarly. When you say, "I am a Socialist" or "I am a Hindu" or "I am a musician" or "I am a woman," the "am" is like an equal sign, and you are saying that your individual sense of being something (an "I") is described by a category that you consider yourself as belonging to. You and the category are not exactly the same thing, but under certain circumstances one can be substituted for the other. In social life, it's often quite important to say what categories you identify with or to call attention to categories you get placed in, whether you identify with them or not. Of course it's possible to have many different, overlapping, or even contradictory personal identities and for people who are significantly different from one another in some ways to be included in the same category.

Identity politics: Although not limited to the United States, identity politics are very important in understanding contemporary US society, given the country's history as a democratic republic. Identity politics have to do with claims for belonging and citizenship in relation to some kind of minority status. They make an appeal to notions of civil society that guard the rights of minorities from abuse by the majority and advance the idea that minority cultural forms, histories, experience, and identities have intrinsic value. In a very real sense, identity politics, which are rooted in the assignment of minority bodies to hierarchical social categories, have always been part of the history of the United States given that it is a nation that has displaced and absorbed native peoples who were categorized as racially different from the settlers, enslaved Africans on the basis of race and non-European origins, controlled immigration by offering preferential entry to some ethnicities while denying entry to others, not allowed women to vote, and criminalized gay and trans people. Minorities have always needed to actively engage in the political process to make their needs known, and their voices heard, in relation to socially dominant groups. Since the mid-twentieth century, many minority identity groups have appealed to notions of justice, civil rights, equality, and cultural pride to contest the ways majority society can discriminate against them either knowingly or unknowingly.

Intersex: Typically, being an egg-producing body means having two X chromosomes, and being a sperm-producing body means having one X and one Y chromosome. When egg and sperm cells fuse (i.e., when sexual reproduction takes place), their chromosomes can combine in patterns (or "karyotypes") other than the typical male (XY) or typical female (XX) ones (such as XXY or XO). Other genetic anomalies can also cause the sex of the body to develop in atypical ways. Other differences of sex development might take place during pregnancy or after birth as the result of glandular conditions that contribute further differences in the typical development of biological sex. Some of these anomalies cause a body that is genetically XY (typically male) to look typically female at birth. Some bodies are born with genitals that look like a mixture of typically male and typically female shapes. Some genetically female bodies (typically XX) are born without vaginas, wombs, or ovaries. All of these variations on the most typical organization of human reproductive anatomy—along with many, many more—are called *intersex* conditions. Intersex used to be called *hermaphroditism,* but that term is now usually considered pejorative. Some intersex people now prefer the medical term *DSD* (for Disorders of Sex Development) to describe their sex status, but others reject this term as unduly pathologizing and depoliticizing. Such people might use *DSD* to refer instead to "differences of sex development," or they might hold on to the word *intersex*—or even *hermaphrodite,* or the slang word *herm*—to signal their sense of belonging to a politicized minority community.

Intersex conditions are far more common than we tend to acknowledge; reliable estimates put the number at about one in two thousand births. Intersex doesn't really have all that much to do with transgender, except for demonstrating that the biology of sex is a lot more variable than most people realize. This becomes significant when you have cultural beliefs about there being only two sexes, and therefore only two genders. These beliefs can lead to intersex people becoming the target of medical interventions such as genital surgery or hormone therapy, often while they are still infants or young children, to "correct" their supposed "abnormality." It is being subjected to the same cultural beliefs about gender, and acted on by the same medical institutions, through the same body-altering techniques that give intersex people and transgender people the most common ground.

Some trans people who think that their need to cross gender boundaries has a biological cause consider themselves to have an intersex condition (current theories favor sex-linked differences in the brain), and some people with intersex bodies also come to think of themselves as being transgender (in that they desire to live in a gender different from the one they were assigned at or after birth).

Still, it's best to think of transgender and intersex identities, communities, and social change movements as being demographically and politically distinct, albeit with some areas of overlap and some shared membership.

Morphology: Morphology means "shape." Unlike genetic sex, which (at least for now) cannot be changed, a person's morphological sex, or the shape of the body that we typically associate with being male or female, can be modified in some respects through surgery, hormones, exercise, clothing, and other methods. A typical adult male morphology is to have external genitalia (penis and testicles), a flat chest (no breasts), and a narrower pelvis. A typical female morphology is to have a vulva, vagina, clitoris, breasts, and a broader pelvis. Morphology can also refer to such aspects of body shape as the size of the hips relative to the waist, the circumference of the wrist relative to the hand, the breadth of the shoulders relative to height, the thickness of the limbs or the torso, whether the fingertips are more tapered or more blunt, the relative prominence or absence of bony eyebrow ridges or to other gender-signifying features of the body.

Queer: In the late 1980s and early 1990s, at the height of the AIDS crisis, some people reclaimed the word *queer,* which had been a derogatory term for homosexuality, and started using it in a positive way. Although it's now often used as a synonym for gay or lesbian, the people who first reappropriated the term were trying to find a way to talk about their opposition to heterosexist social norms; *queer* was less a sexual orientation than it was a political one, what the "queer theorists" of the day called being "antiheteronormative." *Queer* is still usually associated with sexuality, and with gay and lesbian communities, but from the beginning a vocal minority insisted on the importance of transgender and gender-nonconforming practices for queer politics. Many trans people involved in queer cultural politics took to calling themselves "genderqueers."

Secondary sex characteristics: Certain physical traits tend to be associated with genetic sex or reproductive potential such as skin texture, body fat distribution, patterns of hair growth, or relative overall body size. Secondary sex characteristics constitute perhaps the most socially significant part of morphology—taken together, they are the bodily "signs" that others read to guess at our sex, attribute gender to us, and assign us to the social category they understand to be most appropriate for us. Many of these physical traits are the effects of varying levels of hormones, the "chemical messengers" such as estrogen and testosterone that are produced by endocrine glands, at different moments in the body's physical development. Adjusting one's hormone levels can change some (but not all) secondary sex-linked traits. Hormonal treatments to alter secondary sex characteristics have a greater capacity to effect a wider range of change the earlier in life they are undertaken. Testosterone can give a beard to an adult person who had never been able to grow one before, but it will never make that person's hips narrower, just as estrogen can promote breast development on the body of an adult who's never had breasts before but will never make that person shorter. But taken in adolescence, while the body is still maturing, hormones allow trans people's bodies to develop many of the same secondary sex characteristics they would have had had their bodies been of another biological sex.

Sex: For such a small word, *sex* means a lot of different things. We use it as a description of a kind of person (as when we tick off a box on a bureaucratic form), for the act of participating in intercourse ("having sex"), as a synonym for our genitals (imagine the purple prose of a steamy novel that might say that "his sex went limp" or that "her sex burned with desire") as well as to describe biological differences in reproductive capacity (having a body that produces either sperm or eggs).

The Latin root of *sex, sexus,* means "a division." Some species reproduce *asexually,* meaning that each individual organism has all it needs to make another new organism just like it, and some species reproduce *sexually,* meaning that not all of the genetic information needed to make a whole new organism is contained within the body of any one organism of that species: in such cases, reproductive capacity is divided, or *sexed,* between different individual bodies. A few sexed species have more than two divisions, but most, like us, have only two. That much about sex is pretty straightforward, though in practice even this biological understanding of sex can get pretty complicated.

The messiness of *sex* has to do with our cultural beliefs about what those biological differences of reproductive capacity mean. It's a cultural belief, not a biological fact, that having a certain kind of reproductive capacity necessarily determines what the rest of your body is like or what kind of person you are, or that some of these biological differences can't change over time, or that biological differences should be used as a principle for sorting people into social categories, or that these categories should be ordered in a hierarchical way.

This set of cultural beliefs and practices about what biological sex means can be called "gender." It can feel confusing at first to try to think analytically about the difference between sex and gender, and the relationship between them, because one of our strongest unexamined cultural beliefs is that gender and sex are the same thing, which is why most people tend to use *sex* and *gender* interchangeably in everyday speech. A good rule of thumb to keep in mind is that sex is generally considered biological, and gender is generally considered cultural, and that you should use the words *male* and *female* (rather than *man* and *woman*) to refer to sex.

Sexuality: What we find erotic and how we take pleasure in our bodies constitutes our sexuality. For most of us, this involves using our sex organs (genitals), but sexuality can involve many other body parts or physical activities as well as the erotic use of sex toys or other objects. Sexuality describes how and with whom we act on our erotic desires. Sexuality is analytically distinct from gender but intimately bound with it, like two lines on a graph that intersect. The most common terms we use to label or classify our erotic desires depend on identifying the gender of the person or persons toward whom our desire is directed: *heterosexual* (toward members of another gender), *homosexual* (toward members of the same gender), *bisexual* (toward members of either gender in a binary gender system), or *polysexual* or *polyamorous* (toward many people of different genders). These terms also depend on our understanding of our own gender—*homo-* and *hetero-* make sense only in relation to how our gender is the "same as" or "different from" another's gender. We can also be *asexual* (not expressing erotic desire for anyone) or *autosexual* (taking pleasure in our own bodies rather than in interacting with others) or *omnisexual* or *pansexual* (liking it all). Because many transgender people don't fit into other people's sexual orientation categories (or because they don't have a clear sense themselves of where they might fit in), there seems to be a relatively high proportion of asexuality and autosexuality in transgender populations, as well as higher rates of polyamory and pansexuality. Some people are specifically attracted to transgender and gender-nonconforming people. Transgender and nonbinary people may be of any sexual orientation, just like cisgender people.

Subcultural and ethnically specific terms: In an important sense, all the terms mentioned in this section on definitions are subcultural terms—words that originate and circulate within a smaller subset of a larger culture. However, the terms discussed here are also the ones most often used by cultural elites, or within mass media, or within powerful professions such as science and medicine and academia. They are often derived from the experiences of formally educated white transgender people. But there are hundreds, if not thousands, of other specialized words related to the subject matter of this book that could just as easily be listed in this section on terms and definitions. And new terms are emerging all the time, in keeping with the evolving social reality of trans* and nonbinary experience.

A number of these words come out of historic gay and lesbian subcultures; for example, "drag" (clothing associated with a particular gender or activity, often worn in a parodic, self-conscious, or theatrical manner); "drag king" and "drag queen" (people who engage in cross-gender performance, either on the stage or on the street, usually in subcultural spaces such as gay-friendly bars, nightclubs, neighborhoods, or commercial sex zones); "butch" (the expression of traits, mannerisms, or appearances usually associated with masculinity, particularly when expressed by lesbian women or gay men); or "femme" (the expression of traits, mannerisms, or appearances usually associated with femininity, particularly when expressed by lesbian women or gay men). Some words, like "neutrois" (a person with a gender-neutral gender identity; similar to agender) are specific to emerging trans* and gender-nonconforming subcultures and are most prevalent in online communities.

Many terms, such as "bulldagger" or "aggressive" (for a masculine woman or one who takes the lead in initiating sex), originate in queer communities of color. The "house" subcultures of many urban African American, Latino/a, and Asian American communities (such as the ones represented in Jennie Livingston's film *Paris*

Is Burning) have large balls in which participants "walk the categories," competing for the best enactment of a multitude of highly stylized gender designations, such as "butch queen up in pumps."

It becomes quite difficult to use the term *transgender* to talk about gender practices across cultures. On the one hand, the word does circulate transnationally, and many people around the world have taken to using it for themselves in spite of it being an English word that originated in the United States and referred to ways that assigned genders could be moved away from in North America. It is used in a transnational context particularly when using the term helps people in the Global South gain access to NGO-funded health care services or become legible in international human rights discourses. On the other hand, using *transgender* can also function to flatten out and overwrite important cultural differences—even becoming part of the practice of colonization, where Eurocentric ways of making sense of the world are put onto other people. It's not possible to list here all the various ethnically specific forms of gender that often get associated with the term *transgender,* but some of the more common ones in the North American context are "two-spirit" (a catchall term for various indigenous American genders), the Indian *hijra,* the Polynesian *mahu,* and the Latin American *travesti.*

Tranny: Once a self-applied term used within trans communities to signal familiarity, comfort, casualness, informality, affection, and insiderness, many younger trans people now consider it a disparaging term that is most often used by cisgender people to ridicule, trivialize, or sexualize transgender people, particularly trans women. There is a strong generational difference of opinion about the use of the word, with older trans people often still preferring to use it—albeit no longer in public discourse, and usually out of earshot of censorious younger people.

Trans man and trans woman: In trans communities, people commonly use words like *transmen, trans men, transgender men,* or *transsexual men* when they are talking about people who were assigned female at birth but who consider themselves to be men and present themselves as such, or *transmasculine person* when referring to someone assigned female at birth who has some degree of masculine identification or expression. Likewise, the words *transwomen, trans women, transgender women,* and *transsexual women* refer to people assigned male at birth who consider themselves to be women and who live socially as such, while *transfeminine person* refers to someone assigned male at birth who expresses or identifies to some degree with femininity. The "man" and "woman" refer, in keeping with the definition of gender given above, to the social category the person identifies with, lives as, and belongs to, not to biological sex or to birth-assigned gender. When gendered rather than gender-neutral pronouns are used, they similarly refer to social gender and gender identity: *she* and *her* for trans women, and *he* and *him* for trans men. In a lot of the older medical literature, the reverse is often true. Doctors and psychiatrists tend to use "transsexual male" to refer to transgender women (and will often say "he") and "transsexual female" to refer to transgender men (and often say "she"). In keeping with more general social etiquette, it's considered polite to call people what they ask to be called and to use the gender terms that best reflect the person's self-understanding and presentation.

Transgender: As noted earlier, this key term around which the book revolves implies movement away from an assigned, unchosen gender position. *Transgender* entered widespread use in the early 1990s, although the word has a longer history that stretches back to the mid-1960s and has meant many contradictory things at different times. During the 1970s and 1980s, it usually meant a person who wanted not merely to temporarily change their clothing (like a transvestite) or to permanently change their genitals (like a transsexual) but rather to change their social gender in an ongoing way through a change of habitus and gender expression, which perhaps included the use of hormones, but usually not surgery. When the word broke out into wider use in the early 1990s, however, it was used to encompass any and all kinds of variation from gender norms and expectations, similar to what *genderqueer, gender-nonconforming,* and *nonbinary* mean now. In recent years, some people have begun to use the term *transgender* to refer *only* to those who identify with a binary gender other than the one they were assigned at birth—which is what *transsexual* used to mean—and to use other words for people who seek to resist their birth-assigned gender without necessarily identifying with another gender or who seek to create some kind of new gender practice. This book usually privileges the 1990s version of *transgender,* using the word to refer

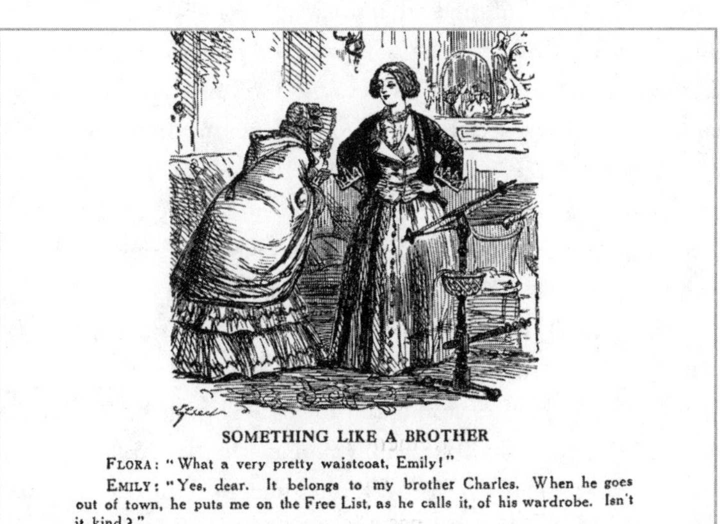

Popular opinion in the nineteenth century sometimes linked feminist dress reform activism with cross-gender dressing. (PHOTO CREDIT: CARTOON STOCK.)

to the widest imaginable range of gender-variant practices and identities. It also relies on abbreviated variants such as *trans* or *trans** to convey that sense of expansiveness and breadth given that contemporary connotations of *transgender* are often more limited.

Transsexual: This term is sometimes traced to the early-twentieth-century German sexologist Magnus Hirschfeld, who wrote of *seelischer transsexualismus,* or "spiritual transsexualism," by which he meant having feelings or emotions or aesthetic sensibilities usually attributed to the binary gender other than the one assigned at birth. For Hirschfeld, what came to be called transsexualism or transsexuality later in the twentieth century was encompassed within his definition of transvestitism (see below). A 1949 article in *Sexology* magazine by Dr. David O. Caldwell, titled "Psychopathia Transexualis," described a person assigned female at birth who thought of himself as a man, but the word *transsexual* was not popularized until Dr. Harry Benjamin starting using it in the 1950s, in the aftermath of the spectacular publicity given to the 1952 surgical "sex change" of Christine Jorgensen. Benjamin used the term to draw a distinction between those "transvestites" (in Hirschfeld's old sense of the word) who sought medical interventions to change their physical bodies (that is, their "sex") and those who merely wanted to change their gendered clothing (the "vestments" in the root of *transvestite*).

Transsexual is now sometimes considered an old-fashioned word, whereas the word *transgender*—which ironically was coined by people who wanted to distinguish themselves from transsexuals—has become more or less synonymous with what transsexuality used to mean: that is, a one-way, one-time, medicalized transition across the gender binary. Some people nevertheless prefer to still use *transsexual* to refer to those trans identities, practices, and desires that require interacting with medical institutions or with legal bureaucracies, in contrast to those trans practices that don't. The terminology becomes even more confusing, however, given that many people who don't consider themselves to be transsexual have increasingly started using the same medicalized body modification practices transsexuals have long used—for example, people assigned female at birth who have mastectomies or take testosterone—without using these practices to make a legal or social claim to being a man. In recent years, facial feminization surgery has become increasingly popular among transsexual women, sometimes undertaken along with genital surgery, and sometimes instead of genital surgery, which raises the intriguing question of whether we now need to think of "face" as a determinant of "sex." To make things even more complicated, trans* activists have worked hard over the last couple of decades to demedicalize the process of changing legal gender—that is, getting rid of requirements that a person must have had genital surgery or taken hormones to change their state-issued IDs or legal gender status. As a result, the boundary between transsexual and transgender has become very blurry indeed.

Transvestite: This is another old word coined by the German sexologist Magnus Hirschfeld. He used it to describe what he called "the erotic urge for disguise," which is how he understood the motivation that led some people to wear clothing generally associated with a social gender other than the one assigned to them at birth. Many people now consider the word to be pejorative or pathologizing, but for some it still retains a neutrally descriptive quality. It's used in this book in its historical sense as well as to refer to people who applied the term to themselves. For Hirschfeld, "transvestites" were one of many different types of "sexual intermediaries," including homosexuals and intersex people, who occupied the middle of a spectrum between "pure male" and "pure female." Initially, this term was used in much the way that *transgender* came to be used in the 1990s and afterward, to convey the sense of a wide range of gender-variant identities and behaviors. Over the course of the last century, however, to the extent that it has not fallen entirely out of favor, *transvestite* refers primarily to people who wear gender-atypical clothing but who do not engage in any kinds of body modification. It usually refers to men rather than women and now usually carries with it the stigmatized connotation of cross-dressing in a fetishistic manner for erotic pleasure.

RELIGION AND TRANSGENDER

Many religious and spiritual traditions incorporate beliefs about changing gender. Shamanic practices in some cultures may involve shamans taking on other-gendered personalities during rituals or being inhabited by the spirit of a differently gendered power or deity; sometimes shamans may live socially in special gender roles. Some religions believe in reincarnation and attribute present-day gender incongruity to past-life experience. Ancient rabbinical texts demonstrate that Judaism once recognized seven distinct genders with different religious, social, and legal obligations. In Islam, the only mention of nonnormative gender in the Qur'an occurs in verse 24:3, in a passage that says Muslim women need not follow the usual rules of modesty when in the presence of male attendants who look and act like women and do not desire them sexually. Although the Hadith (a collection of stories and sayings attributed to the prophet Muhammad by later writers) contains explicitly transphobic content, many feminist, queer, and trans interpreters of the Islamic tradition argue that the Hadith incorporates patriarchal and heterosexist social views that are not found in the more tolerant Qur'an, which is believed to be divinely inspired.

The Judeo-Christian Bible says a lot of things about sexuality and gender that even observant Christians and Jews no longer pay much attention to; for example, that if a married couple has intercourse during the woman's menstrual period, both partners should be executed (Leviticus 18:19). But many people who look for religious justification for their condemnatory views on transgender still point to the following verse, Deuteronomy 22:5: "A woman shall not wear man's

continues

clothing, nor shall a man put on a woman's clothing; for whoever does these things is an abomination to the Lord your God."

As transgender religious scholar Virginia Ramey Mollenkott points out in *Omnigender,* her award-winning overview of religious attitudes toward sex/gender variance, many Christians feel they have a deep stake in maintaining the gender binary. The last several popes, including the current Pope Francis, have been sharply critical of transsexual genital surgeries, which they believe destroy God-given reproductive capacity, and of what they call "gender ideology," which they claim promotes the false secular-humanist belief that gender is a social construct rather than an innate and divinely conferred quality of the body. As Mollenkott's book makes clear, however, many religious traditions, including many denominations and schools of thought within Christianity, adhere to a more tolerant perspective on transgender issues. One organization that promotes acceptance rather than condemnation of gender diversity is the Center for Lesbian and Gay Studies in Religion and the Ministry at the Pacific School of Religion in Berkeley, California (clgs.org).

Transgender Issues in the Spotlight

Why the current obsession with all things trans*, which ticked up sharply in the early 1990s, when gender variance seems to be a pretty persistent part of human cultures across time and around the world? Although the mass media have paid nonstop attention to transgender issues since at least the 1950s, the past couple of decades certainly have witnessed a steady increase in transgender visibility, with a strong trend toward increasingly positive representation. When the first edition of this book was published in 2008, a Google search for the word "transgender" retrieved 7.3 million hits, and a search for "transsexual" retrieved 6.4 million. As of 2017, googling "transgender" retrieves 70.7 million hits, and "transsexual" nets 56.8 million—a tenfold increase in less than ten years. Back in the 1950s, Christine Jorgensen could generate millions of words of press coverage simply for *being* transsexual, whereas now the contemporary media are completely saturated with continual references to and representations of transsexuality and other transgender phenomena—everything from award-winning shows like *Transparent* to innovative series like the Wachowskis' *Sense8* to trans-youth reality shows like *I Am Jazz*—not to mention the wall-to-wall coverage of Caitlyn Jenner's gender transition and mainstream print media outlets like *Time* and *National Geographic* running highly publicized cover stories on trans issues.

A lot of cultural trends, social conditions, and historical circumstances have collided to make trans topics hot. Some people think that the numbers of transgender people are on the rise. Those who favor biological theories point often to environmental factors, like the amount of endocrine-disrupting chemicals in our water, soil, and food. Other observers insist that increased visibility is just an artifact of the Internet age—not really a rise in prevalence, just a new way for previously isolated and socially invisible people to link up and disseminate information about themselves. Others point to gender systems themselves transforming in ways that make cis/trans distinctions feel like relics of the twentieth century. Globalization brings us all into increasingly frequent and extensive contact with people from cultures different from our own, including people who have different experiences of gender and sexuality, which can lead to greater familiarity and comfort with gender variation.

The current fascination with transgender also probably has something to do with new ideas about how representation works in the age of digital media. Back in the analog era, a representation (word, image, idea) was commonly assumed to point to some real thing, the same way a photograph was an image produced by light bouncing off a physical object and causing a chemical change on a piece of paper, or the way a sound recording was a groove cut in a piece of vinyl by sound waves produced by a musical instrument or a person's voice. A person's social and psychological gender was commonly assumed to point to that person's biological sex in exactly the same way: gender was considered a representation of a physical sex. But a digital image or sound is something else entirely. It's unclear exactly how it's related to the world of physical objects. It doesn't point to some "real" thing in quite the same way, and it might in fact be a complete fabrication built up pixel by pixel or bit by bit—but a fabrication that nevertheless exists as an image or a sound as real as any other. Transgender gender representation works similarly. The image and sound of "man" and "woman" are perfectly understandable, however they are produced, whatever material thing they refer to. For the generation that's grown up amid the turn-of-the-century digital media and telecommunications revolution and that is thoroughly immersed in video gaming culture and computer-generated movie special effects, transgender often just makes sense intuitively as a possible way of being, even to people who do not feel transgender themselves. "Self" doesn't map onto the biological body in quite the way it seemed to in the last century, and being trans simply isn't as big a deal as it used to be in many contexts.

Probably half a dozen other things also figure into the equation. The end of the Cold War in the late 1980s and early 1990s ushered in an era when it became politically imperative to think outside the totalizing East-West binaries that shaped mass consciousness in the decades after World War II. In the decentralized and globalized geopolitical era that came after the Cold War, transgender reflected a similar shift in thinking beyond the binaries of "man" and "woman." There was also the sense in the 1990s, so hard to fathom now that we are well into the twenty-first century, that the calendar's impending millennial rollover meant we would soon be living in "the future," when everything would be different, and we would all have flying cars like the Jetsons and Dick Tracy two-way wrist radios (whereas in real life it turned out that we'd have self-driving robot cars and smartphones with video cameras). Transgender in the nineties became one way of imagining that future, where new telecommunications technologies, biotechnology, and medical science promised to remake what it would mean to be human.

But the reality, quite apart from science fiction fantasies, is that technology really is fundamentally transforming the conditions of human life on earth. Stop for a moment to reflect on some recent (and not so recent) developments in biomedicine: cloning, in vitro fertilization, intrauterine surgeries, sperm and egg banking, surrogate baby farms, genetic engineering, gene therapy, plant-animal hybrids, artificial DNA, human embryos with more than two genetic parents. As these and other biomedical developments continue to coalesce, we are finding more and more ways to separate sex (in the sense of biological reproduction) from one's psychological gender identity or social gender role. Contemporary trans issues offer a window into that brave new world.

CHAPTER 2

A HUNDRED-PLUS YEARS OF TRANSGENDER HISTORY

IMAGINE BEING A young female person in the 1850s who can't face a life of marriage and child rearing, who has no practical work skills outside the home, and who dreams of adventure in the military, at sea, or in the mining towns of the mountainous and desert West. Donning your brother's clothes, you slip away in the night and head out to meet your fate. Your life might depend on being taken for exactly what you present yourself as being. Or imagine being a young male person with a fondness for the social companionship of women but no romantic interest in them, whose greatest happiness is in taking care of children. You thrill at the thought of being related to as a woman. You disappear into the streets of a large city, looking for a way of living that feels right to you, but find yourself subjected to all of the indignities that society can visit upon an individual who is feminine, unattached, and unlikely to be offered a job or a home.

Regulating Sexuality and Gender

People who contradicted social expectations of what was considered typical for men or for women have existed since the earliest days of colonial settlement in what is now the United States. Thomas or Thomasine Hall was an indentured servant in Virginia in the 1620s who seems to have had an intersex anatomy, and who lived sometimes as a man and sometimes as a woman. The colony of Massachusetts first passed laws against cross-dressing in the 1690s. In the eighteenth century, numerous women and transmasculine people—most famously, Deborah Sampson—enlisted in the Revolutionary Army as men. Joseph Lobdell, formerly known as Lucy Ann, author of *The Female Hunter of Delaware and Sullivan Counties,* became locally famous in upstate New York during the early years of the Republic not only as an excellent shot with a rifle but as a feminist advocate for marriage reform, before being deemed psychiatrically ill and institutionalized for the rest of his long life. A popular literary magazine, *The Knickerbocker,* even published a short fictional story in 1857 called "The Man Who Thought Himself a Woman," which offered a sympathetic portrait of a person with transgender feelings. And throughout the antebellum period, the institution of slavery often functioned to strip away gender signifiers from enslaved people not just by divorcing them from the traditional social roles for men and women in their African cultures of origin but by attempting to render many of them into interchangeable laboring bodies, whether male or female.

Not until the mid-nineteenth century, however, did social conditions take shape that would foster a mass transgender movement for social change in the century that lay ahead. Starting in the 1850s, a number of US cities began passing municipal ordinances that made it illegal for people to appear in public "in a dress not belonging to his or her sex." There was an even longer history of public regulation of dress dating back to the colonial period, with rules that forbid people from disguising themselves in public or wearing clothes associated with a particular social rank or profession they did not hold, and which criminalized white people for

OUTLAWING CROSS-DRESSING

One of several anti-cross-dressing laws passed in the middle of the nineteenth century, the following San Francisco ordinance was enacted in 1863:

> *If any person shall appear in a public place in a state of nudity, or in a dress not belonging to his or her sex, or in an indecent or lewd dress, or shall make any indecent exposure of his or her person, or be guilty of any lewd or indecent act or behavior, or shall exhibit or perform any indecent, immoral or lewd play, or other representation, he should be guilty of a misdemeanor, and on conviction, shall pay a fine not exceeding five hundred dollars.*

Municipal Laws Prohibiting Wearing Dress of Opposite Sex

Nineteenth Century			
Location	**Year**	**Location**	**Year**
Columbus, Ohio	1848	Dallas, Texas	1880
Chicago, Illinois	1851	Nashville, Tennesee	1881
Wilmington, Delaware	1856	San Jose, California	1882
Springfield, Illinois	1856	Tucson, Arizona	1883
Newark, New Jersey	1858	Columbia, Missouri	1883
Charleston, South Carolina	1858	Peoria, Illinois	1884
Kansas City, Missouri	1860 1889	Butte, Montana	1885
Houston, Texas	1861	Denver, Colorado	1886
Toledo, Ohio	1862	Lincoln, Nebraska	1889
Memphis, Tennessee	1863	Santa Barbara, California	189?
San Francisco, California	1863	Omaha, Nebraska	1890
St. Louis, Missouri	1864	Cheyenne, Wyoming	1892
Minneapolis, Minnesota	1877	Cicero, Illinois	1897
Oakland, California	1879	Cedar Falls, Iowa	1899

Twentieth Century	
Location	**Year**
Cedar Rapids, Iowa	1905
Orlando, Florida	1907
Wilmington, North Carolina	1913
Charleston, West Virginia	1913
Columbus, Georgia	1914
Sarasota, Florida	1919
Pensacola, Florida	1920
Cleveland, Ohio	1924
West Palm Beach, Florida	1926
Detroit, Michigan	195?
Miami, Florida	1952 1956
Cincinnati, Ohio	1974

Compiled by Clare Sears in "A Dress Not Belonging to His or Her Sex: Cross-Dressing Law in San Francisco, 1860–1900" (PhD diss., Sociology Department, University of California, Santa Cruz, 2005), based on data from William Eskridge, Gaylaw: Challenging the Apartheid of the Closet *(Cambridge, MA: Harvard University Press, 1997).*

disguising themselves as Indians (as was common during populist protests like the Boston Tea Party) or black people from impersonating whites—but the wave of local legislation in the 1850s represented a new development specific to gender presentation. Although people with transgender feelings lived in rural as well as urban environments, and in all parts of the country—indeed, historian Peter Boag's book *Re-Dressing America's Frontier Past* notes that stories about cross-dressers are "ubiquitous" in nineteenth- and early twentieth-century newspapers (which are now easily accessible online in searchable digital formats)—these new laws can be interpreted, at least in part, as a response to the growing urbanization of US culture.

Very little historical research helps us explain why cross-dressing became a social issue seemingly so in need of regulation in the 1850s, but an old argument about capitalism and gay identity offers some suggestive parallels. According to historian John D'Emilio, modern gay and lesbian communities weren't possible until the middle of the nineteenth century, with the rise of modern industrial cities and their large working-class populations. It wasn't until men could leave tight-knit rural communities, characterized by intimate and interlocking forms of familial and religious surveillance, that they had the opportunity to form different kinds of emotional and erotic bonds with other men. Cities—where the industrial economy created many wage-paying jobs that allowed single men to be independent from their families of origin and to live in relative anonymity within masses of other people—provided the crucial social circumstances for gay communities to take shape.

Because women were less able than men to free themselves from the constraints of marriage, child care, and the care of aging parents, there was not a similar urban lesbian subculture until the twentieth century, when more women were able to support themselves as independent wage earners. The 1920s were a pivotal decade in this shift. For the first time, the urban population in the United States exceeded the rural population; women wielded historically unprecedented political power through the recently acquired right to vote, and Jazz Age sensibilities embraced more expansive ideas of socially acceptable female sexuality. The greater scope of possibility for independent womanhood came to be seen as an important aspect of a new "modern era." Coalescing after the upheavals of World War I, a number of factors characterized this period, such as new entertainment technologies (for example, motion pictures and sound recordings), modernist styles of art and literature, and electrically illuminated homes and streets that created more opportunities for nighttime socializing.

It is important to recognize that we still know very little about the social history of cross-dressing or the public expression of

Loreta Janeta Velazquez served in the Civil War as Confederate soldier Harry Buford. (PHOTO CREDIT: UNIVERSITY OF WISCONSIN PRESS.)

transgender feeling in earlier periods. And yet, the same circumstances that supported the development of same-sex social worlds also would have applied to people who sought different ways to express their sense of gender. People assigned female at birth who could successfully present themselves as men had greater opportunities to travel and find work. People assigned male at birth who identified as women had greater opportunities to live as women in cities far removed from the communities where they had grown up. In practice, the distinctions between what we now call "transgender" and "gay" or "lesbian" were not always as meaningful back then as they have since become. Throughout the second half of the nineteenth century and the first half of the twentieth century, homosexual desire and gender variance were often closely associated. One common way of thinking about homosexuality back then was as gender "inversion," in which a man who was attracted to men was thought to be acting like a woman, and a woman who desired women was considered to be acting like a man.

First wave feminism and an increasingly ethnically diverse population were also likely factors that sparked new efforts to regulate public gender variance beginning in the 1850s. First wave feminism is usually defined as the wave of reform that spanned the entire nineteenth century, beginning with late-eighteenth-century calls for female emancipation such as Mary Wollstonecraft's *Vindication of the Rights of Woman,* gaining momentum with the Seneca Falls Convention on the rights of women in 1848, and culminating in the suffrage campaigns that won women in the United States the right to vote in 1919. Dress reform was an important focus of first wave feminist activism. Amelia Bloomer, for example, argued in the 1840s that long skirts and cumbersome undergarments were essentially a form of bondage that dragged women down, and she advocated that women wear pants-like clothing instead. Nineteenth-century antifeminist opinion, which saw in feminism a threatened loss of distinction between men and women, considered dress reform to be tantamount to cross-dressing.

On the West Coast, where the California gold rush and subsequent silver strikes attracted many trans-Pacific immigrants from Asia, cultural diversity added another element that upset conventional Euro-American assumptions about gender. Gold rush–era newspapers are full of stories about how difficult it was for European Americans to tell Chinese men apart from Chinese women, because they all wore their hair long and dressed in silky pajama-like costumes. To understand the historical conditions for contemporary transgender activism, we thus have to take into account race, class, culture, sexuality, and sexism, and we have to develop an understanding of the ways that US society has fostered conditions of inequality and injustice for people who aren't white, male, heterosexual, and middle class—in addition to understanding the difficulties particularly associated with engaging in transgender practices.

The Social Power of Medicine

One of the most powerful tools for social regulation in this period was the rapid development of medical science. This is not to suggest that modern medicine hasn't saved many lives and greatly improved the quality of life for untold millions of people—it has. But since the end of the eighteenth century, science has gradually come to replace religion as the highest social authority, and since the middle of the nineteenth century medical science has played an increasingly central role in defining everyday life. It has often been used for very conservative social purposes—"proving" that black people are inferior to white people, or that females are inferior to males. Medical practitioners and institutions have the social power to determine what is considered sick or healthy, normal or pathological, sane or insane—and thus, often, to transform potentially neutral forms of human difference into unjust and oppressive social hierarchies. This particular operation of medicine's social power has been especially important in transgender history.

For those transgender people who have felt compelled to physically change something about their embodiment, medical science has long offered the prospect of increasingly satisfactory surgical and hormonal interventions. Once anesthesia had been invented and a new understanding of the importance of antisepsis had made surgery something other than a likely death sentence (once again, in the middle decades of the nineteenth century), individuals began approaching doctors to request surgical alteration of gender-signifying parts of their bodies. But medical science has always been a two-edged sword—its representatives' willingness to intervene has gone hand in hand with their power to define and judge. Far too often, access to medical services for transgender people has depended on constructing transgender phenomena as symptoms of a mental illness or physical malady, partly because "sickness" is the condition that typically legitimizes medical intervention. It's also important to recognize that many of the genital surgeries that became available to later generations of transgender people were developed by practicing on the bodies of enslaved black women who were subjected to medical experimentation, and that these procedures were used nonconsensually on the bodies of intersex youth.

It's possible to see medical and psychiatric professionals—as well as people seeking relief from gender-related distress (or simply trying to figure themselves out)—groping over the course of the nineteenth century for new words, labels, identity categories, and theories to describe and explain transgender phenomena. In Austria, Karl Heinrich Ulrichs anonymously published a series of booklets in 1864–1865 under the collective title *Researches on the Riddle of "Man-Manly" Love;* in them he developed a biological theory to account for people such as himself, whom he called "Urnings," and whom he described with the Latin phrase *anima muliebris virili corpore inclusa* (meaning "a female soul enclosed within a male body"). It was in correspondence with Ulrichs that the German-born Hungarian citizen Karl Maria Kertbeny first coined the term *homosexual* in 1869, which he also intended to connote same-sex love, minus the element of gender inversion to be found in the term "Urning." Both men considered the respective conditions they described to be physical and inborn, and thus proper objects of medical inquiry. Ulrichs and Kertbeny also thought that because transgender/homosexual feelings had a biological basis, laws against their expression should be reformed in the name of a rational social order that reflected scientific truth. Their efforts represent early instances of social activism based on the idea that people we would now probably label gay or transgender were not by definition sinners or criminals but simply different kinds of people who were equally entitled to full participation in society. The logic of their arguments still informs many transgender and gay social justice efforts; more often than not, however, biological theories about gender variance and homosexuality are used to argue that gay and transgender people are physically and psychologically degenerate, and that these conditions therefore should be corrected or eliminated.

Many other long-gone words for transgender phenomena pop up in the burgeoning medical literature of the late nineteenth and early twentieth centuries, demonstrating the extent to which transgender issues were coming to be seen as a medical problem. The period's leading scientific authority on sexuality, Richard von Krafft-Ebing, supplied a great many terms in the several editions of his influential medical compendium, *Psychopathia Sexualis,* first published in 1886. These included "antipathic sexual instinct" (disliking what one *should* find erotic based on one's sex or gender), "eviration" (a deep change of character in which a male's feelings and inclinations become those of a woman), "defemination" (a deep change of character in which a female's feelings and inclinations become those of a man), and "metamorphosis sexualis paranoica" (the psychotic delusion that one's body was transforming into another sex). Krafft-Ebing also wrote about "insanity among the Scythians" (an ancient nomadic people from the Eurasian steppes who sometimes practiced ritual genital modification as part of their religious observations) and *mujerados,* "male women" noted by the Spanish conquistadors during the colonization of the Americas, whom he believed had become feminized through excessive masturbation, leading to atrophy of the penis and testicles. One early psychiatrist, Albert Moll, wrote about *conträre Geschlechtsempfindung* (contrary sexual feeling) in 1891; another, Max Marcuse, described a *Geschlechtsumwandlungstreib* (drive for sex transformation) in 1913. That same year, British psychologist Havelock Ellis coined "sexo-aesthetic inversion" (wanting to look like the other sex) and later, in 1928, "Eonism," which referred to the Chevalier D'Eon, a member of the court of Louis XVI who, at various stages of life, lived alternately as a man and as a woman. It was in this climate of ever-evolving vocabulary and increasing attention to transgender phenomena that Magnus Hirschfeld coined *transvestite,* the only word of its kind to survive into contemporary usage.

An Early Advocate

Hirschfeld was a pivotal figure in the political history of sexuality and gender. Born in Prussia in 1868, he earned a degree in medicine at the University of Berlin in 1892. His most important theoretical contribution to the study of gender and sexuality was his concept of "sexual intermediaries," the idea that every human being represented a unique combination of sex characteristics, secondary sex-linked traits, erotic preferences, psychological inclinations, and culturally acquired habits and practices. According to his calculations, there were more that forty-three million different combinations of characteristics, and therefore more than forty-three million kinds (or genders) of humans. In 1897, Hirschfeld cofounded the Scientific-Humanitarian Committee, usually regarded as the first organization in the world to effectively devote itself to social reform on behalf of sexual minorities. Like Ulrichs and Kertbeny before him, Hirschfeld thought that variations in human sexuality and gender were rooted in biology, and that a just society was one that recognized the natural order of things. He edited the first scientific journal on "sexual variants"—the *Yearbook for Sexual Intermediaries,* published between 1899 and 1923—and was a founding member of Sigmund Freud's Psychoanalytic Society in 1908 (which he broke with in 1911). In 1919, Hirschfeld founded the Institute for Sexual Science in Berlin, a combination of library, archive, lecture hall, and medical clinic, where he amassed an unprecedented collection of historical documents, ethnographies, case studies, and literary works detailing the diversity of sexuality and gender around the world. In 1928, he became the founding president of the World League for Sexual Reform.

Hirschfeld was a pioneering advocate for transgender people. As early as 1910 he had written *The Transvestites,* the first book-length treatment of transgender phenomena. He worked with the Berlin police department to end the harassment and targeting for arrest of transgender people. Transgender people worked on the staff of the Institute for Sexual Science (albeit as receptionists and maids), though some were part of Hirschfeld's social circle as well, including Dorchen Richter. Richter underwent the first documented male-to-female genital transformation surgery in 1931, arranged on her behalf by Hirschfeld himself. Hirschfeld also played a role in arranging medical care for another early transsexual woman, Lilli Elbe, subject of the (historically inaccurate) novel and film *The Danish Girl.* Hirschfeld was the linchpin, and his institute the hub, of the international network of transgender people and progressive medical experts who set the stage for the post–World War II transgender movement. His colleagues included Eugen Steinach, the Austrian endocrinologist who first identified the morphology-shifting effects of the so-called sex hormones, testosterone and estrogen, in the 1910s, as well as young Harry Benjamin, the German-born doctor who moved to the United States in 1913 and became the leading medical authority on transsexuality in the 1950s.

Hirschfeld's work came to a tragically abrupt end in the 1930s. The World League for Sexual Reform splintered between liberal and radical factions (some members favoring the reform politics of Western democratic capitalism, and others favoring Soviet-style Marxist revolution) and had to cancel planned conferences because of the rise of Stalinism and fascism in Europe. Adolf Hitler personally denounced Hirschfeld, who was a socialist as well as a gay man, as "the most dangerous Jew in Germany." Fearing for his life if he remained in the country, Hirschfeld turned a planned visit to the United States into an around-the-world lecture tour. Between 1930 and 1933 he visited New York, Chicago, San Francisco, Honolulu, the Philippines, Indonesia, Japan, China, Egypt, and Palestine, preaching his vision of politically progressive sexual science. In 1933, fascist vigilantes ransacked and destroyed Hirschfeld's institute in Berlin; the most familiar photo of Nazi book burning depicts Hirschfeld's library of materials on sexual diversity going up in flames, a bust of Hirschfeld himself clearly visible in the bonfire. Unable to return to Germany, Magnus Hirschfeld settled in Nice, on the French Riviera, where he died of a heart attack on his sixty-seventh birthday, in 1935.

By the early twentieth century, some transgender individuals had also sought the legitimation afforded by science to argue for better treatment for themselves. One of the "case studies" for Hirschfeld's 1910 book on transvestites, a German American living in San Francisco, had first come to his attention after writing to a German feminist publication to suggest that mothers should raise their transgender children according to their "mental sex" rather than their "physical sex." Earl Lind, a self-described "androgyne" and "fairy" in New York who also used the names Ralph Werther and Jennie June, and who voluntarily underwent castration, published two autobiographical works, *Autobiography of an Androgyne* (1918) and *The Female Impersonators* (1922). Both were intended to "help the suffering androgyne." The books' publisher, Dr. Alfred Herzog, likewise said he brought them into print because "androgynism was not sufficiently understood" and that "therefore androgynes were unjustly made to suffer." According to Lind, a group of New York androgynes led by one Roland Reeves had formed "a little club" called the Cercle Hermaphroditos as early as 1895 on the basis of their self-perceived need "to unite for defense against the world's bitter persecution."

Midcentury Transgender Social Networks

The Cercle Hermaphroditos was the first known informal organization in the United States to concern itself with what we might now call transgender social justice issues, but it does not appear to have had any lasting influence or to have inspired any direct successors. Not until the middle of the twentieth century did social networks of transgender people begin to interconnect with networks of socially powerful people in ways that would produce long-lasting organizations and provide the base of a social movement.

It's striking that so much of the early networking and organizing on trans issues takes place between transfeminine people and cisgender men, because there were of course many transmasculine people and trans men living interesting and accomplished lives between the 1850s and 1950s. Dr. Mary Walker—one of the first women in the United States to earn a medical degree—was a Civil War–era surgeon, feminist, and dress reformer who often wore masculine attire and who was twice arrested for cross-dressing. Murray Hall was a prominent operative in New York City's Democratic Party political machine who lived, married, and—in the years before female suffrage—voted as a man for more than a quarter century. Jack Garland, whose Californio family was politically prominent in San Francisco before the Anglo conquest in the 1840s, was frequently mentioned in northern California newspapers and served in the Philippines during the Spanish-American War. Alan Hart, an early pioneer in the use of X-rays to diagnose tuberculosis, was also the author of four published novels: *Dr. Mallory, The Undaunted, In the Lives of Men,* and *Dr. Finlay Sees It Through.* Houston-born Willmer Broadnax became a gospel-singing sensation in the 1940s. Pauli Murray, assigned female at birth in Baltimore in 1910, struggled with questions of gender identity in her youth, often passing as a teenage boy and even seeking hormonal masculinization in the 1940s, before reconciling herself to living as a masculine woman. She passed the California bar in 1945, became the state's first black deputy attorney general, and, in 1950, authored the monumental study *States' Laws on Race and Color,* which provided the underpinning evidence and arguments for the landmark *Brown v. Board of Education* Supreme Court decision on school desegregation. Murray's writing on race and gender has been recognized retroactively as foundational for intersectional feminist thought, though the transgender dimension of her perspective is not always acknowledged.

In her book *How Sex Changed: A History of Transsexuality in the United States,* Joanne Meyerowitz describes how the staff and clients of the Langley Porter Psychiatric Clinic at the University of California, San Francisco (UCSF), played an important role in building up networks among trans women seeking medical

CASE 13: THE STORY OF A NINETEENTH-CENTURY TRANSVESTITE

In Magnus Hirschfeld's *The Transvestites,* "Case 13" consists of letters, written in 1909, from a person known variously as Jenny, Johanna, and John, who was born in the Austro-Hungarian Empire and who later moved to the United States. Hirschfeld considered this person to be "a typical representative of the group we are concerned with." These reminiscences are abridged from the original.

I was born in 1862. I did not want any trousers and put up such a fuss, and since my sister was one year older I could wear her clothes until Mother died in 1868. My aunts then forced me to wear boys clothing. I clearly remember that I always only wanted to be a girl, and my relatives and acquaintances would tease me.

I wanted to go to the teachers' seminary because later, I thought, when I finished, I could go around as a governess or a children's teacher. Even at the time I had firm plans to become a woman. When I saw that they were not going to allow me to study to be a teacher, at the first opportunity I stole from a girl who was my size. I put on her things and took her certificate of domicile and burned my boy's things that night. Everything boyish I left behind and went to Switzerland where my relatives would not know where I was.

I first went to work as a nanny and did general housework. At the same time, I learned embroidery. I grew strong and not ugly, so that boys would lie in wait for me. At that time I felt fully a young woman, except when the fellows got fresh with me, and it would occur to me that, unfortunately, I was not one.

At 16½ a man tried to rape me. I protected myself, but he gave me a bad name as being a hermaphrodite, so I had to move away and went to France. I had a friendship with a girl, who, like me, was in opposition to her sex, namely manly, and when she went

continues

CASE 13: THE STORY OF A NINETEENTH-CENTURY TRANSVESTITE *continued*

to St. Quentin to the embroidery factory there, I followed her. There I had the opportunity for the first time to come together with women who with other women lived like married people.

In 1882 I left France and went to New York. Here, I soon found work as a maid on a farm because I thought I would be able to live there inconspicuously, but one day the farmer's wife was away and he became fresh. I was afraid of discovery and left that place and got a good job in Jersey City.

I became acquainted with an embroiderer who found out I was no young woman. He threatened to call the police and tell them I was playing a masquerade. He forced me into sodomy and fellatio and a few months passed during which I got more miserable each day. One morning I packed everything together and, when he was away, sold everything of worth. I went to Montana as a woman cook. There, however, betrayed again, I took myself to San Francisco in 1885, and still live there today.

I am now 47 years old and today it is still my deepest wish to wear a new princess dress, a new flowered hat, and lace petticoats. I decorate my bedroom in the manner of women, and a man seldom enters my room, because I am no friend to men. Conversations with women satisfy me more, and I am envious of educated women, because I look up to them. For that reason I have always been an activist for equal rights.

assistance for their gender transitions. Under the direction of Karl Bowman, a former president of the American Psychiatric Association, the Langley Porter Clinic became a major center of research on variant sexuality and gender in the 1940s and 1950s—in sometimes ominous ways. During World War II, Bowman conducted research on homosexuality in the military, using as test subjects gay men whose sexuality had been discovered while they were serving in uniform, who were being held in a military psychiatric prison at the Treasure Island Naval Base in San Francisco Bay. After the war, he was the principal investigator for a statewide project funded by the California Sex Deviates Research Act of 1950 to discover the "causes and cures" of homosexuality; part of this research involved castrating male sex offenders in California prisons and experimenting on them by administering various hormones to see if it altered their sexual behavior.

In the course of this work, Bowman became acquainted with several individuals living in San Francisco whom we would now call transsexuals, as he noted in his first report to the California state legislature:

> I have records of two males, both of whom have asked for complete castration, including amputation of the penis, construction of an artificial vagina, and the administration of female sex hormones. I also have two cases of females who have requested a panhysterectomy and the amputation of their breasts, together with the giving of male sex hormones, in the hope that in some way the clitoris may finally develop into a penis. Male homosexuals of this type are called "Queens" and seem to differ markedly from the main group of homosexuals who are more nearly like the average man. Here we have an extremely interesting field for further investigation. We are therefore setting up a careful plan to study a group of these so-called "Queens."

One of the transgender people Bowman came in contact with (though not one of the prospective transsexuals) was Louise Lawrence, a person assigned male at birth who began living full-time as a woman in 1942. Lawrence, a native of northern California who had been dressing in feminine attire most of her life, had developed an extensive correspondence network with trans people around the country by placing personal ads in magazines and by contacting people whose arrests for public cross-dressing had been covered in the newspapers. Lawrence frequently lectured on transgender topics to Bowman's colleagues at UCSF.

Lawrence's connections to Bowman, and through him to other sex researchers such as the famed Alfred Kinsey, functioned as a crucial interface between medical researchers and transgender social networks. Her home became a waystation for transgender people from across the country who sought access to medical procedures in San Francisco, and her numerous transgender contacts supplied data that a new generation of sex researchers would use to formulate their theories. In 1949, Bowman and Kinsey, along with transsexual medical pioneer Harry Benjamin and future California governor Edmund G. (Pat) Brown (then California's state attorney general), became involved in a legal case involving one of Lawrence's friends that had long-lasting repercussions for the course of transgender access to medical services in the United States. Brown, on the advice of Bowman and Kinsey but over the objections of Benjamin, offered the legal opinion that transsexual genital modification would constitute "mayhem" (the willful destruction of healthy tissue) and would expose any surgeon who performed such an operation to possible criminal prosecution. That opinion cast a pall, lasting for years, over efforts by US transgender people to gain access to transsexual medical procedures in their own country. In the 1950s, only a few dozen "sex change" operations were performed in the United States, most of them by Los Angeles urologist Elmer Belt (a friend of Benjamin's), under conditions of strict secrecy.

This 1949 "mayhem" case was notable in one further regard: it was Harry Benjamin's first involving a transsexual patient. The case thus helps link the emerging transgender scene in the United States with the earlier one in Europe that revolved around Magnus Hirschfeld. Benjamin was born in Berlin in 1885 and earned his medical degree at the University of Tübingen in 1912. He had become acquainted with Hirschfeld through a mutual friend in 1907, and he had accompanied Hirschfeld on trips into Berlin's transvestite nightclub subculture, but at the time Benjamin's professional interest was in tuberculosis. In the 1920s, after Benjamin had taken up residence in New York, he developed an interest in the new science of endocrinology. He became a devotee of the Austrian pioneer of the field, Hirschfeld's colleague Eugen Steinach, and visited the two men every summer in Vienna and Berlin to learn more about the use of hormones as a life-extension and geriatric rejuvenation therapy. Benjamin, who organized the US leg of Hirschfeld's global tour, refused to travel to Germany after Hitler came to power in 1933. Instead, he began conducting a summer medical practice in San Francisco, where his expertise in endocrinology eventually brought him into contact with Karl Bowman, and with Louise Lawrence and her friends. Benjamin's sympathy toward Lawrence and her circle, and his difference of opinion from that of his

Nazis burn the library of Magnus Hirschfeld's Institute for Sexual Science in Berlin, 1933. (PHOTO CREDIT: NATIONAL ARCHIVES.)

US-trained colleagues in the 1949 case that marked the beginning of his career in transsexual medicine, was no doubt informed by the more progressive attitudes he had encountered at Hirschfeld's Institute for Sexual Science in Berlin.

Meanwhile, through her involvement with the Langley Porter Clinic, Louise Lawrence had met a pharmacologist and postdoctoral researcher at UCSF who, as Virginia Prince, would come to play an important role in transgender history. Born to a socially prominent family in Los Angeles in 1912, Prince was still living as a furtively cross-dressing man when she came in contact with Lawrence in 1942. That encounter quickly brought Prince into the orbit of the leading figures in transgender-oriented medical research. Schooled in transgender issues as part of that emerging network, Prince would eventually found the first enduring organizations in the United States devoted to transgender concerns. In spite of her open disdain for gay people, her frequently expressed negative opinion of transsexual surgeries, and her conservative stereotypes regarding masculinity and femininity, Prince (who began living full-time as a woman in 1968) has to be considered a central figure in the early history of the contemporary transgender political movement.

Pioneering transgender community organizer Louise Lawrence. (Photo credit: Oviatt Library, California State University-Northridge.)

Virginia Prince returned to Los Angeles

by the later 1940s, but she remained in touch with Lawrence and her network of transgender contacts, especially those living in Southern California, to whom Prince added her own growing circle of cross-dressing friends and acquaintances. In 1952, Prince and a group of transvestites who met regularly in Long Beach published an unprecedented newsletter—*Transvestia: The Journal of the American Society for Equality in Dress*—which they distributed to a mailing list consisting largely of Lawrence's correspondents. This little mimeographed publication, which existed for only two issues, is arguably the first overtly political transgender publication in US history. Even its subtitle seems deliberately intended to evoke the dress reform activism of nineteenth-century first wave feminism. The periodical made a plea for the social toleration of transvestitism, which it was careful to define as a practice of heterosexual men, distinct from homosexual drag.

Prince and her fledgling heterosexual transvestite rights movement soon had another identity category from which to distinguish themselves, once Christine Jorgensen burst onto the scene on December 1, 1952. Jorgensen, assigned male at her birth to Danish American parents in the Bronx in 1926, made international headlines with news of her successful genital transformation surgery in Copenhagen. A shy and somewhat effeminate youth, Jorgensen had been drafted into the army for a year after graduating high school. She was pursuing a career as a photographer and film editor without any great success when she learned in 1949 that hormonal and surgical "sex change" was possible—in Europe. Given that the procedures she underwent in Copenhagen had by then been performed numerous times with little fanfare, Jorgensen's instant and worldwide celebrity came as something of a surprise (even though she herself, denials to the contrary, seems to have first called her story to the attention of the press). In a year when hydrogen bombs were being tested in the Pacific, war was raging in Korea, England had crowned a new queen, and Jonas Salk was working on the polio vaccine, Jorgensen was the most written-about topic in the media in 1953.

Part of the extreme fascination with Jorgensen undoubtedly had to do with the fact that she could present herself in public as young, pretty, gracious, and dignified—but another part surely had to do with the mid-twentieth-century awe over scientific technology, which now could not only split atoms but also, apparently, turn a man into a woman. It had something to do with the fact that Jorgensen was the first transgender person to receive significant media attention who happened to be from the United States, which had risen to a new level of international geopolitical importance in the aftermath of World War II. The media made much of the fact that Jorgensen was an "ex-GI," suggesting profound anxieties about masculinity and sexuality. There had been a great deal of attention to male homosexuality in the military during World War II, and maybe, some thought, gender transformation represented a solution to that perceived problem. But if a macho archetype such as "the soldier" could be transformed into a stereotypically feminine "blonde bombshell," what might that mean for a man of average—and now apparently more precarious—virility? A final contributing factor was intense attention to social gender roles. With millions of women who had worked outside the home during the war being steered back toward feminine domesticity, and millions of demobilized military men trying to fit themselves back into the civilian social order, questions of what made a man a man or a woman a woman, and what their respective roles in life should be, were very much up for debate. The feminist movement of the 1960s took shape in reaction to socially conservative solutions to these questions, and transgender issues have been a touchstone for those same debates ever since fate thrust Christine Jorgensen into the spotlight.

Jorgensen, who went on to a successful career in show business, never considered herself a political activist, but she was well aware of the historic role she had to play as a public advocate for the issues that were central to her own life. Thousands of people wrote to her, many of them offering variations on the theme expressed by a French transgender woman who told Jorgensen that her story "touched me deeply and gave me a new hope for the future," or the person in upstate New York who wrote, "May God bless you for your courage so that other people may more clearly understand our problem." One correspondent told Jorgensen, "You are a champion of the downtrodden minorities who strive to live within their God-given rights"; another, in a letter to Jorgensen's parents, noted that there are "hundreds of thousands of people who look to Chris today as a sort of liberation." Jorgensen herself, after her return to the United States in 1953 generated an avalanche of attention from the paparazzi, told her doctors back in Copenhagen that she needed "as much good publicity as possible for the sake of all those to whom I am a representation of themselves."

Christine Jorgensen became the most famous transgender person in the world when news of her 1952 "sex change" surgery made headlines around the world. (PHOTO CREDIT: ROYAL DANISH LIBRARY.)

Jorgensen's fame was a watershed event in transgender history. It brought an unprecedented level of public awareness to transgender issues, and it helped define the terms that would structure identity politics in the decades ahead. Christine Jorgensen was originally identified in the media as a "hermaphrodite," or intersex person, with a rare physical condition in which her "true" femaleness was masked by an only apparent maleness. But she was soon relabeled a "transvestite," in that older sense developed by Hirschfeld, in which the term referred to a wider range of transgender phenomena than it does today. That difference in usage results largely from the efforts of Virginia Prince in the 1950s and 1960s, partly in response to Jorgensen, to redefine *transvestitism* as a synonym for heterosexual male cross-dressing. Harry Benjamin simultaneously started promoting the word *transsexual* to distinguish people such as Jorgensen, who sought surgical transformation, from people such as Prince, who did not.

Both transvestitism and transsexuality came to be seen as something different from either homosexuality or intersexuality. All four categories strove to articulate the complex and variable interrelations between social gender, psychological identity, and physical sex—intellectual labor that informed the concept of a "sex/gender system" that became an important theoretical development within the emerging second wave feminist movement. By the end of the 1950s, the identity labels and border skirmishes between identity-based communities that still inform transgender activism today had largely fallen into place.

Government Harassment

In late 1959, a little event with big implications for transgender political history started to unfold in Los Angeles, when Virginia Prince pursued a friend's suggestion that she begin a personal correspondence with an individual on the East Coast. This third person, who self-represented as a lesbian, had expressed a desire through their mutual acquaintance to be put in written contact with Prince. Prince subsequently received a photograph from her East Coast correspondent (whom neither she nor her friend had ever met face to face) of two women being sexual with one another, which bore the caption "Me and You." Prince's correspondent invited her to "ask anything," and, as the intimacy of the correspondence deepened, Prince sent a letter describing a lesbian sexual fantasy involving the two of them. Prince's correspondent, it soon turned out, was another male cross-dresser, one who happened to be under surveillance by federal postal authorities for soliciting and receiving obscene materials, and whose personal mail was being examined surreptitiously by the government as part of an ongoing criminal investigation. In 1960, postal inspectors questioned Prince and ultimately decided, on the basis of this incident, to prosecute her for the crime of distributing obscenity through the US mail.

The events at the heart of this case—sort of an old-school, paper-based version of online sex—prefigure some of the conundrums about identity that are now routine features of communication in the Internet age. How do you know if that person you met online really is, for example, an eighteen-year-old aspiring female pop vocalist from Portland rather than a balding forty-year-old accountant from Akron, when you have little way of knowing how the self-image that person presents online relates to the way he or she walks around in the world? What does "really" really mean, when you might never meet face to face anyway? And why should the government care in the first place what two adults do in a private communication? Why should incongruence between various presentations of gender, or a frank but personal discussion of sexuality, be considered a matter of state interest or be considered obscene?

That such an incident became the target of a criminal investigation in the mid-twentieth century speaks volumes about the depth of transgender political struggles. What is at stake is not just what conventionally counts as political activity within modern society (such as staging protest rallies, committing acts of civil disobedience, organizing workers, passing laws, registering voters, or trying to change public opinion) but also the very configurations of body, sense of self, practices of desire, modes of comportment, and forms of social relationships that qualify one in the first place as a fit subject for citizenship.

As the Prince prosecution demonstrates, the state's actions often regulate bodies, in ways both great and small, by enmeshing them within norms and expectations that determine what kinds of lives are deemed livable or useful and by shutting down the spaces of possibility and imaginative transformation where people's lives begin to exceed and escape the state's uses for them. This is a deep, structural problem within the logic of modern societies, which essentially perform a cost-benefit analysis when allocating social resources. People are expected to work in the ways demanded by the state—paying taxes, serving in the military, reproducing a population that will serve as the nation's future workforce, and performing socially useful services. Those who don't or can't function this way—whether through physical impairment, denial of opportunity, or personal choice—have a harder time sustaining themselves and justifying their very existence. Their situations—being black or female or disabled or queer—are not deemed to be valuable or worthy in their own right. Transgender lives are similarly devalued; they are considered neither useful nor happy lives to live, nor are they seen as offering any kind of value to society by virtue of their transness.

Such theoretical complexities notwithstanding, Prince's obscenity case, rooted as it was in government surveillance of the mail, helps situate early transgender political history within the anticommunist hysteria about national security at the height of the Cold War. It links particularly closely to the recurrent "lavender scares" of the period, in which gays were witch-hunted out of positions in government, industry, and education, based on the paranoid belief that such "perverts," besides being of dubious moral character, posed security risks because their illegal "lifestyle" made them vulnerable to blackmail or exploitation by enemies of the

LITERATURE AND OBSCENITY

Legal and social definitions of *obscenity* changed rapidly in the decades after World War II in ways that ultimately made information about variant gender and sexual practices (many of which were then deemed obscene) more easily accessible for many people. Cheap paperback books became very popular in this period, and—as long as the publishers could argue that the works had some literary, artistic, or historical significance—they often managed to evade censorship even when dealing with stigmatized topics. Several transgender-themed mass market paperback books were published in the 1950s, most of them trying to cash in on the Christine Jorgensen craze. These included the 1953 intersex saga *Half,* by Jordan Park, and a reissue of the 1933 *Man into Woman,* Niels Hoyer's biography of the Danish painter Lilli Elbe.

Much of the so-called homophile nonfiction periodical literature from this period, which advocated social tolerance for homosexuals, was deemed obscene in the late 1950s and early 1960s. A notable obscenity case involved *ONE* magazine, published by the Los Angeles homophile organization ONE, starting in 1952; *ONE* has the distinction of being the first pro-gay publication to be sold openly at newsstands. In the mid-1950s, a federal district court in California declared it obscene and banned it from the mail. That the US Supreme Court subsequently overturned the decision in 1958 indicates how quickly the legal climate on obscenity issues was beginning to shift, as does another landmark legal decision of this period. H. Lynn Womack, a former Georgetown University professor turned gay erotica publisher, successfully sued the postmaster general in 1961 for confiscating copies of his homoerotic

continues

LITERATURE AND OBSCENITY *continued*

Grecian Guild body-builder magazines. As late as 1964, however, Sanford Aday and Wallace de Ortega Maxey, two mail-order publishers of soft-core "sleaze paperbacks" (including transgender titles such as 1958's *The Lady Was a Man*), were convicted on federal charges of shipping "dirty books" across state lines, fined $25,000 each, and sentenced to a total of forty years in prison. The men were released a few years later, after the Supreme Court embraced a more lenient legal definition of obscenity.

The gradual relaxation of obscenity standards reflected the broader cultural shifts of the "sexual revolution" fomented by Alfred Kinsey's best-selling reports on male and female sexuality (published in 1948 and 1953, respectively), the advent of *Playboy* magazine in 1953, the introduction of oral contraception ("the Pill") in 1960, and the more open-minded ethos of the youth counterculture that took shape among the post–World War II Baby Boomer generation. The first long-running transgender community publications appeared just at this historical juncture, when new possibilities for publishing work on nonnormative gender and sexual expression were first starting to emerge.

state. Consequently, the emerging transgender politics of the late 1950s and early 1960s can't be cleanly separated from the history of official persecution of homosexuals. It needs to be understood as part of an overarching set of struggles about privacy, censorship, political dissent, minority rights, freedom of expression, and sexual liberation. But trans people, particularly those who consistently tried in daily life to present themselves to others as the gender they considered themselves to be, faced additional challenges. To whatever extent they failed to pass flawlessly as a cisgender person, their very presence in public space was criminalized, and they were at greater risk of extralegal violence from the police and some members of the public. Those without political connections, money, or racial privilege were especially vulnerable.

Coincidentally or not—though probably not—between the time Prince wrote the "lesbian letter" that initially brought her to the attention of the authorities and the time she was charged with a serious crime, she had started publishing *Transvestia* magazine, which turned out to be the first long-running transgender-oriented periodical in the United States. Launched in 1960 and published several times a year into the 1980s, *Transvestia* revived the short-lived publication of the same name that Prince and her circle of cross-dressing friends had published in 1952. Like the homophile literature it closely resembled, Prince's *Transvestia* excluded explicit sexual content and focused on social commentary, educational outreach, self-help advice, and autobiographical vignettes drawn from her own life and the lives of her readers. The magazine significantly shifted the political meaning of transvestitism, moving it away from being the expression of a criminalized sexual activity and toward being the common denominator of a new (and potentially political) identity-based minority community. That shift undoubtedly fueled the determination of federal prosecutors to convict Prince of a felony and to halt the distribution of *Transvestia,* just as they had tried to halt the distribution of *ONE* magazine and other homophile publications.

In such a volatile legal landscape, things could have turned out much worse than they did when Virginia Prince's case went to trial in Los Angeles Federal Court in February 1961. She pleaded guilty to a lesser charge and avoided serving time in prison by accepting five years of probation, during which time she agreed to refrain from public cross-dressing and from using the mail for indecent purposes. Although postal authorities tried to ban distribution of *Transvestia,* the court, reflecting the trend toward increasingly lenient definitions of obscenity, did not find it to be obscene, and postal inspectors never pursued charges against the publication's subscribers. In 1962, with the tacit consent of high-level US Postal Service bureaucrats with whom Prince had been pleading her case, the federal judge declared Prince's probationary sentence to be fulfilled; she never had another brush with the law.

The First Modern Transgender Organizations

While her obscenity case was working its way through court, Virginia Prince founded the first long-lasting transgender organizations in the United States. In 1961, she convened a clandestine meeting in Los Angeles of several local *Transvestia* subscribers—instructing them all, unbeknownst to one another, to rendezvous at a certain hotel room, each carrying a pair of stockings and high heels concealed in a brown paper bag. Once the men were assembled, Prince instructed them all to put on the shoes she had asked them to bring—simultaneously implicating all of them in the stigmatized activity of cross-dressing and thereby forming a communal (and self-protective) bond. This group became known as the Hose and Heels Club and began meeting regularly. In 1962, once Prince's legal troubles were behind her, her community-organizing efforts kicked into high gear. She transformed the Hose and Heels Club into the "Alpha Chapter" of a new national organization, the Foundation for Personality Expression (FPE), which she modeled on the collegiate sorority system and which soon had several chapters across the country.

Prince used FPE, later known as the Society for the Second Self, or Tri-Ess, as a platform to promote her personal philosophy about gender, which she outlined in books such as *How to Be a Woman Though Male* and *The Transvestite and His Wife*. Prince believed that cross-dressing allowed men to express their "full personality" in a

DRAG BALLS

While white suburban transgender people were sneaking out to clandestine meetings, many transgender people of color were highly visible parts of urban culture. "Miss Major" came out as trans as a teenager in the late 1950s in Chicago. In this 1998 interview, she describes the African American drag ball subculture of her youth.

> *We had the balls then, where we could go out and dress up. You had to keep your eyes open, had to watch your back, but you learned how to deal with that, and how to relax into it, and how to have a good time. It was a pleasure, a wonder—even with the*

Four "queens" arrive at a San Francisco drag ball in 1965. (PHOTO CREDIT: HENRI LELEU, GLBT HISTORICAL SOCIETY, SAN FRANCISCO.)

continues

DRAG BALLS *continued*

confusion. We didn't know at the time that we were questioning our gender. We just knew that this felt right. There wasn't all this terminology, all this labeling—you know what I mean?

[The balls] were phenomenal! It was like going to the Oscars show today. Everybody dressed up. Guys in tuxedos, queens in gowns that you would not believe—I mean, things that they would have been working on all year. There was a queen in the South Side who would do the South City Ball. There was one on the North Side who would do the Maypole Ball. There were different ones in different areas at different times. And the straight people who would come and watch, they were different than the ones who come today. They just appreciated what was going on. They would applaud the girls when they were getting out of one Cadillac after another. It was just that the money was there, and the timing was right, and the energy was there to do this thing with an intensity that people just don't seem to have today. It seems to have dissipated. Then it was always a wonder—whether you participated, whether you watched, whether you just wore a little cocktail dress and a small fur coat—it was just a nice time.

world that required a strict division between the masculine and the feminine. FPE meetings, which were highly secretive affairs held in private homes or hotel rooms, tended to involve the conduct of organizational business, a presentation by an invited speaker, and time for socializing. Prince personally controlled membership in these groups well into the 1970s, and she limited members to married heterosexual men, excluding gays, male-to-female transsexuals, and individuals who had been assigned female at birth.

The membership restrictions of FPE, and the form and content of its meetings, demonstrate a familiar pattern in minority identity politics in US history: it is often the most privileged elements of a population affected by a particular civil injustice or social oppression who have the opportunity to organize first. In organizing around the one thing that interferes with or complicates their privilege, their organizations tend to reproduce that very privilege. This was certainly true of FPE, which was explicitly geared toward protecting the privileges of predominantly white, middle-class men who used their money and access to private property to create a space in which they could express a stigmatized aspect of themselves in a way that didn't jeopardize their jobs or social standing. Prince herself took the leading role in driving wedges between transvestite, transsexual, gay and lesbian, and feminist communities, and she did not envision an inclusive, expansive, progressive, and multifaceted transgender movement. And yet, she unequivocally played a key role in founding just such a movement. After beginning to live full-time as a woman in 1968, Prince worked vigorously for many years to promote various transgender causes, such as the ability to change gender designation on state-issued identification documents. Her legal troubles in the early 1960s were potentially quite serious, and if for nothing else she should be honored in transgender political history for the personal courage she showed in facing a felony conviction and federal prison sentence all for the ostensible crime of "using the mail while transgender."

CHAPTER 3

TRANS LIBERATION

AS TRANSGENDER PHENOMENA came under mounting social and medical regulation in the United States between the 1850s and the 1950s, daily life for some trans people shifted into increasingly distinct public and private spheres. Class and race privilege encouraged white people with transgender feelings, especially if they enjoyed a measure of social respectability or financial security, to construct their identities in isolation, to engage in cross-dressing only furtively, and to form networks with others like themselves only at great risk, unless they were willing to present themselves as people in need of medical or psychiatric help. Ironically, it was the most closeted and least political segment of the transgender population that first formed sustainable organizations and first became targets of federal prosecution. At roughly the same time as Virginia Prince's run-in with the postal inspectors, however, another form of transgender political history began to take shape among people who lacked many of the privileges enjoyed by members of Prince's Foundation for Personality Expression. These transgender people had a very different relationship to (or membership in) gay communities and communities of color, as well as to public space and to

STREET QUEENS

John Rechy, born in 1934 in El Paso, Texas, is the author of more than a dozen books, many of which revolve around his youthful involvement in the world of male hustlers. *City of Night,* excerpted below, paints a vivid portrait of "Miss Destiny" and other "street queens" in Los Angeles in the early 1960s.

> *As I stand on the corner of 6th and Main, a girlish Negro Youngman with round eyes swishes up: "Honey," she says—just like that and shrilly loudly, enormous gestures punctuating her words, "you look like you jest got into town. If you aint gotta place, I got a real nice pad. . . . " I only stare at her. "Why, baby," she says, "dont you look so startled—this is L.A.!—and thank God for that! Even queens like me got certain rights!*
>
> *" . . . Well," she sighs, "I guess you wanna look around first. So I'll jest give you my number." She handed me a card, with her name, telephone number, address: Elaborately Engraved. "Jest you call me—anytime!" she said. . . .*
>
> *Looking at Chuck and Miss Destiny—as she rushes on now about the Turbulent Times—I know the scene: Chuck the masculine cowboy and Miss Destiny the femme queen: making it from day to park to bar to day like all the others in that ratty world of downtown L.A. which I will make my own: the world of queens technically men but no one thinks of them that way—always "she"—their "husbands" being the masculine vagrants—fleetingly and often out of convenience sharing the queens' pads—never considering theyre involved with another man (the queen), and only for scoring (which is making or taking sexmoney, getting a meal, making a pad)—he is himself not considered "queer"—he remains, in the vocabulary of that world, "trade."*

It was real-life people such as Rechy's character Miss Destiny who, in the 1960s, were among the first gender-nonconforming people to

continues

become militant at places such as Cooper Do-Nut. However, claiming figures such as Miss Destiny as part of transgender history is controversial in some quarters, because some people say that the word *transgender* didn't exist back then, or that some queens considered themselves gay men rather than trans women. But some queens from this period did move on to live their lives as women, and they do look back on their experiences as being part of transgender history—and many contemporary trans people certainly find inspiration in the fierce determination exhibited by people decades ago who lived lives in public that challenged conventional expectations for what it meant to be a man or a woman, whatever those people thought of themselves.

For a good history of male hustler culture, including the involvement of transwomen, see Mack Friedman's *Strapped for Cash: A History of American Hustler Culture,* published in 2003. Hubert Selby Jr. delivers an emotionally devastating portrait of working-class queer sexuality in post–World War II America in his *Last Exit to Brooklyn* (first published in 1964), which integrates the story of a trans character, Georgette, into the overarching story of life in a gritty urban neighborhood.

the police. They confronted on a daily basis all the things that FPE's membership worked so hard to avoid.

Militant Foreshadowings

In a 2005 interview, John Rechy, author of *City of Night* and other classic mid-twentieth-century novels set in the gritty urban underworlds where sexual outlaws and gender nonconformists carved out spaces they could call their own, spoke of a previously undocumented incident in May of 1959, when transgender and gay resentment of police oppression erupted into collective resistance. According to Rechy, it happened at Cooper Do-Nut, a doughnut and coffee hangout that stayed open all night on a rough stretch of Main Street in Los Angeles and that happened to be situated between two popular gay bars. An ethnically mixed crowd of drag queens and male hustlers, many of them Latino or African American, frequented Cooper's, as the business was colloquially known, along with the people who enjoyed their company or bought their sexual services. Police cars regularly patrolled the vicinity and often stopped to question people in the area for no reason at all. The police would demand identification—which, for trans people whose appearance might not match the name or gender designation on their IDs, often led to arrest on suspicion of prostitution, vagrancy, loitering, or many other so-called nuisance crimes. On that night in May 1959, when the police came in and arbitrarily started rounding up the drag queens milling around Cooper's, they and others on the scene spontaneously resisted arrest en masse. The incident started with customers throwing doughnuts at the cops and ended with fighting in the streets, as squad cars and police wagons converged at the site to make arrests. In the ensuing confusion, many people who had been arrested, including Rechy, managed to escape.

The disturbance at Cooper Do-Nut was an unplanned outburst of frustration, and it was no doubt typical of other unrecorded and unremembered acts of spur-of-the-moment resistance to antitrans and antigay oppression. A similar though nonviolent incident took place in Philadelphia in 1965 at Dewey's, a lunch counter and late-night coffeehouse that appealed to a crowd similar to the one that frequented Cooper's. Since the 1940s, it had been popular with gays, lesbians, drag queens, and street sex workers as a place to go after the bars had closed, as well as a place for cheap food all day long. In April 1965, Dewey's started refusing to serve young customers who wore what one gay newspaper of the day euphemistically described as "nonconformist clothing," claiming that "gay kids" were driving away other business. Customers rallied to protest, and on April 25, more than 150 patrons were turned away by the management. Three teenagers refused to leave after being denied service in what appears to be the first act of civil disobedience over anti-transgender discrimination; they, along with a gay activist who advised them of their legal rights, were arrested and subsequently found guilty on misdemeanor charges of disorderly conduct. During the next week, Dewey's patrons and members of Philadelphia's homophile community set up an informational picket line at the restaurant, where they passed out thousands of pieces of literature protesting the lunch counter's treatment of gender-variant young people. On May 2, activists staged another sit-in. The police were again called in, but this time made no arrests. The restaurant's management backed down and promised "an immediate cessation of all indiscriminate denials of service."

Compton's Cafeteria in San Francisco's Tenderloin neighborhood was the scene of an early episode of transgender resistance to social oppression when transgender women, gay men, and sex workers fought back against police harassment in August 1966. (Photo credit: Jonathan Price.)

The Dewey's incident, like the one at Cooper Do-Nut, demonstrates the overlap between gay and transgender activism in the working-class districts of major US cities. Historian Marc Stein, in *City of Sisterly and Brotherly Loves: Lesbian and Gay Philadelphia, 1945–1972,* tells how the Janus Society, Philadelphia's main gay and lesbian organization at the time, issued the following statement in its newsletter after the events of May 2, 1965:

> All too often, there is a tendency to be concerned with the rights of homosexuals as long as they somehow appear to be heterosexual,

> whatever that is. The masculine woman and the feminine man often are looked down upon . . . but the Janus Society is concerned with the worth of an individual and the manner in which she or he comports himself. What is offensive today we have seen become the style of tomorrow, and even if what is offensive today remains offensive tomorrow to some persons, there is no reason to penalize non-conformist behavior unless there is direct anti-social behavior connected with it.

The Dewey's incident further illustrates the extent to which the tactics of minority rights activism cross-fertilized different movements. Lunch counter sit-ins had been developed as a form of protest to oppose racial segregation in the South, but they proved equally effective when used to promote the interests of sexual and gender minorities. It would be a mistake, however, to think that the African American civil rights struggle simply "influenced" early gay and transgender activism at Dewey's, for to do so would be to assume that all the gay and transgender people involved were white. Many of the queer people who patronized Dewey's were themselves people of color, and they were not "borrowing" a tactic developed by another movement.

The Compton's Cafeteria Riot of 1966

By the middle of the 1960s, life in the United States was being transformed by several large-scale social movements. The post–World War II Baby Boomer generation was coming into young adulthood at the very moment the US war in Vietnam was beginning to escalate. A youth-oriented cultural rebellion began to unfold in which countercultural styles in music and fashion—rock and roll, psychedelic drugs, mod clothing, free love—offered significant challenges to an older generation's notion of acceptable gender and sexual expression. Long hair on men and button-fly blue jeans on women actually made political statements about the war, the military draft, and the general drift of mainstream society. The African American civil rights movement was reaching a crescendo, buoyed by passage in 1964 of the Civil Rights Act and the Voting Rights Act in 1965, as well as by the birth of a radical new Black Power movement. Similar ethnic pride and liberation movements were beginning to vitalize Chicano/a, Asian American, and Native American people. To a certain extent, the simultaneous white gay liberation and radical feminist movements modeled themselves on these ethnic movements, conceptualizing gay people and women as oppressed social minority groups. National political life, which had been thrown into turmoil after the 1963 assassination of President John F. Kennedy, reached a tragic low point with the 1968 assassinations of his brother Robert F. Kennedy and the Reverend Martin Luther King Jr. The most militant phase of the transgender movement for social change, from 1966 to 1973, was part of this massive social upheaval.

The 1966 Compton's Cafeteria Riot in San Francisco's seedy Tenderloin neighborhood was similar to the incidents at Cooper Do-Nut and Dewey's. For the first time, however, direct action in the streets by trans people resulted in long-lasting institutional change. One weekend night in August—the precise date remains tantalizingly unrecovered—Compton's, a twenty-four-hour cafeteria at the corner of Turk and Taylor Streets, was buzzing with its usual late-night crowd of drag queens, hustlers, slummers, cruisers, runaway teens, and down-and-out neighborhood regulars. The restaurant's management became annoyed by a noisy young crowd of queens at one table who seemed to be spending a lot of time without spending a lot of money. So they called in the police to roust them—as they had been doing with increasing frequency throughout the summer. A surly police officer, accustomed to manhandling

Vanguard, founded in 1965, was the first gay and transgender youth organization in the United States. The members published a psychedelically illustrated magazine (also called Vanguard*) from the mid-1960s until the early 1970s.* (PHOTO CREDIT: *VANGUARD* MAGAZINE.)

Compton's clientele with impunity, grabbed the arm of one of the queens and tried to drag her away. She unexpectedly threw her coffee in his face, and a melee erupted. Plates, trays, cups, saucers, and silverware flew through the air at the startled police officers, who ran outside and called for backup. Compton's' customers turned over the tables and smashed the plate-glass windows before pouring out of the restaurant and into the streets. The police wagons arrived, and street fighting broke out in the vicinity of Compton's, all around the corner of Turk and Taylor. Drag queens beat the police with their heavy purses and the sharp stiletto heels of their shoes. A police car was vandalized, a newspaper stand was burned to the ground, and—in the words of the best available source on what happened that night, a retrospective account by gay liberation activist Reverend Raymond Broshears, published in the program of San Francisco's first Gay Pride march in 1972—"general havoc was raised that night in the Tenderloin." The small restaurant had been packed when the fighting broke out, so the riot probably involved fifty or sixty patrons, plus police officers and any neighborhood residents or late-night passersby who joined the fray.

Contextualizing Compton's

Although the exact date of the riot remains a mystery—none of the mainstream San Francisco daily newspapers covered the story; police reports have conveniently disappeared; surviving participants who were interviewed decades later remembered only that it happened on a summer weekend night; and Broshears's account (written six years after the fact) said only that the riot took place in August—its underlying causes are clear. Understanding why the riot happened where and when it did reveals a great deal about the issues that have historically motivated the transgender social justice struggle and helps us understand similar dynamics at work today.

The location of the riot was by no means random. San Francisco's downtown Tenderloin neighborhood had been a sex-work district since the early 1900s. In fact, if you look up the word *tenderloin* in many dictionaries, you'll find that one slang meaning is actually an inner-city "vice" district controlled by corrupt police officers. As large cities formed in the United States in the nineteenth century, they typically developed certain neighborhoods in which activities that weren't tolerated elsewhere—prostitution, gambling, selling and consuming criminalized drugs, and sexually explicit entertainment—were effectively permitted. Police often turned a blind eye to this illicit activity, often because the cops on the beat, and sometimes their superiors in the station house, were getting a cut of the profits in exchange for not arresting the individuals engaged in those activities. Only occasionally, when civic or religious groups mounted a morality crusade or some sex scandal implicated a high-ranking politician, did police make "sweeps" of

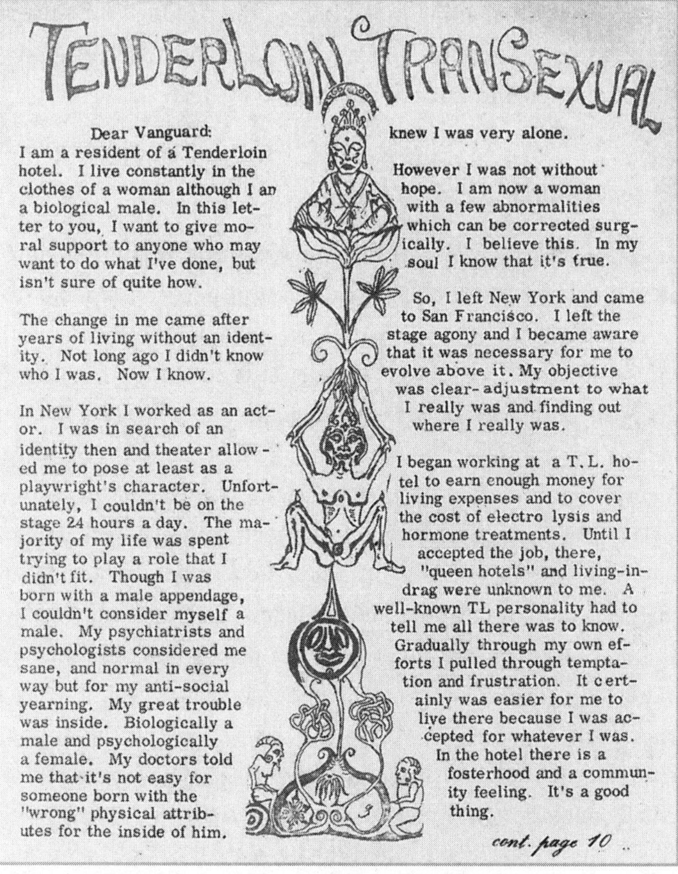

TENDERLOIN TRANSEXUAL

Dear Vanguard:
I am a resident of a Tenderloin hotel. I live constantly in the clothes of a woman although I an a biological male. In this letter to you, I want to give moral support to anyone who may want to do what I've done, but isn't sure of quite how.

The change in me came after years of living without an identity. Not long ago I didn't know who I was. Now I know.

In New York I worked as an actor. I was in search of an identity then and theater allowed me to pose at least as a playwright's character. Unfortunately, I couldn't be on the stage 24 hours a day. The majority of my life was spent trying to play a role that I didn't fit. Though I was born with a male appendage, I couldn't consider myself a male. My psychiatrists and psychologists considered me sane, and normal in every way but for my anti-social yearning. My great trouble was inside. Biologically a male and psychologically a female. My doctors told me that it's not easy for someone born with the "wrong" physical attributes for the inside of him. knew I was very alone.

However I was not without hope. I am now a woman with a few abnormalities which can be corrected surgically. I believe this. In my soul I know that it's true.

So, I left New York and came to San Francisco. I left the stage agony and I became aware that it was necessary for me to evolve above it. My objective was clear- adjustment to what I really was and finding out where I really was.

I began working at a T. L. hotel to earn enough money for living expenses and to cover the cost of electro lysis and hormone treatments. Until I accepted the job, there, "queen hotels" and living-in-drag were unknown to me. A well-known TL personality had to tell me all there was to know. Gradually through my own efforts I pulled through temptation and frustration. It certainly was easier for me to live there because I was accepted for whatever I was. In the hotel there is a fosterhood and a community feeling. It's a good thing.

cont. page 10

Transgender people faced serious housing and employment discrimination in the 1960s, forcing many to live in dangerous and impoverished neighborhoods. (PHOTO CREDIT: *VANGUARD* MAGAZINE.)

the neighborhood. Soon enough, however, it would be business as usual again.

The Tenderloin was just this sort of neighborhood. Much of the so-called vice trade in the neighborhood was supported by non-residents of one sort or another: downtown office workers getting a "massage" on their lunch breaks, bar-hoppers looking for a place to sober up after last call, teenage thrill seekers and out-of-town tourists eager for some racy big-city entertainment, suburban heroin junkies looking to score a fix. But the neighborhood's resident population tended to be those who could least afford to live elsewhere or who were prevented from doing so: released convicts and parolees, old-timers on small pensions, recent immigrants, pimps, prostitutes, drug addicts, alcoholics—and trans women.

Housing and employment discrimination against transgender people is still prevalent in the United States, and this discrimination was even more common in the past than it is now. In the 1960s, even more so than today, a person who looked transgender would be less likely to be rented to and would have a great deal of trouble finding work. As a result, a great many transgender women lived in the Tenderloin in cheap residential hotels, many of them along Turk Street near Compton's. To meet their basic survival needs they often worked as prostitutes or as maids in the hotels and bars where their friends sold sex. Although most people who participated in the Tenderloin's underground economy of sex, drugs, and after-hours entertainment were free to come and go, the neighborhood functioned as more of an involuntary containment zone, or ghetto, for transgender women. Police actually helped concentrate a population of transgender women in the Tenderloin by directing them to go there when they were picked up in other parts of the city.

The police could be especially vicious to "street queens," whom they considered bottom-of-the-barrel sex workers and who were the least able to complain about mistreatment. Transgender women working the streets were often arrested on suspicion of prostitution even if they were just going to the corner store or talking with friends; they might be driven around in squad cars for hours, forced to perform oral sex, strip-searched, or, after arriving at the jail, humiliated in front of other prisoners. Transgender women in jail often would have their heads forcibly shaved or, if they resisted, be placed in solitary confinement in "the hole." And because they were legally men (with male genitalia in spite of their social lives as women, and often in spite of having breasts and no facial hair) they would be placed in the men's jail, where their femininity made them especially vulnerable to sexual assault, rape, and murder.

This chronically bad situation became even worse in the mid-1960s, when US involvement in the war in Vietnam escalated. Wartime is typically a time of heightened surveillance of commercial sexual activity in cities where large numbers of troops are being mobilized for deployment. Military and civilian police, along with public health officials, cooperate to prevent troops (many of them quite eager to escape thoughts of battlefield death with wild sexual escapades) from acquiring sexually transmitted infections that might compromise their combat readiness and which might even be spread within the ranks by homosexual activity. There were wartime crackdowns on prostitution in San Francisco during the Spanish-American War in the Philippines in the 1890s, during World War II in the 1940s, and during the Korean conflict in the 1950s. Among the hardest-hit establishments in San Francisco during the crackdown associated with the 1964–1966 escalation of US troops in Vietnam were the gay and drag bars.

Yet another factor that changed an already grim situation from bad to worse for transgender women in the Tenderloin was the effect of urban renewal and redevelopment. Their increasingly serious plight was directly related to very broad-scale social and economic changes. As in other major US cities, San Francisco's built environment underwent a major transformation in the two decades after World War II as the city "modernized." Some of this redevelopment was driven by needs created during the war years. Many working-class and poor people had left small towns for war-related work in the major coastal cities in the 1940s and had been housed temporarily in quickly constructed housing projects. When the war was over, many soldiers came home from overseas to find their families living in new cities rather than their old hometowns, putting a further burden on city housing. Complicating things even more, many of these new urban residents were people of color, who were not well integrated or welcomed into the fabric of white-dominated cities once the need for their wartime labor had passed. Part of the government's response to the problems of postwar adjustment was to fund big new housing projects for working-class people and to help former soldiers buy suburban homes with low-interest home loans.

San Francisco business elites and city planners, like their counterparts elsewhere, tried to turn the necessity of solving pressing urban problems into an opportunity to reenvision the city in ways that reflected their own interests. They imagined a new and improved San Francisco Bay Area, with San Francisco itself functioning as the center of finance, culture, high-tech industry, and tourism for the entire region. Surrounding San Francisco to the east and south would be a semicircle of heavy industry and, beyond that, residential suburbs. New freeways and public transportation systems would have to be built to bring office workers from the suburbs to the center of business downtown.

In the process of reorganizing the entire fabric of daily urban life, old neighborhoods had to be destroyed or relocated. To one side of the Tenderloin were the Fillmore and Western Addition neighborhoods that had become mostly black during the war years (after first being emptied of Japanese American residents who had been sent to internment camps); residents there were forcibly removed to new housing projects on the edge of the city, in Bayview and Hunters Point, and entire blocks bulldozed for newer higher-density apartments. To the other side of the Tenderloin was the South of Market neighborhood (sometimes called Skid Row), which had revolved around the maritime economy—lots of short-term residential hotels and rooming houses for sailors who would stay in town for only a few weeks or months, working-class bars and restaurants, and industries related to shipping and commerce. During post–World War II redevelopment, San Francisco's port was shut down and moved across the bay to Oakland; doing so required breaking the waterfront labor unions, which created less favorable economic conditions for many working-class people. The waterfront-oriented district itself started to become derelict and was then condemned and slated for redevelopment as museums, convention facilities, and other tourist-oriented establishments. The physical destruction of these important black and working-class neighborhoods in the 1950s and 1960s left the Tenderloin as the last remaining enclave of affordable housing in central San Francisco. New residents coming in from adjacent areas began to displace the Tenderloin's most vulnerable and at-risk residents—transgender women who worked as street prostitutes and lived in the cheapest hotels.

In response to the massive social dislocations of urban renewal and redevelopment, Tenderloin residents launched a grassroots campaign for economic justice in 1965. They were inspired in equal measures by the socially progressive gospel preached by the Reverend Martin Luther King Jr. and other ministers in the civil rights struggle, by the federal government's new War on Poverty programs, and by the vision of radically participatory democratic social movements outlined by Saul Alinsky in his activist handbook *Reveille for Radicals.* Neighborhood activists, including many members of San Francisco's homophile organizations and street-outreach ministers from Glide Memorial United Methodist Church, went door to door in the Tenderloin, organizing the neighborhood and mobilizing it for social change. Their immediate goal was to establish needed social services by qualifying the neighborhood for federal antipoverty funding. Through a quirk of circumstances, the

Tenderloin, one of the poorest areas of the city, was initially excluded from plans to direct more federal funding toward eradicating poverty in San Francisco because of the fact that its residents in the 1960s were almost all white. The coalition of grassroots groups that oversaw the local distribution of federal grant money was based in the black neighborhoods of Bayview, Hunters Point, the Fillmore, and the Western Addition, in the predominantly Latino/a Mission District, and in Chinatown. The Tenderloin organizers not only had to document economic need in their neighborhood but also had to persuade poor communities of color that adding an additional antipoverty target zone predominately populated by white people would be the right thing to do, even if that meant the already existing zones got a smaller slice of a fixed amount of money. Compounding matters even further, most of the white people were queer, and most of the people of color were straight. The eventual establishment of the Central City Anti-Poverty Program thus represented a singular accomplishment in the history of US progressive politics: the first successful multiracial gay-straight alliance for economic justice.

Tenderloin activists involved in the antipoverty organizing campaign were striving to create conditions in which people could truly participate in structuring the society they lived in instead of just reacting to changes created by others. One unexpected consequence of neighborhood mobilization was the formation of Vanguard, an organization made up mostly of young gay hustlers and transgender people. Vanguard, formed in 1965 with the encouragement of a young minister named Adrian Ravarour, is the earliest known queer youth organization in the United States. Its name, which signaled members' perception that they were the cutting edge of a new social movement, shows how seriously they took the ideals of radical democracy. The group's second leader even took a nom de guerre, Jean-Paul Marat, after a famous figure in the French Revolution.

By the summer of 1966, Vanguard was holding informal meetings at Compton's Cafeteria. The restaurant functioned as a chill-out lounge for the whole neighborhood, but for young people who often had no homes, families, or legal employment, who were marginalized by their gender or sexuality, it provided an especially vital resource.

Just a block away from Compton's, Glide Memorial United Methodist Church had been a hotbed of progressive social change since the early 1960s, and it played an important role in weaving together many different strands of Tenderloin activism. It was founded in 1929 by Lilly Glide, the daughter of a prominent family of philanthropists in San Francisco, as a "working man's mission," a place where down-and-out folks could go for a bowl of soup in exchange for listening to a sermon. The congregation had dwindled by the late 1950s, but the church still had a large endowment from the Glide family, prompting the national Methodist leadership to transform Glide Memorial into a model for a new kind of urban Christian ministry, of the sort inspired by the Reverend Martin Luther King Jr.'s civil rights activism. Under the leadership of the Reverend Cecil Williams, who became head pastor in 1966, Glide has become one of the most famous liberal Christian churches in the United States, supported by the likes of Maya Angelou, Oprah Winfrey, and Bill Clinton.

One of the most daring social initiatives launched by Glide in the early 1960s was to establish the Council on Religion and the Homosexual (CRH), the first ecumenical organization to bring the problem of antigay discrimination to the attention of the liberal Protestant churches. Activist ministers at Glide worked with leaders of the early homophile, or gay rights, organizations, to shift the focus of religious concern away from condemning the supposed sin of homosexuality toward ministering to the daily needs of people who suffered—through the loss of family, friends, work, or sense of emotional well-being—because of their sexual orientation. A police raid on a 1965 costume ball, a fund-raiser for the CRH that featured a lot of drag and was attended by many politically progressive San Franciscans, is widely credited with putting gay rights on the agenda of straight civil rights activists in the Bay Area. That same commitment to loving and compassionate attention to stigmatized expressions of sexuality and gender also led activist ministers connected with Glide to support the gay and trans youth group Vanguard.

Vanguard described itself as "an organization of, by, and for the kids on the streets." Its goals were to promote a sense of self-worth among its members, to offer mutual support and companionship, to bring youth issues to the attention of older people, and to assert its presence in the neighborhood. One of the group's early flyers urged people to think past racial divisions and focus instead on shared living conditions. "You've heard about Black Power and White Power," the flyer said before telling its readers to "get ready for Street Power." Vanguard members' basic approach was to treat the street as their home. They cleaned it up, challenged people coming into the neighborhood for sex and drugs to pick up their dirty needles and empty bottles, and intervened with people acting in inappropriate ways. Vanguard's first major political action, however, was to confront the management of Compton's Cafeteria over its poor treatment of trans women and street queens.

Over the summer of 1966, tensions had been on the rise at Compton's between management and customers. As the restaurant's customers increasingly claimed its turf as their own, the management asserted its property rights and business interests more and more strongly. It instituted a "service charge" for each customer to make up for income lost to tables of young people "camping out" and not buying any food, but it applied the charge in a discriminatory and arbitrary manner. It hired security guards to harass the street kids and shoo them outside, particularly the transgender youth. And with greater and greater frequency, it called the cops. In July, Vanguard worked with ministers from Glide and with older members of San Francisco's homophile organizations to set up a picket line protesting the mistreatment of its members, much as the customers and gay activists in Philadelphia had done at Dewey's. In San Francisco, however, the restaurant's management turned a deaf ear to the complaints. Soon after the picket failed to produce any results, frustration boiled over into militant resistance.

One thing that made the incident at Compton's different from similar incidents at Cooper Do-Nut and Dewey's was a new attitude toward transgender health care in the United States. Doctors in Europe had been using hormones and surgery for more than fifty years to improve the quality of life for transgender people who desired those procedures; doctors in the United States had always been reluctant to do so, fearing that to operate or administer hormones would only be colluding with a deranged person's fantasy of "changing sex" or would be enabling a homosexual person to engage in perverse sexual practices. And after 1949, California Attorney General Pat Brown's legal opinion against genital modification created legal vulnerabilities for doctors who performed genital surgery. This situation began to change in July 1966, just before the Compton's Cafeteria riot, when Dr. Harry Benjamin published a pathbreaking book, *The Transsexual Phenomenon*. In it, he used the research he had conducted with transgender patients during the past seventeen years to advocate for the same style of treatment that Magnus Hirschfeld had promoted in Germany before the Nazi takeover. Benjamin essentially argued that a person's gender identity could not be changed and that the doctor's responsibility was thus to help transgender people live fuller and happier lives in the gender they identified as their own. Benjamin's book helped bring about a sea change in medical and legal attitudes. Within a few months of its publication, the first "sex change" program in the United States was established at the Johns Hopkins University Medical School.

The sudden availability of a new medical paradigm for addressing transgender health care needs undoubtedly played a role in creating a flashpoint at Compton's, where long-standing grievances finally erupted into collective resistance. When people struggling against an injustice have no hope that anything will ever change, they use their strength to survive; when they think that their actions matter, that same strength becomes a force for positive change. Because Benjamin worked in San Francisco for part of every year, some of his patients were the very Tenderloin street queens who would soon start fighting back to improve their lives. They were intimately familiar with his work. Of course, not every person assigned male at birth who lived and worked in women's clothes in the Tenderloin wanted surgery or hormones, and not all of those who did thought of themselves as women or as transsexuals. But many of them did. And for those who did, the changes in medical service provision that Benjamin recommended must have been an electrifying call to action. The next time the police raided their favorite neighborhood hangout, they had something to stand up for.

Looking back, it's easy to see how the Compton's Cafeteria riot in 1966 was related to large-scale political, social, and economic developments and was not just an isolated little incident unrelated to other things that were going on in the world. The circumstances that created the conditions for the riot continue to be relevant in trans movements today: discriminatory policing practices that target members of minority communities, urban land-use policies that benefit cultural elites and displace poor people, the unsettling domestic consequences of US foreign wars, access to health care, civil rights activism aiming to expand individual liberties and social tolerance on matters of sexuality and gender, and political coalition building around the structural injustices that affect many different communities. Collective resistance to the oppression of trans people at Compton's Cafeteria did not automatically solve the problems that trans people in the Tenderloin faced daily. It did, however, create a space in which it became possible for the city of San Francisco to begin relating differently to its transgender citizens—to begin treating them, in fact, as citizens with legitimate needs instead of simply as a problem to get rid of. That shift in awareness was a crucial step for contemporary transgender social justice movements—the beginning of a new relationship to state power and social legitimacy. It would not have happened the way that it did without direct action in the streets on the part of transgender women who were fighting for their own survival.

A New Network of Services and Organizations

Several important developments for the transgender movement took place in San Francisco in the months after the Compton's Cafeteria riot. The Central City Anti-Poverty Program Office opened that fall as a result of the Tenderloin neighborhood organizing campaign. This multiservice agency included an office for the police community-relations liaison officer to the homophile community, a police sergeant by the name of Elliott Blackstone. One afternoon shortly after the agency opened, a transgender neighborhood resident named Louise Ergestrasse came into Blackstone's office, threw a copy of Benjamin's *The Transsexual Phenomenon* on his desk, and demanded that Blackstone do something for "her people." Blackstone was willing to be educated on the matter, and he soon took a leading role in changing police treatment of transgender people. Another group of transgender Tenderloin activists, led by a trans woman named Wendy Kohler, a patient of Harry Benjamin, started working with activist doctor Joel Fort at a unit of the San Francisco Public Health Department called the Center for Special Problems.

A few months later, in early 1967, a group of transgender people began meeting at Glide Memorial Methodist Church, where they formed the first known trans support group, Conversion Our Goal (COG).

Between 1966 and 1968, these groups and individuals formed an interlocking network of transgender activists, allies, and services. COG, which published the short-lived *COG Newsletter,* provided an initial point of contact for transgender people seeking medical services, who were then steered toward the Center for Special Problems, which offered additional group support sessions, psychological counseling, hormone prescriptions, and, eventually, when a "sex change" clinic was established at nearby Stanford University Medical School, surgery referrals. Perhaps most important, however, the center provided ID cards for transgender clients that matched their social genders. It was a simple laminated piece of orange paper, signed by a public health doctor, bearing the name actually used by the client, the client's home address, and the statement: "[Client's name] is under treatment for transsexualism at the Center for Special Problems." Although the ID card did "out" those carrying it as transsexual, it nevertheless allowed people to open bank accounts and do other things that required identification. Without that card, transsexuals living in a social gender other than the one assigned to them at birth were essentially "undocumented workers" who had great difficulty finding legal employment.

Meanwhile, the Central City Anti-Poverty Program offered transgender women in the Tenderloin the opportunity to leave prostitution, teaching them clerical skills through the Neighborhood Youth Corps training programs. Elliott Blackstone worked to dissuade his colleagues in the police department from arresting transgender people on charges of cross-dressing or for using the "wrong" toilets, and he promoted many other reformist attitudes toward transgender issues. Significantly, a California State Supreme

Court ruling in 1962 had struck down laws that criminalized cross-dressing, but the practice of arresting transgender individuals based on those laws nevertheless persisted. Police attitudes, as well as laws, needed to change, and Blackstone played a vital role in challenging the actual practices of law enforcement.

Although most of the city-funded aspects of the San Francisco–based transgender support network that developed in the mid-1960s continue to operate even now, the community-based organizations proved ephemeral, as such groups often are. COG split into two competing factions within a year of its founding. The major faction regrouped as the equally short-lived National Sexual-Gender Identification Council (NSGIC) under the leadership of Wendy Kohler, whose main accomplishment was holding a one-day conference on transsexual issues at Glide. The minor faction, which never emerged as an effective organization and which existed primarily on paper, regrouped as CATS (California Advancement for Transsexuals Society) under the leadership of Louise Ergestrasse. The divisions within COG may well have reflected the split between Kohler's more assimilationist, upwardly mobile mind-set and Ergestrasse's orientation toward transgender street cultures. Far more successful than either was the National Transsexual Counseling Unit (NTCU), which, in 1968, brought together many of the players in San Francisco's mid-1960s transgender activist scene. The NTCU's success resulted in large measure from the financial support provided by one of the most influential figures in US transgender history—wealthy female-to-male transsexual philanthropist Reed Erickson.

A Behind-the-Scenes Benefactor

Before Reed Erickson became a major voice on transgender matters, most of the significant figures in transgender political history

Millionaire philanthropist Reed Erickson was a trans man who funded the revolutions in transgender health care and social services that blossomed in the 1960s. (Photo credit: Aron Devor.)

were cisgender men and transgender women. A community of trans men would become increasingly organized, active, and visible by the 1970s, but transgender men before Erickson tended to disappear into the woodwork of mainstream society and tended not to participate in groups and organizations. One reason for this difference lay in the fact that it was often easier for a mature female to pass as a young man than it was for a mature male to pass as a woman (with or without the use of hormones and surgery). Because visually perceiving someone to be transgender is one of the main triggers for antitransgender discrimination and violence, transgender women have been disproportionately affected by denials of employment and housing, and by violent crimes against them, and have had greater needs to take political and self-protective action. Transgender women who survive by participating in sexual street subcultures have long banded together for mutual support, whereas transgender men often lived without being part of a larger trans community. As a result, the political histories of transgender men and women, which have grown increasingly intertwined since the 1990s, sprang from very different social conditions.

Reed Erickson was assigned female at his birth in El Paso, Texas, in 1917 and grew up near Philadelphia, where his father owned a successful lead-smelting company, Schuylkill Industries. Erickson attended Philadelphia High School for Girls and Temple

University, where he ran with a left-wing lesbian crowd. His father subsequently moved the family business to Baton Rouge, Louisiana, and Erickson attended graduate school at Louisiana State University, where in 1946 he became the first person assigned female at birth to get a master's degree in engineering there. Because of his political leanings and sexual orientation, Erickson came under FBI surveillance as a suspected communist during the McCarthy era and was reputedly blacklisted from several jobs. Consequently, he worked for the family business and started companies of his own, including ones that manufactured metal folding chairs and stadium bleacher seating. Interestingly, Schuylkill Industries owned a large yacht, the *Granma,* that the company sold in the 1950s to Fidel Castro, who sailed it from Mexico, filled with scores of armed supporters, to launch the Cuban Revolution.

When Erickson's father died in 1962, Erickson inherited the family businesses and ran them successfully until selling them to Arrow Electronics in 1969 for roughly $5 million. Erickson's wealth, which by the time of his death exceeded $40 million, gave him the means to pursue many idiosyncratic projects. In addition to being a successful businessman, he was a nudist (and owned his own nudist colony in Florida), a New Age spiritualist, and a recreational psychedelic drug user with an interest in interspecies communication and mental telepathy. He considered his best friend to be a leopard named Henry, and he lived most of the time in a gated residential compound in Mazatlán, Mexico, that he named the Love Joy Palace. Erickson, who eventually became addicted to the party drug ketamine ("Vitamin K") and who was under indictment in the United States on several drug-related charges, fled to the Love Joy Palace permanently in 1972. He died there in 1992 after many years of deteriorating health.

Within a year of his father's death, Erickson had contacted Harry Benjamin and soon became his patient. He started masculinizing his body in 1963 and began to live socially as a man at that time. In 1964, he established the Erickson Educational Foundation (EEF) to support his many interests, as well as a separate foundation that specifically supported the work of Harry Benjamin, and a third entity, the Institute for the Study of Human Resources (ISHR), that quietly funded numerous other academic and medical research programs. The EEF developed a series of educational pamphlets that gave basic advice to transsexuals on such matters as how to legally change one's name or where to find a competent surgeon. It was Erickson's behind-the-scenes money that funded Benjamin to write *The Transsexual Phenomenon* and greased the wheels at prestigious educational institutions such as Johns Hopkins, Stanford, the University of Minnesota, UCLA, and the medical campus of the University of Texas on Galveston Island, all of which established major clinical research programs to develop transsexual medicine. Erickson was also a major benefactor of the ONE Institute, an educational organization that grew out of the homophile activist group in Los Angeles that published *ONE* magazine.

In funding the medical-legal-psychotherapeutic institutional framework within which transgender concerns have been addressed in the United States for more than fifty years, Erickson pursued the same strategy the homophile organizations of the day pursued: providing direct support to members of oppressed minority communities while marshaling the powers of social legitimation to speak about the issues in a new way. Although that model of activism (and the institutions it helped build) has come under criticism from later generations, Erickson seems to have accomplished what was possible for him to accomplish at the time. In spite of his wealth and great range of opportunity, he faced many of the same issues other transgender people faced, such as being denied employment and having to educate his service providers about his own health care needs. The name Erickson chose for ISHR, his foundation to promote the study of "human resources," was grounded in his own perception of having more potential for making a positive contribution to the world than circumstances would allow. He thought that transgender people such as himself represented a vastly underused resource of talent, creativity, energy, and determination. Although he was able to work on a scale that most people can only dream of, Erickson in fact did what most transgender people find themselves needing to do—working to create the conditions of daily life that allow them to meet their needs and pursue their dreams.

Reed Erickson became aware of the unprecedented social and political developments in San Francisco through his close contact with Harry Benjamin, and after watching the situation there develop for a couple of years, he decided to fund the National Transsexual Counseling Unit. The EEF paid the rent and provided office furnishings for the NTCU, and it also paid the salaries of two full-time peer counselors who did street outreach, provided walk-in counseling, and answered a steady stream of mail from gender-questioning people around the world. For the most part, the NTCU directed its clients to the Center for Special Problems for additional services. San Francisco police officer Elliott Blackstone, in an unusual administrative arrangement, managed the NTCU office as part of his responsibilities in the police community-relations program but drew no salary from the EEF. Blackstone did, however, travel to police professional development meetings and criminal justice conferences in the United States and Europe at EEF's expense to promote his unusually critical views on police treatment of transgender people. At the NTCU office, he worked with individual transgender people to resolve conflicts they had with the law or with employers, and with social service agencies to encourage them to be more responsive to transgender needs. He also conducted sensitivity training on gay and transgender issues for every San Francisco Police Academy class. By the end of the 1960s, the combined efforts of politically mobilized transgender communities, sympathetic professionals and public servants, and a generous infusion of private money made San Francisco the unquestioned hub of the transgender movement in the United States.

Stonewall

Meanwhile, across the continent, another important center of transgender activism was taking shape in New York City, where, not coincidentally, Harry Benjamin maintained his primary medical practice. In 1968, Mario Martino, a female-to-male transsexual, founded Labyrinth, the first organization in the United States devoted specifically to the needs of transgender men. Martino and his wife, who both worked in the health care field, helped other transsexual men navigate their way through the often-confusing maze of transgender-oriented medical services just then beginning to emerge, which (despite being funded primarily by Reed Erickson) were geared more toward the needs of transgender women than transgender men. Labyrinth was not a political organization but rather one that aimed to help individuals make the often-difficult transition from one social gender to another.

Marsha P. (for "Pay It No Mind") Johnson was a veteran of the 1969 Stonewall Riots in New York and cofounder, with Sylvia Rivera, of STAR—Street Transvestite Action Revolutionaries. (PHOTO CREDIT: AMY COLEMAN.)

Far overshadowing the quiet work of Martino's Labyrinth Foundation, however, were the dramatic events of June 1969 at the Stonewall Inn, a bar in New York's Greenwich Village. The "Stonewall Riots" have been mythologized as the origin of the gay liberation movement, and there is a great deal of truth in that characterization, but—as we have seen—gay, transgender, and gender-nonconforming people had been engaging in militant protest and collective actions against social oppression for at least a decade by that time. Stonewall stands out as the biggest and most consequential example of a kind of event that was becoming increasingly common, rather than as a unique occurrence. By 1969, as a result of many years of social upheaval and political agitation, large numbers of people who were socially marginalized because of their sexual orientation or gender identity, especially younger people who were part of the Baby Boomer generation, were drawn to the idea of "gay revolution" and were primed for any event that would set such a movement off. The Stonewall Riots provided that very spark, and they inspired the formation of Gay Liberation Front groups in big cities, progressive towns, and college campuses all across the United States. Ever since the summer of 1969, various groups of people who identify with the people who participated in the rioting have argued about what actually happened, what the riot's underlying causes were, who participated in it, and what the movements that point back to Stonewall as an important part of their own history have in common with one another.

Although Greenwich Village was not as economically down-and-out as San Francisco's Tenderloin, it was nevertheless a part of the city that appealed to the same sorts of people who resisted at Cooper Do-Nut, Dewey's, and Compton's Cafeteria: drag queens, hustlers, gender nonconformists of many varieties, gay men, lesbians, and countercultural types who simply "dug the scene." The Stonewall Inn was a small, shabby, Mafia-run bar (as were many

RADICAL TRANSSEXUAL

Suzy Cooke was a young hippie from upstate New York who lived in a commune in Berkeley, California, when she started transitioning from male to female in 1969. She came out as a bisexual transsexual in the context of the radical counterculture.

I was facing being called back up for the draft. I had already been called up once and had just gone in and played crazy with them the year before. But that was just an excuse. I had also been doing a lot of acid and really working things out. And then December 31, 1968, I took something—I don't really know what it was—but everything just collapsed. I said, "This simply cannot go on." To the people that I lived with, I said, "I don't care if you hate me, but I'm just going to have to do something. I'm going to have to work it out over the next couple of months, and that it doesn't matter if you reject me, I just have to do it."

As it was, the people in my commune took it very well. I introduced the cross-dressing a few days later as a way of avoiding the draft. And they were just taken aback at how much just putting on the clothes made me into a girl. I mean, hardly any makeup. A little blush, a little shadow, some gloss, the right clothes, padding. I passed. I passed really easily in public. This is like a few months before Stonewall. And by this point I was dressing up often enough that people were used to seeing it.

I was wallowing in the happiness of having a lot of friends. Here I was being accepted, this kinda cool/sorta goofy hippie kid. I was being accepted by all these heavy radicals. I had been rejected by my parental family, and I had never found a family at college, and now here I was with this family of like eight people all surrounding me. And as it turned out, even some of the girls that I had slept with were thinking that this was really cool. All the girls would donate clothes to me. I really had not been expecting this. I had been expecting rejection, I really had been. And I was really very pleased and surprised. Because I thought that if I did this then I was going to have to go off and live with the queens. And I didn't.

of the gay-oriented bars in New York back in the days when being gay or cross-dressing were crimes). It drew a racially mixed crowd and was popular mainly for its location on Christopher Street near Sheridan Square, where many gay men "cruised" for casual sex, and because it featured go-go boys, cheap beer, a good jukebox, and a crowded dance floor. Then as now, there was a lively street scene in the bar's vicinity, one that drew young and racially mixed queer folk from through the region most weekend nights. Police raids were relatively frequent (usually when the bar was slow to make its payoffs to corrupt cops) and relatively routine and uneventful. Once the bribes were sorted out, the bar would reopen, often on the same night. But in the muggy, early morning hours of Saturday, June 28, 1969, events departed from the familiar script when the squad cars pulled up outside the Stonewall Inn.

A large crowd of people gathered on the street as police began arresting workers and patrons and escorting them out of the bar and into the waiting police wagons. Some people in the crowd started throwing coins at the police officers, taunting them for taking "payola." Eyewitness accounts of what happened next differ in their particulars, but some witnesses claim a transmasculine person resisted police attempts to put them in the police wagon, while others noted that African American and Puerto Rican members of the crowd—many of them street queens, feminine gay men, transgender women, or gender-nonconforming youth—grew increasingly angry as they watched their "sisters" being arrested and escalated the level of opposition to the police. Both stories might well be true. Sylvia Rivera, a transgender woman who came to play an important role in subsequent transgender political history, long maintained that, after she was jabbed by a police baton, she threw the beer bottle that tipped the crowd's mood from mockery to collective resistance. In any case, the targeting of gender-nonconforming people, people of color, and poor people during a police action fits the usual patterns of police behavior in such situations.

Bottles, rocks, and other heavy objects were soon being hurled at the police, who, in retaliation, began grabbing people from the crowd and beating them. Weekend partiers and residents in the heavily gay neighborhood quickly swelled the ranks of the crowd to more than two thousand people, and the outnumbered police barricaded themselves inside the Stonewall Inn and called for reinforcements. Outside, rioters used an uprooted parking meter as a battering ram to try to break down the bar's door, while other members of the crowd attempted to throw a Molotov cocktail inside to drive the police back into the streets. Tactical Patrol Force officers arrived on the scene in an attempt to contain the growing disturbance, which nevertheless continued for hours until dissipating before dawn. That night, thousands of people regrouped at the Stonewall Inn to protest. When the police arrived to break up the assembled crowd, street fighting even more violent than that of the night before ensued. One particularly memorable sight amid the melee was a line of drag queens, arms linked, dancing a can-can and singing campy, improvised songs that mocked the police and their inability to regain control of the situation: "We are the Stonewall girls / We wear our hair in curls / We always dress with flair / We wear clean underwear / We wear our dungarees / Above our nellie knees." Minor skirmishes and protest rallies continued throughout the next few days before finally dying down. By that time, however, untold thousands of people had been galvanized into political action.

Stonewall's Transgender Legacy

Within a month of the Stonewall Riots, gay activists inspired by the events in Greenwich Village formed the Gay Liberation Front

(GLF), which modeled itself on radical Third World liberation and anti-imperialist movements. The GLF spread quickly through activist networks in the student and antiwar movements, primarily among white young people of middle-class origin. Almost as quickly as it formed, however, divisions appeared within the GLF, primarily taking aim at the movement's domination by white men and its perceived marginalization of women, working-class people, people of color, and trans people. People with more liberal, less radical politics soon organized as the Gay Activists Alliance (GAA), which aimed to reform laws rather than foment revolution. Many lesbians redirected their energy toward radical feminism and the women's movement. And trans people, after early involvement in the GLF (and being explicitly excluded from the GAA's agenda), quickly came to feel that they did not have a welcome place in the movement they had done much to inspire. As a consequence, they soon formed their own organizations.

In 1970, Sylvia Rivera and another Stonewall regular, Marsha P. Johnson, established STAR—Street Transvestite Action Revolutionaries. Their primary goal was to help street kids stay out of jail, or get out of jail, and to find food, clothing, and a place to live. They opened STAR House, an overtly politicized version of the "house" culture that already characterized black and Latino queer kinship networks, where dozens of trans youth could count on a free and safe place to sleep. Rivera and Johnson, as "house mothers," would hustle to pay the rent, while their "children" would scrounge for food. Their goal was to educate and protect the younger people who were coming into the kind of life they themselves led—they even dreamed of establishing a school for kids who'd never learned to read and write because their formal education was interrupted by discrimination and bullying. Some STAR members, particularly Rivera, were also active in the Young Lords, a revolutionary Puerto

Rican youth organization. One of the first times the STAR banner was flown in public was at a mass demonstration against police repression organized by the Young Lords in East Harlem in 1970, in which STAR participated as a group. STAR House lasted for only two or three years and inspired a few short-lived imitators in other cities, but its legacy lives on even now.

A few other transgender groups formed in New York in the early 1970s. A trans woman named Judy Bowen organized two extremely short-lived groups: Transvestites and Transsexuals (TAT) in 1970 and Transsexuals Anonymous in 1971. More significant was the Queens' Liberation Front (QLF), founded by drag queen Lee Brewster and heterosexual transvestite Bunny Eisenhower. The QLF formed in part to resist the erasure of drag and trans visibility in the first Christopher Street Liberation Day march, which commemorated the Stonewall Riots and is now an annual event held in New York on the last Sunday in June. In many other cities, this weekend has become the traditional date to celebrate LGBTQ Pride. The formation of the QLF demonstrates how quickly the gay liberation movement started to push aside some of the very people who had the greatest stake in militant resistance at Stonewall. QLF members participated in that first Christopher Street Liberation Day march and were involved in several other political campaigns through the next few years—including wearing drag while lobbying state legislators in Albany. QLF's most lasting contribution, however, was the publication of *Drag Queen* magazine (later simply *Drag*), which had the best coverage of transgender news and politics in the United States, and which offered fascinating glimpses of trans life and activism outside the major coastal cities. In New York, QLF founder Lee Brewster's private business, Lee's Mardi Gras Boutique, was a gathering place for segments of the city's transgender community well into the 1990s.

Angela K. Douglas

One other burst of trans activist energy during this period that deserves particular mention revolved around Angela K. Douglas. Douglas had been involved in the countercultural scene in Los Angeles in the mid-1960s, where she mingled with many soon-to-be-famous filmmakers and rock musicians. She herself, before her transition in 1969, played in the obscure psychedelic rock band Euphoria. Douglas covered the birth of gay liberation politics for the Los Angeles underground press and joined GLF-LA, which she soon left because of the transphobia she perceived in that organization. (It should also be noted that Morris Kight, the principal architect of the gay liberation movement in Los Angeles, suspected Douglas of being an FBI informant.) She subsequently formed TAO (Transsexual Activist Organization) in 1970, which published the *Moonshadow* and *Mirage* newsletters—always-interesting hodgepodges of eccentric political manifestos, psychedelic art, photographs, activist news, and occult beliefs. TAO was the first truly international grassroots transgender community organization, with a worldwide mailing list and loosely affiliated chapters in various cities, including one in Birmingham, England, that shaped the sensibilities of activist attorney and professor of law Stephen Whittle, who would later lead a successful campaign for transgender legal reform in the United Kingdom in the 1990s and establish himself as one of the leading international authorities on transgender legal and human rights issues.

Douglas, who suffered several psychotic breaks as a young adult, would spend most of her life living in poverty and ill health in rural Florida until her death in 2007. During this later period, she wrote a poignant autobiography, *Triple Jeopardy* (self-published in 1982), penned a few songs, and churned out a prodigious amount of paranoid writings directed at people she accused of "stealing her life." Throughout the 1970s, however, Douglas tirelessly criss-crossed the United States and wrote extensively for radical, counter-cultural, and transgender community publications. She was briefly involved in the New York radical scene, and her involvement there was mentioned in Donn Teal's as-it-happened history, *The Gay Militants.* Douglas moved her base of operations to Miami in 1972, where a significant part of TAO's membership was drawn from Cuban refugees and other Caribbean immigrants. She was always more of a gadfly and provocateur than a movement builder, and from her alternative perspective she ceaselessly criticized the doctors, lawyers, and psychiatrists associated with Harry Benjamin, the EEF, and the "police-run" NTCU in San Francisco. In spite of her growing psychiatric difficulties, Douglas's political writings offered important countercultural critiques of the emerging transgender establishment.

By the early 1970s, transgender political activism had progressed in ways scarcely imaginable when the 1960s had begun. On one front, privileged white male transvestites were making community with one another in the nation's suburbs, while on another front, multiracial groups of militant cultural revolutionaries were claiming space for themselves in the streets of America's major cities. Transsexuals had taken the first crucial steps toward redefining the relationship between their needs and life goals and state-sanctioned medical care, social services, and legal accommodation of their identities. In spite of those remarkable accomplishments, however, the decade ahead would be one of the most difficult and frustrating periods of transgender history in the United States.

CHAPTER 4

THE DIFFICULT DECADES

BY THE EARLY 1970s, US American culture—especially popular culture—had undergone some startling transformations as a result of the upheavals of the 1960s. One of the most visible differences was a sudden proliferation of gender styles that broke free from the more rigid codes still in place in the early 1960s. In those earlier years, a woman wearing pants in public would still raise eyebrows, and a man with hair long enough to touch the collar of his shirt would be looked at with suspicion. After a decade of "sex, drugs, and rock and roll," more unisex fashions had become common, and there was a greater acceptance of traditionally masculine clothing on women. Men did not have the same license to embrace traditionally feminine clothing, but even so, society allowed them a greater range of expression in their appearance. On the cultural fringe, avant-garde transgender theatrical and musical acts such as the Cockettes and Sylvester (on the West Coast) and Wayne (later Jayne) County and the New York Dolls (on the East Coast) inspired the better-known gender-bending styles of glam rocker David Bowie and filmmaker John Waters's cult movie star Divine. High art and low-life swirled around pop artist Andy Warhol's Factory, helping popularize countercultural icons such as Lou Reed and the transgender

Warhol superstars Candy Darling, Jackie Curtis, and Holly Woodlawn, and infusing the glam, glitter, and early punk music scenes in venues such as Max's Kansas City and CBGB. What could be described as a "transgender aesthetic," a new relationship between gendered appearance and biological sex, was becoming hip and cool for countercultural audiences. But these stylistic innovations did little to alter institutionalized forms of sexism and social oppression based on gender. Even as transgender styles began inching into the cultural mainstream, people who lived transgender lives from day to day began to experience a profound backlash against the recent gains made by people like themselves.

Backlash and Watershed

Transgender people were not alone in experiencing a political backlash. By the early 1970s, reactionary tactics by the government had violently shut down many countercultural tendencies that had emerged in the 1960s. The escalation of the war in Vietnam continued; antiwar activism and racial unrest roiled the streets of the nation from coast to coast, and the FBI's domestic surveillance program infiltrated many antiestablishment groups and movements. Members of the Black Panther Party were murdered by the police in Chicago, and antiwar student protesters were killed by National Guard troops at Kent State University in Ohio. In San Francisco, the National Transsexual Counseling Unit was wrecked by reactionary members of the police department, who entrapped one of the peer counselors there in a drug bust; a police informant pretended to be sexually and romantically interested in the NTCU employee and then, after dating her for a few weeks, asked her to score cocaine for him and to bring it to work, where he would buy it from her. Once the drugs were on the premises, officers swooped in for the arrests. They also planted narcotics in Elliott Blackstone's desk, unsuccessfully attempting to frame him. The peer counselor was convicted on drug charges and spent two years in jail, and Blackstone, though he remained on the police force for a few more years until qualifying for his retirement pension, was reassigned to a new job in which he didn't interact with the city's transgender scene. The NTCU limped along for a while longer, but the agency closed in 1974, when the Erickson foundation stopped funding it.

The rise of university-based sex change programs during the late 1960s and early 1970s illustrates the complex cultural politics of transgender issues at this historical juncture. Some university-based research on transgender identification had been conducted at the University of California in the early 1950s, and the Gender Identity Research Clinic had been established on the UCLA campus in 1962. Within months of the publication of Harry Benjamin's *The Transsexual Phenomenon* in 1966, however, Johns Hopkins University opened the first medical program in the United States to combine scientific research into the biology and psychology of gender with the expert evaluation of transgender individuals for hormone treatment and genital surgery. Similar programs quickly followed at other major research universities. These years, between the mid-1960s and the late 1970s, represent what could be called the "Big Science" period of transgender history.

On the one hand, this heightened level of attention represented a welcome development for transgender people in the United States who wanted to physically change their sex. Before the development of these programs, US trans people who sought surgery usually had to leave the country to find services overseas or in Latin America, and many simply could not afford to do so. These new programs, some of which were free of charge to qualified research participants, made "sex change" domestically available for the first time. On the other hand, as trans people seeking surgery and hormones quickly discovered, the new university-based scientific research programs were far more concerned with restabilizing the gender system, which seemed to be mutating all around them in bizarre and threatening directions, than they were with helping that cultural revolution along by further exploding mandatory relationships between sexed embodiment, psychological gender identity, and social gender role. Access to transsexual medical services thus became entangled with a socially conservative attempt to maintain traditional gender configurations in which changing sex was grudgingly permitted for the few seeking to do so, to the extent that the practice did not trouble the gender binary for the many.

The elaboration of an elite university-based medical research culture around "sex change" had significant consequences for transgender political activism. Transgenderism and homosexuality had been conceptually interrelated since the nineteenth century, and transgender politics, the homophile movement, and gay liberation had run alongside one another and sometimes intersected throughout the 1950s and 1960s. The early 1970s, however, represented a watershed moment in this shared history when the transgender political movement lost its alliances with gay and feminist communities in ways that did not begin to be repaired until the early 1990s and that, in many ways, have yet to be fully overcome. Although gay liberation and feminism are typically considered politically progressive developments, for transgender people they often constituted another part of the backlash, in large part because of the different relationships these movements and identities had to institutionalized medical, scientific, and legal powers and to minority civil rights discourse.

Consider, for example, how the course of the war in Vietnam affected gay male and transgender community dynamics. Direct US involvement in Southeast Asian military conflicts began to escalate after the 1964 Gulf of Tonkin incident in which communist North Vietnamese boats were accused of firing on the vessels of

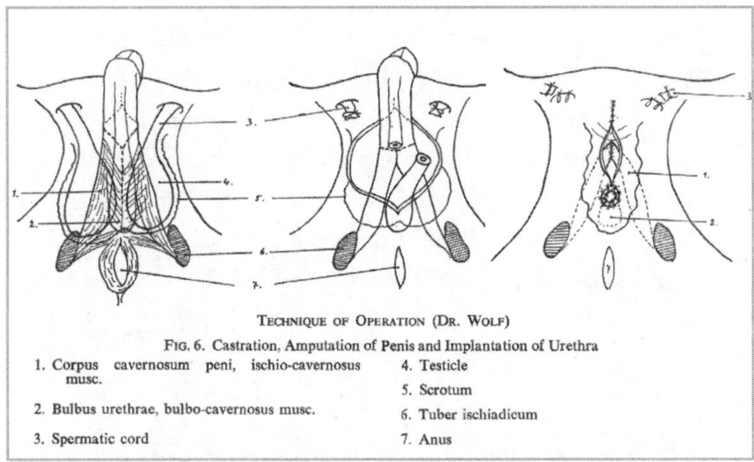

Medical drawing of a male-to-female genital conversion operation (1958), included in the text Homosexuality, Transvestitism, and Change of Sex, *by Eugene de Savitsch.* (Photo credit: Heinemann Books.)

US military advisers; major commitments of US ground troops followed in 1965. The countercultural hippie style popular among both gays and straights—with its bright, flowing fabrics, long hair, and love beads—represented a deliberate reversal of the gender conventions of militaristic masculinity and signaled political opposition to the war. One popular sexual liberation slogan from the height of the antiwar movement was "Fuck, Don't Fight"; an unstated but equally apropos slogan for many draft-age men would have been "Genderfuck, Don't Fight." It should not be surprising that the period when transfeminine people made their most significant political gains overlapped with a period in which public gender transgression by cisgender men had the broadest and deepest sense of political urgency. Significantly, however, when major US involvement in Vietnam began to wind down, after the 1973 Paris Peace Accords, the gender coding of men's clothing styles simultaneously began to shift. In gay male culture, 1973 was the year that the masculine "clone look" of denim, plaid, and short haircuts replaced radical hippie or fairy chic, signaling the return of a more gender-normative expression of male homosexuality. It is possible to trace the current "homonormativity" of mainstream gay culture (an emphasis on being "straight-looking and straight-acting"), as well as the perceived lack of meaningful connection to transgender communities among mainstream gays and lesbians, to the shifts of 1973.

TRANS LIB

In the early 1970s, trans people voiced their hopes for a liberation movement, using the same language and arguments as other liberation struggles. Militant trans liberationists rejected the idea that they were simply enacting gender stereotypes, and they resented the idea that they were expendable "shock troops" in feminist and gay liberation struggles. The following article, though it contains a few errors of historical fact, captures the spirit of early trans liberation sentiment; it documents both the nationwide scope of organizing and the perception among some trans people that their struggles were part of a larger movement for social change. The article originally appeared in 1971 in the *Trans Liberation Newsletter.*

Transvestite and Transsexual Liberation

The oppression against transvestites and transsexuals of either sex arises from sexist values and this oppression is manifested by homosexuals and heterosexuals alike in the form of exploitation, ridicule, harassment, beatings, rapes, murders and the use of us as shock troops and sacrificial victims.

We reject all labels of "stereotype," "sick," or "maladjusted" from non-transvestic and non-transsexual sources and defy

continues

any attempt to repress our manifestations as transvestites or transsexuals.

Trans Lib began in the summer of 1969 when Queens formed in New York and began militating for equal rights. In 1970 the Transvestite-Transsexual Action Organization (TACO) formed in Los Angeles, the Cockettes in San Francisco, Street Transvestite Action Revolutionaries (STAR) in New York, Fems Against Sexism and Transvestites and Transsexuals (TAT) also formed in New York. Radical Queens formed in Milwaukee—all in 1970. Queens became Queens Liberation Front.

Transvestism, transsexuality, and homosexuality are separate entities. Sexist values incorrectly classify any male who wears feminine attire as a homosexual, and to a lesser degree, any female who wears masculine attire is also classified as a homosexual.

We share in the oppression of Gay women. Trans Lib includes transvestites, transsexuals, and hermaphrodites of any sexual manifestation and of all sexes—heterosexuals, homosexual, bisexual, and asexual. It is becoming a separate movement as the great majority of transvestites are heterosexual, and many transsexuals (post-operative) are also heterosexual, and because the oppression directed toward us is due to our transvestism and transsexualism and for no other reason. We unite around our oppression, as all oppressed groups unite around their particular oppression. All power to Trans Liberation.

WE DEMAND

1. *Abolition of all cross-dressing laws and restrictions of adornment.*
2. *An end to exploitation and discrimination within the gay world.*
3. *An end to exploitation practices of doctors and physicians in the fields of transvestism and transsexualism.*

continues

TRANS LIB *continued*

4. *Free hormone treatment and surgery upon demand.*
5. *Transsexual assistance centers should be created in all cities with populations of one million inhabitants, under the direction of postoperative transsexuals.*
6. *Full rights on all levels of society and full voice in the struggles for liberation of all oppressed peoples.*
7. *Immediate release of all persons in mental hospitals or prison for transvestism or transsexualism.*

Transvestites who exist as members of the opposite anatomical gender should be able to obtain full identification as members of the opposite gender. Transsexuals should be able to obtain such identification commensurate to their new gender with no difficulty, and not be required to carry special identification as transsexuals.

Another marker of the growing divergence of trans and gay communities can be seen in the campaign to depathologize homosexuality, which was considered a psychological illness in the United States until the early 1970s. Starting in the 1950s, homophile groups had worked with sympathetic straight or closeted members of the legal, medical, and psychiatric professions to delist it from the American Psychiatric Association's *Diagnostic and Statistical Manual of Mental Disorders (DSM).* One of the first major accomplishments of the gay liberation movement that took shape in the wake of Stonewall was to achieve this long-term goal. Building on the foundation of homophile activism, gay psychologists who "came out" within their profession succeeded in having their peers remove homosexuality from the *DSM* in 1973. As a result, because gays were now "liberated" from the burden of psychopathology, gay and trans communities no longer had a common interest in working to address how they were each treated by the mental health establishment. Gay liberationists who had little familiarity with transgender issues came to see transgender people as "not liberated" and lacking in political sophistication, as being still mired in an old-fashioned "preliberation" engagement with the establishment, as still trying to fit in with the system when what they should really be doing was freeing themselves from medical-psychiatric oppression.

In many respects, the transgender movement's politics toward the medical establishment were more like those of the reproductive justice movement than those of the gay liberation movement. Transgender people, like people seeking abortion or contraception, wanted to secure access to competent, legal, respectfully provided medical services for a nonpathological need not shared equally by every member of society, a need whose revelation carried a high degree of stigma in some social contexts, and for which the decision to seek medical intervention in a deeply personal matter about how to live in one's own body was typically arrived at only after intense and often emotionally painful deliberation. The US Supreme Court ruled on the landmark *Roe v. Wade* case in 1973, guaranteeing a woman's right to an abortion; transgender medical needs, however, were not viewed through the same set of rationales that won *Roe,* in large part because an emerging feminist position on transgender issues proved even more hostile to transgender interests than the gay liberation perspective.

The second wave of feminist activism in the United States is generally considered to have begun in the early 1960s, with the publication of Betty Friedan's *Feminine Mystique* in 1963 and the formation of the National Organization for Women (NOW) in 1966. Simone de Beauvoir's *Second Sex,* published in France in 1949, had prepared the ground by placing the question of feminism squarely at the forefront of post–World War II intellectual life. Early second wave feminism quickly came to be seen by those on the cultural and political left as white, middle class, heterosexual, and establishment-oriented in its worldview, however, and more radical, race-conscious, and countercultural versions of feminism critiqued the feminist mainstream almost from the beginning. In 1973, black feminists in New York, some of whom had been involved in the civil rights movement, the Black Panthers, and the Black Lesbian Caucus of the GLF, recognized the necessity of forming a separate group, the National Black Feminist Organization. Inspired by this activism, Boston-area black feminists formed the Combahee River Collective the next year. The Combahee River Collective Statement, crafted over the next few years, remains a touchstone of black and intersectional feminism and provides an important foundation for trans-inclusive feminist politics. Collective members noted that they felt "a great deal of criticism" of male sexism and "loathed" that many men were socialized to be macho and oppressive toward women, but they also stated: "We do not have the misguided notion that it is their maleness per se—i.e., their biological maleness—that makes them what they are. As black women, we find any kind of biological determinism a particularly dangerous and reactionary basis on which to build a politic."

Such cautions notwithstanding, some strains of second wave feminism developed a pronounced biologically determinist politic. New Yorker Robin Morgan played an important role in launching WITCH (Women's International Terrorist Conspiracy from Hell) in 1968, a loose network of socialist-feminist collectives, and her views would have a powerful influence on early white radical feminist views of transgender issues. Many lesbians associated with gay liberation began meeting in feminist consciousness-raising groups. One of these groups, the Radicalesbians, which included Rita Mae Brown, Karla Jay, and others, played a pivotal part in the political development of lesbian feminism through its influential pamphlet, "The Woman-Identified Woman."

At the Second Congress to Unite Women, held in New York in 1970, the Radicalesbians and their paradigm-shifting pamphlet burst onto the scene in response to recent pejorative comments by Betty Friedan about the "lavender menace"—the question of lesbian participation in feminist politics. Friedan opposed associating lesbian concerns with feminism because she feared that society's homophobia would limit feminism's appeal and hamper its progress. The Radicalesbians staged what has come to be known as the "Lavender Zap" when, just as the conference was about to begin, they cut power to the microphones, killed the lights, and stormed the stage. When the lights came back up and the microphones came back on a few moments later, Radicalesbians members wearing Lavender Menace T-shirts had commandeered the attention of all present. They passed out copies of "The Woman-Identified Woman" and facilitated a discussion of feminism, homophobia, and lesbian-baiting that changed the direction of feminist politics in the United States.

"The Woman-Identified Woman" famously begins with the statement, "A lesbian is the rage of all women condensed to the point of explosion." Its major conceptual accomplishment was to create linkages between straight and lesbian women through a shared understanding of gender oppression—for all feminist women, in other words, to be "woman-identified," to give strength to each other, rather than reflecting back to each other the "self-hate and the lack of real self" that were "rooted in our male-given identity" as patriarchally defined women. The idea of women having their primary emotional ties to each other, regardless of their sexual orientation, rather than to men, was a major milestone in the historical development of feminist consciousness, as was the sense that gender roles were male-defined and functioned strictly as a form of repression to keep women in a subordinate position relative to men.

As vital, however, as these moves were for nourishing an incipient feminist sense of pride and strength, and however much they cleared conceptual space for redefining and politicizing gender, they nevertheless also precipitated a significant recontextualization of some lesbian sexual subcultures, a development not necessarily beneficial for all concerned. The traditional organization of lesbian erotic life around "butch" and "femme" identities fell under suspicion as examples of "male identification" and "patriarchal gender" that pathetically imitated heterosexual male-female couplings and that did not further the revolutionary goal of overthrowing gender itself. As a result, butches, who expressed an unwelcome masculinity, as well as femmes, who embraced a feminine gender presentation deemed politically reactionary, were marginalized within a lesbian feminist political community whose "androgynous" style was seen as gender neutral.

One consequence of this shift away from "roles" and toward androgyny in lesbian and feminist culture was the foreclosure of social space that tolerated—or even celebrated—transmasculine people (some of whom might now be characterized as transgender), along with the women who loved them, who previously had had a place in women's and lesbian communities. The erosion of that space directly influenced the formation of FTM (female-to-male) transgender communities by the middle years of the 1970s. Before pursuing that story, however, it seems important to document the emergence of new transphobic discourses based on gay liberation and lesbian feminist analyses of gender. Most initially addressed male-to-female transsexuals who were involved in feminist communities, but, as the female-to-male community grew in the 1980s and 1990s, older arguments were revised, expanded, and adapted to take greater account of gender variance among people assigned female at birth.

Transsexual lesbian singer and activist Beth Elliott in the 1970s. (Photo credit: Richard McCaffrey.)

Feminist Transphobia

As already noted, 1973 represented an inflection point in US transgender political history. Trans people, when they transitioned from one gender to another, still routinely faced loss of family and friends, housing and employment discrimination, high levels of social stigma, and greater risks for experiencing violence. Long-standing antitransgender prejudices meshed with new levels of medical attention to make pathologization the readiest path to health care services and a better quality of life. Progressive political movements, rather than critiquing the medical system that told transgender people they were sick, instead insisted that transgender people were politically regressive dupes of the patriarchal gender system who, at best, deserved to have their consciousnesses raised. A perfect storm of hostility toward transgender issues was beginning to gather force.

Some transgender people of the post–World War II Baby Boom had been drawn to gay liberation, radical feminism, and New Left politics, just like other members of their generation, but their welcome there tended to be short-lived. San Francisco's first Gay Pride parade in 1972 (which commemorated the Compton's Cafeteria riot along with Stonewall and welcomed drag participation) degenerated into fistfighting when the Reverend Raymond Broshears, one of the gay male organizers, punched a member of a lesbian separatist contingent that insisted on carrying signs that said "Off the Pricks!" in violation of the parade's "no violence" policy. At the postparade rally, feminists and some of their gay male supporters denounced the fight as an example of stereotypical gender roles and patriarchal oppression of women, and they announced that they never again would participate in a Gay Pride event organized by Broshears or in one that permitted drag queens to "mock" women. In 1973, two separate San Francisco Pride events were organized, one by Broshears, and the other by gays and lesbians who opposed drag and expressly forbid transgender people from participating. Broshears never organized another Gay Pride event, while the anti-drag event became the forerunner of the current San Francisco LGBTQ Pride celebration. That same year, across the continent in New York, event organizers tried to prevent Sylvia Rivera, the founder of Street Transvestite Action Revolutionaries, from addressing the annual commemoration of Christopher Street Liberation Day. Rivera took the stage anyway and issued a devastating critique of the cisgender whiteness of the gay and feminist movements:

> I've been trying to get up here all day. I have been to jail. I have been raped and beaten many times, by men, heterosexual men. I will no longer put up with this shit. I have had my nose broken. I have lost my job. I have lost my apartment. For gay liberation. And you all treat me this way? What the fuck's wrong with you?

> I believe in gay power. I believe in us getting our rights, or else I would not be out there fighting for our rights. That's all I wanted to say to you people. Come and see the people at STAR House. The people there are trying to do something for all of us, not [just] men and women that belong to a white, middle-class club. And that's what you all belong to. Revolution! Gay Power!! (Edited from the original)

Another consequential incident in the rising tide of hostility toward transgender people in the summer of 1973 was directed against transsexual lesbian singer Beth Elliott, by Robin Morgan, at the West Coast Lesbian Feminist Conference. Elliott discovered her feminism, lesbianism, and womanhood in the context of a college friendship in the late 1960s with a young woman who was also in the process of coming out. After transitioning from man to woman in her late teens, Elliott subsequently threw herself into community activism by participating in the hippie folk music scene, becoming an antiwar activist, and serving as vice president of the San Francisco chapter of the pioneering lesbian organization the Daughters of Bilitis. Her formative teenage relationship came back to haunt her in the early 1970s, however, when her former college friend, by now a member of the lesbian separatist Gutter Dykes Collective, publicly accused Elliott of having sexually harassed her years earlier—a charge Elliott vigorously and vehemently denied, but which, by the very nature of things, could never be extricated from the circular round of "she said/she said" accusations, denials, and counteraccusations. In retrospect, these accusations of harassment appear to be an early instance—perhaps the first—of an emerging discourse in feminism that held all male-to-female transsexuals to be, by definition, violators of women, because they represented an "unwanted penetration" into women's space. Elliott, for her part, claims her former friend made false accusations to save face within her separatist clique once her adolescent friendship with Elliott became known. Whatever the circumstances might have been, the public accusation of sexual misconduct served as a lightning rod for discharging years of gathering unease about the participation of transgender women in lesbian and feminist spaces. It devastated Elliott, derailed her career in the early women's movement and music scene, and became the basis for one of the most pernicious and persistent characterizations of transgender people to be found in feminism.

The fallout began in December 1972 when Elliott was ousted from the Daughters of Bilitis, not because of any accusations against her but on the grounds that she wasn't "really" a woman; several other members resigned in protest over that decision. Meanwhile, Elliott also served on the organizing committee of the West Coast Lesbian Feminist Conference, planned for April of 1973 in Los Angeles, and she had been asked to perform as a singer in the conference's entertainment program. The Gutter Dykes leafleted the conference to protest the presence there of a "man" (Elliott), and keynote speaker Robin Morgan, recently arrived from the East Coast, hastily expanded her address to incorporate elements of the brewing controversy. All of her incorporations came from the separatist perspective, and none from Elliott and her supporters. Morgan's speech, titled "Lesbianism and Feminism: Synonyms or Contradictions?" was subsequently published in her memoir *Going Too Far: The Personal Chronicle of a Feminist* and was widely reprinted in the feminist press. More than twelve hundred women at the conference—which turned out to be the largest lesbian gathering to date—listened to the speech firsthand. For many attendees, the controversy over Beth Elliott's participation in the West Coast Lesbian Feminist Conference was their first encounter with the "transgender question," and what transpired there would inform opinions nationwide.

"All hell broke loose that very first night, caused by the gate-crashing presence of a male transvestite who insisted that he was 1) an invited participant, 2) really a woman, and 3) at heart a lesbian," Morgan wrote in her introductory notes to the keynote speech in *Going Too Far*. "It was incredible that so many strong angry women should be divided by one smug male in granny glasses and an earth-mother gown." In the 1973 speech itself, Morgan asked her audience why some of them felt compelled to defend the "obscenity of male transvestism" and to "permit into our organizations . . . men who deliberately *re*emphasize gender roles, and who parody female oppression and suffering." "No," she continued, "I will not call a male 'she'; thirty-two years of suffering in this androcentric society and of surviving, have earned me the title 'woman'; one walk down the street by a male transvestite, five minutes of his being hassled (which he may enjoy), and then he dares, he dares to think he understands our pain? No, in our mothers' names and in our own, we must not call him sister."

Morgan then went on to identify Elliott as "the same man who four years ago tried to pressure a San Francisco lesbian into letting him rape her; the same man who single-handedly divided and almost destroyed the San Francisco Daughters of Bilitis Chapter." She accused Elliott of "leeching off women who have spent entire lives *as women* in women's bodies" and ended her personal attack by declaiming: "I charge him as an opportunist, an infiltrator, and a destroyer—with the mentality of a rapist." Morgan then called upon the conference attendees to vote on ejecting Elliott, saying, "You can let him into your workshops—or you can *deal* with him." According to writers for the *Lesbian Tide,* more than two-thirds of those present voted to allow Elliott to remain, but the antitranssexual faction refused to accept the popular results and promised to disrupt the conference if their demands were not met. Eventually, after much rancorous debate, Beth Elliott went on to perform but thereafter left the remainder of the conference.

Conference attendees brought news of the Elliott controversy (and, of course, much else) back to women's communities across the country, and, throughout the middle years of the 1970s, the "transsexual rapist" trope began to circulate in grassroots lesbian networks as the most extreme version of an antipathy toward transgender people rooted in the concepts of "woman identification" and "women-only space." In 1977, for example, Sandy Stone, a male-to-female transsexual recording engineer who had worked with Jimi Hendrix and other rock luminaries before joining the Olivia Records collective to help launch the women's music industry, became the target of an antitranssexual campaign among some women who threatened to boycott Olivia if Stone did not resign. They argued that consumers were being deceived in the claim that Olivia was "women-only." Although the collective was willing on principle to stick by Stone, she voluntarily left to pursue other opportunities in order not to damage Olivia's business. By 1978, Boston University feminist theologian Mary Daly had elevated transphobia to a metaphysical precept by labeling transsexuality a "necrophilic invasion" of vital women's space in the section of her book, *Gyn/Ecology,* called "Boundary Violation and the Frankenstein Phenomenon." But it was Daly's doctoral student, Janice G. Raymond, who, in 1979, consolidated the many strands of antitransgender discourse circulating within feminist communities into one grand narrative, published as *The Transsexual Empire: The Making of the She-Male.*

Because Raymond's book has played such an important role in transgender political history—serving both as a sourcebook for antitransgender opinion as well as a goad for transgender countertheorizing—it merits discussion here at some length. As the debates about transgender issues shifted during the 1990s and the 2000s, Raymond's attitudes—never representative of all feminist opinion—have been caricatured and derided by people friendly to transgender concerns, while those hostile to transgender interests hold her work up as a sound argument in their favor. Because what she actually wrote has been obscured by the heated arguments of others, and because her own arguments continue to be referenced in contemporary feminist debates, it seems useful to discuss Raymond extensively.

First, Raymond explicitly identifies the practice of transsexuality with rape, unequivocally stating: "All transsexuals rape women's bodies by reducing the real female form to an artifact, appropriating this body for themselves;" she asserts that the mere presence of male-to-female transsexuals in women's space "violates women's sexuality and spirit." Rape, she claims, is usually accomplished by force, but it can also be accomplished by deception; male-to-female transsexuals who seek to be involved in women's and feminist communities "merely cut off the most obvious means of invading women," but they continue to rape women, as she claims Sandy Stone did via her work at Olivia, whenever they do not declare themselves to be transsexuals.

Furthermore, Raymond claims that male-to-female transsexuals are agents of the patriarchal oppression of women, comparing them to the eunuchs (castrated males) who once guarded the harems of Eastern potentates. "Will the acceptance of transsexually constructed lesbian-feminists who have lost only the outward appendages of their physical masculinity lead to the containment and control of lesbian-feminists?" Raymond asks. "Will every lesbian-feminist space become a harem?" Just because some "men" are castrated doesn't make them "un-men," she continues; it just means they can be used as "'keepers' of woman-identified women when the 'real men,' the 'rulers of patriarchy,' decide that the women's movement . . . should be controlled and contained." In this way, she claims, eunuchs, too, "can rise in the Kingdoms of the Fathers."

Combining Orientalist stereotypes with a thinly veiled Islamophobia, Raymond thus constructs the transsexual as a tool of alien powers bent on the subjugation of progressive Western feminism.

One of the more lurid and logically incoherent sections of *The Transsexual Empire* is called "Learning from the Nazi Experience." "In mentioning the Nazi experiments," Raymond writes, "it is not my purpose to directly compare transsexual surgery to what went on in the camps but rather to demonstrate that much of what went on there can be of value in surveying the ethics of transsexualism." She then constructs a string of false syllogisms, inferences, and analogies that work to associate transsexuality with Nazism without actually asserting that transsexuals are Nazis or Nazi collaborators. Raymond quotes countercultural antipsychiatry guru Thomas Szasz to the effect that sometimes profit-hungry doctors have collaborated with governments and corporations in ways that seem to violate their professional ethics to "first do no harm," and then she notes that Nazi science was government funded. "Not so incidentally," she points out, "some transsexual research has been funded by government grants." Nazi doctors conducted experiments such as comparing the skulls of Aryans and non-Aryans to gain racial knowledge, whereas doctors in the 1970s experimented on transsexual bodies to learn whether it was "possible to construct a functional vagina in a male body" to gain sexual knowledge; therefore, Raymond claims, "What we are witnessing in the transsexual context is a science at the service of patriarchal ideology of sex-role conformity in the same way that breeding for blond hair and blue eyes became a so-called science at the service of Nordic racial conformity." The section ends with a series of associations bearing little logical relationship to one another: the Nazis were Germans; the first physician on record to perform a sex conversion surgery was a German who worked at Hirschfeld's institute in Germany; Harry Benjamin, a German, visited the Hirschfeld institute many times in the 1920s; the institute's confidential files reputedly held compromising information on prominent homosexual or cross-dressing Nazis; and Nazis conducted medical experiments in the concentration camps that sometimes involved castration and hormone treatments aimed at "curing" homosexuality. Therefore? Transsexuality has something to do with Nazism.

Raymond, who has just spent so many words condemning eugenic arguments, begins the "Suggestions for Change" appended to her book with the statement: "I contend that the problem of transsexualism would best be served by morally mandating it out of existence." She does not want to actually outlaw transsexual surgeries but rather to control and limit access to them (the way one would regulate methadone access to heroin addicts) and to promote legislation against sex-role stereotyping, "where it would be possible for the law to step in at the beginning of a destructive sexist process that leads ultimately to consequences such as transsexualism." In *The Transsexual Empire* and related presentations shortly after its publication, Raymond further recommended gender reorientation for transsexuals by means of feminist consciousness-raising therapy, which would explore "the social origins of the transsexual problem and the consequences of the medical-technical solution," and public education campaigns in which ex-transsexuals would speak of their dissatisfactions with changing sex, and in which former providers of medical services to transsexuals would discuss why they decided to stop providing services.

Transgender community members have asked since the 1970s how anyone could fail to see that Raymond's rhetoric and policy recommendations replicate arguments made by ex-gay ministries, religious fundamentalists, antiabortion activists, and bigots of many stripes. In spite of these protestations, antitransgender discourses continued to proliferate in the 1980s, when it became common to denounce transsexuality as a "mutilating" practice and, if anything,

TRANS-POSITIVE SECOND WAVE FEMINISM

Second wave feminism was not uniformly, or even predominantly, hostile to transgender and transsexual people. Shulamith Firestone, a socialist feminist, was involved in some of the same radical feminist groups as Robin Morgan but broke with her over numerous political differences. Firestone took a different stance on the relationship between feminism and biomedical science from the views presented by Janice Raymond in *The Transsexual Empire*. In her book, *The Dialectic of Sex: A Case for Feminist Revolution*, Firestone writes:

> *Just as to assure elimination of economic classes requires the revolt of the underclass (the proletariat) and . . . their seizure of the means of production, so to assure the elimination of sexual classes requires the revolt of the underclass (women) and the seizure of control of reproduction. . . . And just as the end goal of socialist revolution was not only the elimination of the economic class privilege but of the economic class distinction itself, so the end goal of feminist revolution must be, unlike that of the first feminist movement, not just the elimination of male privilege but of the sex distinction itself. . . . The reproduction of the species by one sex for the benefit of both would be replaced by (at least the option of) artificial reproduction: children would be born to both sexes equally, or independently of either.*

In the controversy about Beth Elliott's participation at the West Coast Lesbian Feminist Conference, *Lesbian Tide* publisher Jeanne Cordova drew parallels between antitransgender prejudice and other forms of discrimination such as sexism, homophobia, and racism. She and lesbian activist the Reverend Freda Smith of Sacramento "stepped up," in the words of Candy Coleman, to speak "loud and strong in defense of Beth Elliott." Coleman, who identified herself as a "Gaysister," deplored the attacks on Elliott, whom she considered "right-on" and of whom she said, "I, like so many other women and Gaysisters, am proud to call her sister."

continues

Psychologist Deborah Feinbloom and her colleagues in Boston wrote an article for the *Journal of Homosexuality,* "Lesbian/Feminist Orientation among Male-to-Female Transsexuals," in which they interviewed transgender women involved in lesbian feminism and found them to be not significantly different from cisgender women in their political beliefs, activist philosophies, and gender ideology.

In the controversy about Sandy Stone's involvement with the all-women Olivia Records collective, C. Tami Weyant wrote to the feminist publication *Sister* and asserted that asking both MTF and FTM transsexuals to struggle against male privilege "as part of their feminist consciousness" was "fair," but that "rejecting them as transsexuals, period, will make us part of the oppression. . . . I strongly believe," she noted, "that only feminism can offer them safe harbor from that oppression, and that the shared issues they have struggled with demand that we struggle to accept all transsexuals who desire to be feminist."

As the foregoing statements suggest, there was nothing monolithic about second wave feminist attitudes toward trans issues. The feminist second wave simultaneously espoused some of the most reactionary attitudes toward trans people to be found anywhere while also offering a vision of transgender inclusion in progressive feminist movements for social change.

the level of vitriol directed against transgender people actually increased. A 1986 letter to the editor published in the San Francisco lesbian newspaper *Coming Up* captures the vehemence with which transsexuals could be publicly vilified:

> One cannot change one's gender. What occurs is a cleverly manipulated exterior: what has been done is mutation. What exists beneath the deformed surface is the same person who was there prior to the deformity. People who break or deform their bodies [act] out the sick farce of a deluded, patriarchal approach to nature, alienated from true being. . . . When an estrogenated man with breasts loves women, that is not lesbianism, that is mutilated

> perversion. [Such an individual] is not a threat to the lesbian community, he is an outrage to us. He is not a lesbian, he is a mutant man, a self-made freak, a deformity, an insult. He deserves a slap in the face. After that, he deserves to have his body and his mind made well again.

Raymond herself has remained completely convinced of the correctness of her position. When *The Transsexual Empire* was reissued in 1994, with a "New Introduction on Transgender," Raymond reasserted her key points that "transsexualism constitutes a sociopolitical program that is undercutting the movement to eradicate sex-role stereotyping and oppression," that transsexuals are "so alienated from their bodies that they think little of mutilating them," and that accepting transsexual people as members of the social genders they live in and are perceived to be by others amounts to collusion with a "falsification of reality." When transgender people accuse some feminists of transphobia, it is to attitudes and statements such as these that they refer.

GID and HIV

Medical attention to transgender issues culminated in the creation of a new category of psychopathology, Gender Identity Disorder (GID), which was first listed in the fourth revised edition of the American Psychiatric Association's *Diagnostic and Statistical Manual of Mental Disorders* in 1980—the first edition published after the 1973 version that had removed homosexuality. The move toward creating this new category had begun many years earlier with the work of Harry Benjamin. In 1966, after the publication of *The Transsexual Phenomenon,* Benjamin's friends and colleagues had organized HBIGDA—the Harry Benjamin International Gender Dysphoria Association. HBIGDA became the main organization for medical, legal, and psychotherapeutic professionals who worked with transgender populations, and its membership consisted primarily of the surgeons, endocrinologists, psychiatrists, and lawyers affiliated with the big university-based programs that provided transgender health care and conducted research into gender identity formation. By the later 1970s, a decade of research had produced a set of treatment protocols for transgender patients, called the "Standards of Care," as well as a set of diagnostic criteria, which became formalized as GID.

GID was very controversial within transgender communities. Most people with transgender feelings resented having their sense of gender labeled as a sickness and their identities classified as disordered; others took great comfort from believing they had a medical condition that could be cured with proper treatment. Until recently, people who have wanted to use hormones and surgery to change their appearance, and to gain access to changing state-issued IDs and legal gender, have had to be diagnosed with GID and abide by the Standards of Care. This has required a psychological evaluation and a period of living in the desired gender role before access has been granted for medically regulated treatments, which then enabled a legal change in gender status. Some transgender people have questioned why gender change needed to be medicalized in the first place, while others have argued that they should have access to health care services without having their need to do so be considered pathological. In spite of it being recognized by psychomedical professionals as a legitimate and diagnosable psychopathology, treatments for GID were not covered by health plans in the United States because they were considered "elective," "cosmetic," or even "experimental." This was a truly inexcusable double bind—if GID was a real psychopathology, its treatment should have been insurable as a legitimate health care need; if treating it was not considered medically necessary, it should not have been listed as a disease.

With the "problem" of transsexuality seemingly solved and contained within the new diagnostic category, several of the university-based programs—notably the one at Johns Hopkins—closed down, and those at several other universities—such as Stanford—spun off into privately run clinics operated by doctors affiliated with the universities' medical schools. Responsibility for ensuring that professional standards of care were being met devolved onto a second tier of psychotherapists in private practice who were members of HBIGDA. Thus, by 1980, a routine set of procedures and protocols for medically managing transgender populations had fallen into place. Transgender access to government-funded social services, which had been more readily available during the Democratic administrations of Johnson and Carter, were drastically curtailed under Nixon and Reagan, in part, it seems, in the latter case, in response to antitransgender feminist arguments that dovetailed with conservative politics. When antipornography feminists in this period, such as Catharine MacKinnon and Andrea Dworkin, allied themselves with conservative government policies in order to criminalize pornography (which they considered violence against women), Janice Raymond hammered home the connections with transgender issues by suggesting that the "same socialization that enables men to objectify women in rape, pornography, and 'drag' enables them to objectify their own bodies," treating a penis a thing to "get rid of" and a vagina as something to acquire.

In briefly tracing the history of the emergence of GID, it is possible to see how the social power of science shifted, during the course of a few years in the 1970s, from a concern with sexual orientation to a preoccupation with gender identity. To a certain degree, the effectiveness of gay liberation and the successes of lesbian and gay civil rights activism had made it politically impossible for responsible medical professionals to continue treating homosexuality as a mental illness. At the same time, the success of feminism in destabilizing conventional means of social control over women's bodies made gender—rather than sexuality—into an even more important social battleground. The intensified interest of medical science in trying to understand, engineer, and "fix" gender in these years needs to be seen, in part, as an attempt to stuff the feminist genie back into its bottle. The result, for transgender people, was a lose-lose situation. All across the political spectrum, from reactionary to progressive and all points in between, the only options presented to them were to be considered bad, sick, or wrong. Consequently, transgender communities became very inwardly focused by the 1980s. They tended to concentrate more on providing mutual aid and support to their members than on broader social activism.

On top of this dismal situation, a devastating new threat to transgender communities appeared in 1981—the first visible manifestation of the AIDS pandemic. Transgender populations that relied on sex work for survival, that shared needles for injecting hormones, or that participated in the gay male sexual subcultures where the epidemic first gained widespread attention in the United States were especially hard hit. Poor access to health care services because of poverty, stigma, and social isolation, as well as additional barriers to access created by the fear many transgender people have of disclosing their transgender status to health care providers (which could potentially reexpose them to social vulnerabilities they had worked hard to overcome), only served to compound the problem. As a result, transgender people—especially African American trans women—now suffer one of the highest HIV infection rates in the world.

FTM Communities

The shifts in lesbian and feminist gender ideology that focused on "woman identification" and provided the conceptual underpinnings for some women to engage in transphobic attacks also encouraged some former butches and femmes to maintain the erotic dynamics of their relationships by leaving the homosexual subcultures they had once considered home and to blend into the dominant heteronormative population once the former butch had transitioned to life as a man. This is not to suggest that trans men would be lesbians given the opportunity but rather to point out that as one possible way of life for transmasculine people was becoming less available, other possibilities were expanding. These changes in the cultural landscape unavoidably affected the life paths that many gender-questioning people followed. It's also important to note that not all trans men have a lesbian history and that many people assigned female at birth who were oriented toward men also found their way into female-to-male communities in increasing numbers by the mid-1970s, and they sometimes embraced gay male identities as they continued to be involved with men after transitioning. Jude Patton, with the Renaissance group in Los Angeles, and Rupert Raj of Toronto, with his *Metamorphosis* magazine, provided support for hundreds of trans men in the 1970s and 1980s. In 1977, their fellow trans activist Mario Martino's memoir *Emergence* became the first full-length autobiography of a trans man to be published in the United States.

One of the first media pieces to draw attention to civil injustices encountered by trans men—and a key moment in the politicization of a US FTM community—involved Steve Dain, an award-winning former high school physical education teacher in Emeryville, California. In 1976, Dain had informed his principal that he would be transitioning genders during the school's summer vacation, and he asked to be reassigned to teach science rather than girls' gym. The request was granted, but because of a change in the school's administration, a new vice principal was unaware of Dain's plan. During the first day of classes, the administrator panicked when he learned that the new science teacher was none other than the old

PE teacher, and he had Dain arrested in his classroom—in front of his students—for "disturbing the peace." Dain successfully sued the Emeryville school district for a large but undisclosed sum and subsequently left teaching to pursue a career as a chiropractor. He became a highly visible spokesperson for FTM issues, appearing in the 1985 HBO documentary *What Sex Am I?* and serving as a lay counselor for many gender-questioning transmasculine people.

One of Dain's most significant protégés was Lou Sullivan, who became the hub of the organized FTM community in the United States in the 1980s. Born in 1951, Sullivan started keeping a journal as a ten-year-old girl growing up in the Milwaukee suburbs and continued journaling regularly until a few days before his untimely death at age thirty-nine, in 1991. In his journal, Sullivan described his early childhood thoughts of being a boy, his confusing adolescent sexual fantasies of being a gay man, and his teenage participation in Milwaukee's countercultural scene. He read John Rechy's novels and dreamed of running away to live with the drag queens of Los Angeles. By the time he graduated high school, he was dressing in men's clothes and was active in the Gay People's Union (GPU) at the University of Wisconsin, Milwaukee, where he found a job as a secretary in the Slavic Languages department.

By 1973, Sullivan self-identified as a "female transvestite" who was sexually attracted to gay and bisexual men. That same year, he launched a career of transgender community activism with the publication of "A Transvestite Answers a Feminist," an article that appeared in the *GPU News,* in which he recounted his conversations with a coworker who was critical of his masculine style of dress. The argument Sullivan laid out—that all people represent their sense of themselves to others by means of certain recognizable gender conventions, and that transgender representations of masculine or feminine identities are no more or no less "stereotypical" than those of anyone else—anticipated a line of thinking that became well

LOU SULLIVAN: RECORDING A LIFE

Lou Sullivan's journals constitute one of the most complete, and one of the most compelling, accounts of a transgender life ever set to page. These excerpts, from ages eleven to twenty-two, chart the trajectory of his emerging gay male identity.

When we got home, we played boys.

—JANUARY 6, 1963, AGE ELEVEN

My problem is that I can't accept life for what it is, like it's presented to me. I feel that there is something deep and wonderful underneath it that no one has found.

—DECEMBER 12, 1965, AGE FOURTEEN

No one looks deeper than the flesh.

—FEBRUARY 22, 1966, AGE FOURTEEN

I want to look like what I am but don't know what someone like me looks like. I mean, when people look at me I want them to think, there's one of those people . . . that has their own interpretation of happiness. That's what I am.

—JUNE 6, 1966, AGE FIFTEEN

My heart and soul is with the drag queens. This last week or so I've wanted to go and leave everything and join that world. But where do I fit in? I feel so deprived and sad and lost. What can become of a girl whose real desire and passion is with male homosexuals? That I want to be one? I still yearn for that world, that world I know nothing about, a serious, threatening, sad, ferocious stormy, lost world.

—NOVEMBER 22, 1970, AGE NINETEEN

I know now that I can get exactly what I want—to fantasize is no longer enough. Before it was beyond my dreams. It was the worst perversion that I wished I had a penis, to fuck a boy, to be on top and inside! But now it's only a matter of time.

—DECEMBER 11, 1973, AGE TWENTY-TWO

established in transgender community discourses in the decades ahead. Another article, "Looking Towards Transvestite Liberation," published in the *GPU News* in 1974, was widely reprinted in the gay and lesbian press. Sullivan continued to contribute reviews and articles to the *GPU News* through 1980, many of them historical vignettes of people assigned female at birth who lived their lives as men. In doing so, Sullivan became an important community-based historian of FTM experience.

Sullivan had come to self-identify as a female-to-male transsexual by 1975, and he moved to San Francisco to seek a medically assisted gender transition at the Stanford University gender dysphoria program. He found work, as a woman, as a secretary for the Wilson Sporting Goods Company, but he spent most of his nonworking hours dressed as a young man, cruising the Castro neighborhood's gay enclave for anonymous sex with men. In 1976, Sullivan was rejected by the Stanford program on the basis of his openly declared gay male identity, and he spent the next four years continuing to live as a woman. During these years, in which he tried to make peace with his female embodiment, he participated in feminist consciousness-raising sessions (which he admits helped him work through some internalized misogyny but never caused him to waver in his gay male identity), learned to repair cars in an effort to combat

Lou Sullivan, the leading organizer of the female-to-male (FTM) community in the 1980s. (Photo credit: Mariette Pathy Allen.)

limiting female stereotypes, and became active in San Francisco Bay Area MTF cross-dresser groups, where he worked to develop peer support for female-to-male individuals. Sullivan had read and been inspired by the 1976 newspaper coverage of Steve Dain's tribulations, but he first had a chance to meet his hero in 1979, after meeting a psychotherapist at a cross-dresser support organization who happened to know Dain.

Steve Dain offered Sullivan important validation and encouraged him to pursue transitioning if it was what he really wanted to do. By 1979, as noted earlier, the framework for transgender medical services was shifting away from university-based research programs and becoming considerably more decentralized. As a result, Sullivan was able to find psychotherapists, endocrinologists, and surgeons in private practice who were not concerned with his identification as a gay man and who were willing to help him transition. Sullivan started hormones in 1979, had chest surgery in 1980, and thereafter starting living full-time as a man. At this point, he threw himself even more fully into transgender community activism. He volunteered as the first FTM peer counselor at the Janus Information Facility, a private organization that took over the Erickson Educational Foundation's transgender information and referral activities after the NTCU folded (and which had changed its name to the Transsexual Counseling Service shortly before it went out of business). As a result, Sullivan found himself in contact with a multitude of gender-questioning people who had been assigned female at birth.

Sullivan simultaneously redoubled his efforts as a community-based historian. He gathered the vignettes he had published through the years in the *GPU News* and incorporated them into the guidebook he developed based on his work at Janus, *Information for the Female-to-Male Cross-Dresser and Transsexual,* which remained the go-to self-help book for trans men well into the 1990s. In 1986,

Sullivan became a founding member (and newsletter editor) of the Gay and Lesbian Historical Society (now the GLBT Historical Society), whose archives comprise one of the best collections of material on gay, lesbian, bisexual, and transgender history anywhere in the world. As a result of Sullivan's early involvement, the organization's transgender holdings are particularly rich. Sullivan also started work on a book-length biography of Jack B. Garland, the nineteenth-century San Franciscan also known as Babe Bean, who had been born female but who lived as a man in the Tenderloin. Sullivan noted that Garland eroticized his relationships with the young men he met in the Tenderloin and that he helped them out by offering food, shelter, and gifts of money. Seeing antecedents to his own trans-gay identity, in his book, published in 1991, Sullivan argued that contrary to the then-prevailing wisdom in gay and feminist scholarship, Garland did not live as a man to escape the conventional limitations of womanhood but rather because of his identification as a man and his homoerotic attraction to other men.

In 1986, while Sullivan was working to establish the GLBT archives in San Francisco, he also organized the second FTM-only support and education organization in the United States. Called simply "FTM," the organization held monthly "FTM Gatherings" featuring educational programs and opportunities to socialize and also published the *FTM Newsletter,* which quickly became the leading source of information in the nation for female-to-male issues. Because of Sullivan's leadership role and his own gay identity, the San Francisco FTM group always attracted a sexually diverse membership and avoided many of the divisions over sexual orientation that had plagued similar MTF organizations since the 1960s. This openness was reflected in the newsletter's editorial slant and helped shape group sensibilities in the community of trans men that started blossoming in the 1980s with Sullivan's support. The organization Sullivan founded became FTM International, now the oldest continuing FTM group in the world. The San Francisco chapter became known as the Lou Sullivan Society, which is now an independent web-based resource for trans men in the Bay Area.

Lou Sullivan's life was cut tragically short by an opportunistic illness contracted as a result of HIV infection. Lou did not live up to the promiscuous stereotype of a gay man in San Francisco in the 1980s, but he did visit gay sex clubs after having his chest surgery in 1980, and in 1985—in an experimental phase—he dated trans women who supported themselves through commercial sex work at a Tenderloin bar called the Black Rose; other than those brief episodes of sexual adventurousness, Sullivan could count his long-term sex partners on one hand. Whenever and however it was that Lou became infected, he remained asymptomatic until 1986, when complications from the genital surgery he had finally decided to pursue stressed his immune system. In the course of his postsurgical recovery, Sullivan developed *Pneumocystis jiroveci* pneumonia (formerly known as *Pneumocystis carinii* pneumonia, PCP), an especially virulent form of pneumonia closely associated with AIDS. At the time his diagnosis was confirmed, survival rates for people with AIDS averaged somewhere in the vicinity of two years. Sullivan survived for five, in reasonably good health until the very end. In his final years he participated in AIDS drug trials, finished his book on Jack Garland, and continued to nurture the FTM group and the Historical Society. Sullivan's final campaign, however, was to persuade HBIGDA members and the committee revising the definition of GID for the next edition of the *Diagnostic and Statistical Manual* to drop "homosexual orientation" as a contraindication in the diagnostic criteria, which was based on the assumption that homosexual transgender people did not exist. Sullivan did not live to see that change take place in 1994, but he took comfort in knowing that his efforts were contributing to a revision of the sexological literature.

In one of his journal entries after his AIDS diagnosis, Lou mused about writing to the staff of the Stanford gender dysphoria program to say, "You told me I couldn't live as a gay man, but now I am going to die like one." He left this life surrounded by friends and family on March 6, 1991, just as a new phase of transgender history was beginning to erupt.

CHAPTER 5

THE MILLENNIAL WAVE

THE TREMENDOUS BURST of new transgender activism that began around 1990 came on the heels of a generally dispiriting decade or two in which transgender people made only small, erratic strides toward a better collective existence. After years of court rulings in which discrimination against transsexuals was found not to be illegal under Title VII of the Civil Rights Act (most notably in the Supreme Court case *Ulane v. Eastern Airlines,* 1984), the 1989 decision in *Price Waterhouse v. Hopkins,* which held sex stereotyping to be illegal after the well-known accounting firm denied a partnership to Ann Hopkins for being "too masculine," opened up important lines of argumentation for trans rights in the decades ahead. The Americans with Disabilities Act (ADA) passed in 1990 could have been interpreted as covering transgender people, who, after all, were considered to have an officially recognized psychopathological debility, except for the fact that "transsexualism" was specifically exempted from coverage. A number of states had come to recognize legal change of sex on birth certificates, change of name and gender on driver's licenses, and the rights of postoperative transsexuals to marry in their current gender by the early 1990s. A few (Illinois, Arizona, and Louisiana) had done so as early as the 1960s; several others (Hawaii, California, Connecticut, Massachusetts, Michigan, New Jersey, Virginia, North Carolina, and Iowa) had followed suit in the 1970s; and several more (Colorado, Arkansas, Georgia, Missouri, New Mexico, Oregon, Utah, Wisconsin, and the District of Columbia) had done so by the 1980s. In addition, three municipalities—Minneapolis, Minnesota; Harrisburg, Pennsylvania; and Seattle, Washington—had enacted human and civil rights protections for transgender people before the end of the 1980s. The Southern California chapter of the American Civil Liberties Union (ACLU) had formed the Transsexual Rights Committee in 1980, which had won a few modest victories pertaining to the treatment of trans people by the Veterans Administration, the California prison system, and government-funded vocational rehabilitation programs, but the committee disbanded around 1983. Althea Garrison was revealed as the first trans person to have been elected to a state legislature when she won a seat in the Massachusetts statehouse in 1992; she was publicly outed two days later, effectively ending her political career. Transgender-related policy, legislative, and electoral victories were few and far between until the 1990s.

A few transgender organizations and service agencies had soldiered on through the bleakest stretches of the 1970s and 1980s. The oldest ongoing transgender gathering in the nation, Fantasia Fair, first met in Provincetown, Massachusetts, in 1975, under the leadership of Ari Kane, a transgender mental health educator who that same year also founded the Outreach Institute of Gender Studies. The weeklong Fantasia Fair, a retreat initially geared toward male-to-female cross-dressers, has tried with some success to broaden its appeal to transsexuals and transmasculine people in recent years. Boston's transgender community also spawned the International Foundation for Gender Education (IFGE) in 1987. Like Fantasia Fair, it initially focused on the needs and interests of MTF cross-dressers but aimed for an increasingly general transgender constituency during the course of its existence. IFGE's magazine, *Tapestry,* was once the most widely circulated transgender publication in the United States. The Janus Information Facility, which had taken over the education and outreach work of the Erickson Educational Foundation in the mid-1970s, itself ceased operations in the mid-1980s and transferred its mission to two stalwarts of the transgender community, Jude Patton and Joanna Clark, who ran the cryptically named transsexual information clearinghouse J2PC (derived from the initials of their names) in San Juan Capistrano, California. Such small-scale, largely self-financed homegrown resources, which enjoyed a few years of influence and significance before sinking beneath the waves of time, characterized the bulk of transgender community organizations into (and even beyond) the 1990s.

But just as transgender social justice activism made gains in the 1960s when transgender issues resonated with larger cultural shifts related to the rise of feminism, the war in Vietnam, sexual liberation, and youth countercultures, the transgender movement bolted forward again in the early 1990s for reasons having little to do directly with transgender issues. As suggested earlier, a variety of novel historical factors—the new political concept of queerness, the AIDS epidemic, the rapid development of the Internet, the end of the Cold War, the maturation of the first post–Baby Boomer generation, and the calendrical millennial turn—all played their parts in revitalizing transgender politics in the last decade of the twentieth century. The wave of change that began at that time continued for a quarter century.

The New Transgender and Queer Feminist Theory

Around 1990, transgender issues experienced a rapid evolution and expansion—indeed, it's about this time that the word *transgender* first started to acquire its current definition as a catchall term for all nonnormative forms of gender expression and identity. Variants of the word had been popping up since the early 1960s in both sexological literature and male cross-dresser communities, where words such as "transgenderal," "transgenderist," and "transgenderism" were used by people like Ari Kane and Virginia Prince to describe individuals, such as themselves, who occupied a different gender category from either transvestites or transsexuals. Throughout the 1970s and 1980s, a "transgenderist" was most likely somebody born with a penis and who kept it in spite of living socially as a woman. Trans activist Holly Boswell made an important contribution toward the expansion of the term with her 1991 article "The Transgender Alternative," published in the community-based journal *Chrysalis Quarterly,* which claimed *transgender* was a word that "encompasses the whole spectrum" of gender diversity and lumps together rather than splits apart the many subgroups within a large, heterogeneous set of communities. Leslie Feinberg gave this expansive sense of *transgender* a political charge with their influential 1992 pamphlet, *Transgender Liberation: A Movement Whose Time Has Come.* Feinberg, who had begun transitioning from female to male in the 1980s before deciding to live again as a masculine woman with some surgical body alterations, became one of the chief architects of the new transgender sensibility, as s/he struggled to define and occupy a space on the borders and intersections of conventional gender categories. Their pamphlet took a Marxist approach to the question of the social, political, and economic oppression of nonnormative expressions of gender, and s/he called for a "transgender" movement that would link many struggles against specific gender-based oppressions together into one radical movement. Feinberg's autobiographically grounded novel *Stone Butch Blues* (1991) communicated the emotional flavor of hir transgender vision to a large and appreciative international audience.

Yet another contribution to the redefinition of *transgender* came in the form of a 1992 academic article by Sandy Stone, "The 'Empire' Strikes Back: A Posttranssexual Manifesto." Stone, who had first gained notoriety in transgender circles as the male-to-female transsexual recording engineer who inspired Janice Raymond to lead a boycott of the all-women Olivia Records collective, had since gotten a PhD in cultural studies, and she made brilliant use of some of the new theories of gender just then beginning to circulate in the academy, which she used to help shift the old trans-exclusionary feminist debates into a productive new register. In calling for "posttranssexual" theorizing capable of reframing the common narratives through which trans people were marginalized, Stone helped give the nascent "transgender" movement an intellectual as well as a political agenda.

There is more than one intellectual genealogy of what came to be called "queer studies." One story has it emerging from the work of literary critics Eve Kosofsky Sedgwick and Michael Moon at Duke University. Stone, however, was more grounded in the version of queer feminism that blossomed in Santa Cruz, where she earned her PhD at the University of California while studying under feminist science studies scholar Donna Haraway. West Coast queer theory was more indebted to feminists of color, primarily the writers in the anthology *This Bridge Called My Back,* and most especially to Gloria Anzaldúa's *Borderlands/La Frontera: The New Mestiza.* Two crucial insights in this body of work were to be found in its intersectional analyses of race/class/gender/sexuality oppressions—no one of which could be privileged over the others in the lives of the women writing about their situations—and in its attention to "hybridity." White feminism often (and often unconsciously) claimed its moral strength based on some concept of "purity"—notably (especially in the first wave) some notion of female sexual purity, but also, more abstractly, in the second wave, on the idea of an essential womanhood to be recovered or restored from the taint of patriarchal pollution. In contrast, Anzaldúa's brand of feminism valued the power to be found in being mixed, in crossing borders, of having no one clear category to fit into—of being essentially impure. Haraway drew on this evolving frame of reference in her famous "Cyborg Manifesto," which described a "post-gender" world of "technocultural" bodies, and added machine/human and animal/human to the kinds of boundary and mixing questions with which feminism should be concerned. Stone's "posttranssexual manifesto," attentive as it was to technologically altered transgender bodies, was deeply influenced by Haraway's approach to the intersectionality of gender, embodiment, and technology. However, it also drew from another new way of thinking about gender then being explored by another feminist faculty member at the University of California, Santa Cruz, Teresa de Lauretis, who coined the term "queer studies" for a conference she organized under that name in Santa Cruz in 1991.

The new "queer" version of gender espoused by de Lauretis and other like-minded feminist scholars, which de Lauretis laid out most succinctly in her essay "Technologies of Gender," discarded the older feminist idea that gender was *merely* repressive—that it was *only* a system for holding women down, turning them into second-class citizens, exploiting their labor, and controlling their reproductive capacities. Without denying that gender systems indeed produced systematic inequalities for women, the new queer take on gender also talked about gender's *productive* power—how "woman" was also a cultural or linguistic "site" or "location" that its occupants identified themselves with, understood themselves through, and acted from. The new queer feminism drew heavily from French philosopher Michel Foucault's concept of social power as decentralized and distributed rather than flowing from a single source;

that is, that each of us has a power particular to our situation, and that power is not just something vested "up there" somewhere in the law or the military or capital or the "patriarchy." Queer feminism reimagined the status "woman" as not simply a condition of victimization to be escaped from, and it reconceptualized gender as a network of "relations of power" that, like language, we don't ever get outside of but always express ourselves through and work within—a situation that gives feminist women a "dual vision" and "split subjectivity." Sometimes womanhood is a binding-in-place that needs to be resisted and worked against, and sometimes, de Lauretis said, women want womanhood to stick to them "like a wet silk dress."

TRANSSUBJECTIVITY AND REALITY HACKING

A 1995 issue of *Wired* magazine included an interview with trans theorist Sandy Stone, who has had an amazingly varied career. Among other things, she has conducted early research on digital telephones at Bell Labs and on neural implants for the National Institutes for Health (NIH), worked as sound engineer for Jimi Hendrix, helped found the women's music scene while working at Olivia Records (where she was the target of a transphobic boycott by trans-exclusionary lesbian feminists), and earned a PhD in History of Consciousness at the University of California, Santa Cruz. Her article "The 'Empire' Strikes Back: A Posttranssexual Manifesto," a scathing rebuttal to Janice Raymond's *The Transsexual Empire,* helped launch the new interdisciplinary field of transgender studies. Stone taught for many years at the University of Texas in Austin, where she established the Advanced Communication Technology Laboratory (ACT Lab). Most of what Sandy and the *Wired* interviewer said to each other wound up on the cutting room floor—the conversation below draws on different parts of the conversation than that which was ultimately published.

continues

TRANSSUBJECTIVITY AND REALITY HACKING *continued*

Wired: You worked in technical fields for many years but now study how that work is done by others. What led you to cultural studies of science?

Stone: It gave me that common language I'd always dreamed of. I could bring to it much of my experience with neurology and telephony and sound recording and computer programming, my studies of classics, and my brief encounters with critical theory. I could find ways in which all of those things fit together. It started with a piece called "Sex and Death among the Cyborgs." I set out to write an essay on data compression and wound up writing about phone sex. Sex usually involves as many of the senses as possible—taste, touch, smell, sight, hearing. Phone sex workers translate all those modalities of experience into sound, then boil that down into a series of highly compressed tokens. They squirt those tokens down a voice-grade line and someone at the other end just adds water, so to speak, to reconstitute the tokens into a fully detailed set of images and interactions in multiple sensory modes. "Sex and Death among the Cyborgs" was an attempt to explore boundaries and prostheses and everything that interests me now.

Wired: What do you mean when you say "boundaries and prostheses"?

Stone: Subjective boundaries and bodily boundaries. We're a culture that likes to preserve the illusion that they're fixed in place. But they move around all the time. For example, where's the boundary of an individual human body? Is it skin? Is it clothes? It's different in different circumstances. I use Stephen Hawking as an example of how body boundary issues interact with technology. Because Hawking can't speak, he lectures with a computer-generated voice. Hawking's computerized voice generator is a prosthesis, from the Greek word for "extension."

continues

It's an extension of his person. It extends his will across the boundaries of flesh and machinery, from the medium of air molecules in motion to the medium of electromagnetic force.

Wired: It seems to me that being transsexual significantly informs your work. Transsexuality could be considered a form of reality hacking—you "change sex" by using for your own purposes the codes that regulate how we understand the meaning of identity through the body. Hormones and surgery are prostheses that extend a sense of self into a set of physical signs that mean identity in social interactions. Experiencing the transformation of your body through transsexual technologies gives one an acute sense of the issues that come up in trying to understand virtual systems, cyberspace, interface, agency, interaction, and identity. It's hard for many people to grasp this aspect of transsexuality because of the way it's been stigmatized, pathologized, exoticized, and eroticized.

Stone: I want to move away from the sexuality model for very much those reasons—that's why I want to talk about transsubjectivity rather than transsexuality. This term better helps us see that the body is an instrument for involvement with others. When I wrote in an essay called "A Posttranssexual Manifesto" that transsexuality was a genre rather than a gender, I meant that the body is a site for the play of language, a generator of symbolic exchange.

Without saying so in quite so many words, de Lauretis and other queer feminists found a useful way to acknowledge that feminist women could be committed to feminist politics without therefore necessarily being forced to concede that "woman" was nothing more than a patriarchal trap for female bodies. This opened a line of argument that led directly to Stone's essay, which called upon transsexual people simultaneously to resist the old ways that medical science had encouraged them to behave as the price for providing services—creating false biographies to conceal their sex change from others, for example, or trying to pass as a cisgender person—while also soliciting them to speak out in a "heteroglossic," Babel-like profusion of tongues about all the imaginable genres of gender difference there could be, if only the homogenizing tendencies of the medically dominated discourse of transsexuality were shattered. In doing so, trans people could simultaneously circumvent the pernicious perspective that had become entrenched over the preceding decade, that transsexuals were either duplicitous, dupes of the patriarchy, or mentally ill. All genders—all genres of personhood—would be on the same plane.

Two other developments internal to feminism shook open spaces within political activism, scholarship, and community formation and allowed transgender feminism to expand and grow in the 1990s. The first was the so-called sex wars, a pivotal episode of which was the 1982 Barnard conference on women, which aired long-standing differences within feminism about female sexuality. Fierce debates raged around the topics of pornography, prostitution, and consensual sadomasochism. Could there be feminist positions on these issues that were not simply condemnatory; that is, could there be feminist pornography, feminist sex work, feminist practices of sexual kink, or were such ideas rooted in "internalized misogyny" and did they constitute "violence against women"? The "sex-positive" and "sex-negative" camps were every bit as polarized as those names suggest, and the sex wars—like earlier disputes within feminism about heterosexism, class, and color—further fragmented a movement that was never as homogeneous as some feminists wanted to believe.

The "sex-negative" camp consigned cross-dressing and transsexual genital modification to the same discredited territory occupied by fetish, prostitution, incest, and rape, while the "sex-positive" camp resisted the idea that some sexual practices condemned by mainstream society were intrinsically antifeminist or that criticizing some aspects of those practices necessarily entailed a condemnation of the women who practiced them. The warring perspectives are succinctly summarized in the names of two feminist publications: *Off Our Backs,* which advocated a resistance to sexist oppression of women, and *On Our Backs,* a frank celebration of female sexual pleasure. Some of the same arguments that the sex-positive feminists made in defense of women who take money in exchange for sex or who engage in bedroom bondage scenarios or rape fantasies or intergenerational desire would open a path whereby transgender practices and perspectives could similarly contest the censure of certain kinds of feminists.

Sex-positive feminism had the disadvantage, however, of regarding being trans as an erotic practice rather than an expression of gender identity. Feminist anthropologist Gayle Rubin's influential article "Thinking Sex," first delivered at the Barnard conference and published in the anthology of conference-related work, *Pleasure and Danger,* clearly demonstrates this point. In charting out the "moral sex hierarchy" shared by "sex-negative" feminism and mainstream US society, Rubin distinguishes between forms of sexuality clearly labeled "good" (such as reproductive heterosexual monogamy) and those clearly labeled "bad" (such as fetishistic cross-dressing, transsexuality, or street prostitution), and she identifies a "major area of contest" between these poles that encompasses sexual practices that are morally ambiguous within the dominant culture (such as promiscuous heterosexuality or long-term, stable, romantic homosexual couplings). Through time, a practice might move from a very marginalized position, to one where its status was contested, to one where it was largely accepted—exactly the path followed by homosexuality in the aftermath of the gay liberation movement.

One of the main goals of Rubin's argument was to challenge the way that some schools of feminism (those drawing on the "purity" tradition) set up hierarchies that placed their own perspective at the top and claimed the power to judge and condemn other positions they deemed morally suspect. Rubin's article noted how early second wave feminism floundered when it tried to apply the economic concept of "class" to the category "woman," which has many noneconomic attributes, and succeeded only when it developed a set of analytical tools that were specific to the situation of women—that is to say, a gender analysis. She then proposed that feminism, as the study of gender, was in turn not a sufficient frame of reference for the analysis of sexuality, and she proposed a new "sexuality studies" that, without abandoning feminism any more than feminism had abandoned economic concerns, would take up a new set of questions about sex. This argument eventually came to be seen as foundational to the intellectual project of queer studies. In making that important argument, however, Rubin clearly categorized transgender practices as sexual or erotic acts rather than expressions of gender identity or sense of self. As a revitalized transgender movement began to gather force in the early 1990s, it posed a challenge to the new queer theory similar to the one posed by sexuality to feminism: it asked whether the framework of queer sexuality could adequately account for transgender phenomena, or whether a new, additional frame of analysis was also required. These are the questions that led, in the years ahead, to the development of the new interdisciplinary academic field of transgender studies.

No account of the new transgender movement and its relation to feminism in the early 1990s would be complete without mentioning the impact of philosopher Judith Butler's work. In her 1990 book, *Gender Trouble: Feminism and the Subversion of Identity*, Butler promoted the concept of "gender performativity," which became central to the self-understandings of many transgender people (along with many cisgender people, too). The main idea is that "being something" consists of "doing it," a point often misunderstood in some quarters of the transgender community as an assertion that gender is a merely a performance and therefore not real. For trans people, who often suffer a great deal to actualize for others the reality of their gender identifications, the idea that gender was a game with no skin in it, just a wardrobe full of possible gender costumes to be put on or taken off at will, felt galling. But that actually was never Butler's point; rather, it was that the reality of gender for *everybody* is the "doing of it." Rather than being an objective quality of the body (defined by sex), gender is constituted by all the innumerable acts of performing it: how we dress, move, speak, touch, look. Gender is like a language we use to communicate ourselves to others and to understand ourselves. The implication of this argument is that transgender genders are as real as any others, and they are achieved in the same fundamental way.

Butler clarified and extended some of her arguments in her next book, *Bodies That Matter: On the Discursive Limits of "Sex."* She argued there that the category of sex, which is conventionally considered the physical foundation of gender difference (that is, male and female biology respectively generate the social roles and personal identities "man" and "woman"), is actually produced by how culture understands gender. The way a gender system points to the body as a form of evidence that proves its truth is just a discourse, a story we tell about what the evidence supplied by the body means. Even what "counts" as sex is up for grabs. This discursive truth achieves its reality by being perpetually "cited" (referred to over and over again in medicine, law, psychiatry, media, everyday conversation, and so forth) in ways that, taken all together, make it real in practice, in the performative sense mentioned above. This way of thinking about sex, gender, and reality opened up for theorists within the new transgender movement the prospect that new "truths" of transgender experience, new ways of narrating the relationship between gendered sense of self, social role, and embodiment, could begin to be told—precisely what Sandy Stone had called for in her "posstranssexual" manifesto.

AIDS and the New Transgender

The shifting paradigms of gender and sexuality that emerged from the intellectual workplaces of academe by the 1990s were informed by the course of the AIDS epidemic, which also played an important role in revitalizing the transgender movement. From a public health perspective, transgender populations had come to be seen as "vulnerable" populations—ones more prone to infection because of the confluence of poverty, social stigma, job discrimination, survival prostitution, fewer educational resources, lack of access to medical information or health care, and other contributing factors. To prevent vulnerable populations from becoming vectors of infection for other larger and healthier populations, AIDS funding entities directed money to "culturally competent" prevention and harm-reduction strategies aimed at trans people. AIDS funding thus became an important mechanism for bringing needed social and financial resources to trans communities. Particularly in communities of color, AIDS agencies and service organizations became centers of transgender activism, hosting support groups, facilitating community gatherings, and providing employment to trans people engaged in health outreach and peer support work. Even strictly social events for trans people who were not HIV-positive were sometimes financially supported through AIDS funding, with the idea that such events could help provide important safer-sex education opportunities and could help build self-esteem and cultural pride that would encourage healthy decision making about potentially risky behaviors. Several organizations and programs established in San Francisco in the early to mid-1990s reflected this national trend, including Projecto ContraSIDA por Vida, the Asian and Pacific Islander Wellness Center, and the transgender program at Brothers Network, an agency primarily serving African American men and transgender women.

The history of the AIDS epidemic significantly reshaped sexual identity politics. When the epidemic first emerged in the United States, it surfaced among gay men who were mostly white. One early name for the syndrome was in fact GRID—Gay-Related Immune Deficiency. But epidemiologists and public health workers knew that the mysterious new disease was not confined to white gay populations and, however much it affected them, to paint the immune deficiency syndrome as "gay related" could serve only to

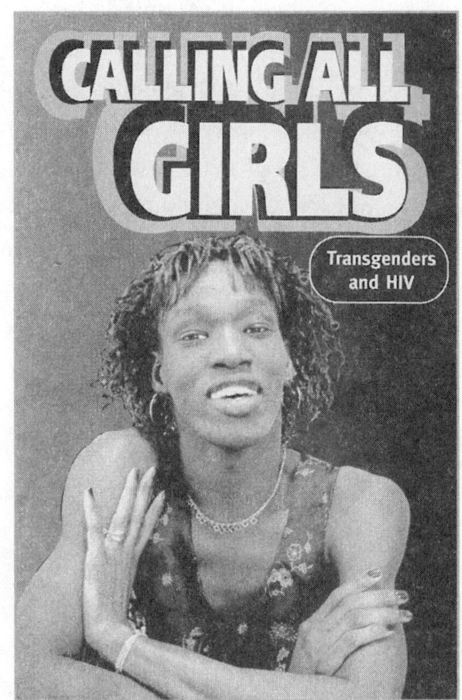

AIDS prevention and educational outreach funding accelerated transgender community formation, especially in communities of color. (Photo credit: GLBT Historical Society.)

impede an adequate public health response. AIDS also affected hemophiliacs, injection drug users, and Haitian immigrants in disproportionate numbers, regardless of their sexual orientation or gender. It soon became clear that AIDS could pass from person to person through heterosexual intercourse and that in fact it was the exchange of bodily fluids, rather than the type of sexual act per se, that created risk of infection. It also quickly became clear that the prevalence of HIV infection was not uniformly distributed but rather was structured at the population level by racism and poverty: poor people of color, particularly African American people, were far more likely to become infected and far less likely to be able to access the best life-prolonging health care. Black transgender women living at the intersection of transphobia, misogyny, homophobia, racism, poverty, and higher rates of incarceration—particularly if they were involved in commercial sex work—were especially vulnerable. The AIDS health crisis thus required gay men, and many lesbians, to rethink the cultural politics of homosexuality and the ways in which homosexual communities related to and intersected with broader social structures—in the same way that it required many nonhomosexuals to relate differently to gay communities and subcultures. To adequately respond to the AIDS epidemic demanded a new kind of alliance politics in which specific communities came together across the dividing lines of race and gender, class and nationality, citizenship and sexual orientation. It also required gay liberation politics and feminist public health activism to take transgender issues far more seriously than they had in the past.

The name for this new kind of unabashedly pro-gay, nonseparatist, antiassimilationist alliance politics to combat AIDS, which did not organize itself around identity categories but instead took aim at the overarching social structures that marginalized those infected by HIV, was *queer*. The new politics resonated with the new intellectual paradigms taking shape in the academy, but it drew its forces from unapologetic, confrontational, and media-savvy protest groups such as ACT UP (AIDS Coalition to Unleash Power), which reclaimed an old epithet for gay people, "queer," and turned it into an in-your-face "So what?" retort to anti-AIDS prejudice. ACT UP was one of the most successful radical direct action political groups in US history, successfully taking on a criminally negligent federal government under President Ronald Reagan, as well as the multi-billion-dollar pharmaceuticals industry, to develop treatments, fund programs, challenge prejudice, and save lives. This newly politicized sense of "queer" first appeared on flyers handed out by militant AIDS organizations at New York's Gay Pride march in June 1990, which were emblazoned with the headline "Queers Read This!" and urged "an army of lovers" to take to the streets. Within days, and for many months, autonomous "Queer Nation" chapters started springing up in cities all across the United States, just as had happened with the Gay Liberation Front in the 1960s. In the two short years that encompassed its waxing and waning, 1990–1992, Queer Nation transformed public perceptions of AIDS and homosexuality and shifted internal gay, lesbian, and bisexual community politics in ways that allowed transgender issues to come back into the community's dialogue—just as transgender issues were simultaneously reentering feminism with a new voice.

LGB(T) (and Sometimes I)

The most direct link between the new queer politics and the transgender movement was the formation in 1992 of Transgender Nation, organized by Anne Ogborn as a focus group within the San Francisco chapter of Queer Nation. QN-SF was a "group of groups" that met monthly so that members of its constituent groups could share ideas, publicize activities, and gather support from other groups for their own actions. Individual groups within QN varied from the women's focus group LABIA (Lesbians and Bisexuals in Action) to SHOP (Suburban Homosexual Outreach Project), and actions varied from staging queer kiss-ins at shopping malls to playing a lead role in massive demonstrations against the Gulf War. If there was an underlying unity to QN's disparate action strategies, it was to be found in the sense of urgency driven by the AIDS crisis and in the conviction that queer people needed to engage immediately in practices that would disrupt the smooth functioning of the heterosexist state and its deadly indifference to queer lives. One strategy was simply to erupt into visibility in the everyday spaces of city life through how one dressed. Typical QN styles included (once shocking, now thoroughly commodified and depoliticized) black leather biker jackets, Doc Martens boots, T-shirts with provocative or cryptic political messages printed on them, tattoos, facial piercings, and copious amounts of Day Glo–colored stickers plastered on any available surface (including the backs of black leather biker jackets), with slogans such as "We Are Everywhere" and "We're Here, We're Queer, Get Used to It." Anne Ogborn had seen a Queer Nation member at a large public protest wearing another popular sticker—"Trans Power/Bi Power/Queer Nation"—with the words "Trans Power" torn off. She asked the woman wearing the sticker if those words had been accidentally or purposefully removed and was told that they had been deliberately ripped away because the wearer didn't consider trans people to be part of *her* queer movement. Ogborn went to the next monthly QN meeting to protest transphobia within the group and, in typical QN fashion, was invited to organize a focus group devoted to transgender concerns.

The announcement in San Francisco's gay and lesbian press of Transgender Nation's formation set off a firestorm of protest in the editorial pages, most of it authored by the same now-aging subset of lesbian feminists who had attacked Beth Elliott at the West Coast Lesbian Feminist Conference nearly twenty years earlier. Although the term TERF (trans-exclusionary radical feminist) had not yet been coined, this is precisely the mind-set that informed the lesbian feminist attack on Transgender Nation. What was different this time around was that their antitransgender rhetoric had come to be seen as a reactionary rather than a progressive stance. A new generation of post–Baby Boomers was reaching adulthood, a generation whose political sensibilities had been formed by the feminist sex wars, the AIDS crisis, and emerging theoretical perspectives on the sex-gender relationship. Many people who embraced the queer vision of the early 1990s readily accepted transgender as part of the "anti-heteronormative" mix. Of course, not all self-identified queers were trans inclusive, nor were all transgender people queer friendly. But a large and previously nonexistent area of overlap between transgender and queer community formations quickly emerged.

Loren Cameron's Body Alchemy *was a prominent part of the new wave of visibility for transgender men in the 1990s.* (PHOTO CREDIT: LOREN CAMERON.)

Transgender Nation erupted with a bang in late 1992, just as QN was falling apart. It initially drew scores of people to its meetings, although it quickly dwindled to a small core of regulars. During its brief existence, its members staged an attention-grabbing protest at the 1993 annual meeting of the American Psychiatric Association that landed three activists in jail; provided courtroom support for transgender women arrested on sex-work charges; inspired the formation of a few Transgender Nation chapters in other cities; informed the political sensibilities of an early transgender studies article on "transgender rage"; and made the rounds of LGB groups in San Francisco, demanding that they take a stand on transgender inclusion (thereby demonstrating whether those groups were part of the new queer movement or the old gay and lesbian movement).

During the next few years, members of variously constituted queer groups and organizations in cities across the United States replicated those lively and sometimes heated debates about the relationship between transgender and lesbian, gay, and bisexual communities. The 1993 March on Washington for Lesbian, Gay, and Bi Equal Rights became a particular flashpoint for trans-inclusion struggles after some local organizing committees voted to add "transgender" to the title of the march, but a trans-inclusion resolution failed to pass at the national organizing committee level. Members of Transgender Nation who thereafter showed up in Washington, DC, to protest the march introduced their new hybrid style of in-your-face queer/transgender politics to transgender and gay communities alike—and in doing so helped accelerate subsequent transgender organizing nationwide. By 1994, transgender people played a much larger role in the twenty-fifth anniversary commemoration of the Stonewall Riots, although they were still relegated to the "alternative" march and rally rather than the "official" one. By 1995, however, many formerly "gay and lesbian" or "gay, lesbian, and bisexual" organizations and events were beginning to add the *T* to their names. In the decades ahead, any number of other initials representing other identities were added to the alphabet soup, and their order was perpetually rearranged.

This shift in nomenclature toward an "LGBT+" community, rather than a "queer" one, marked the beginning of a new phase in the social history of sexual and gender identity politics in the

United States. It represented a retreat from the more radical concept of alliance, resistance, and rebellion by different groups against the same oppressive structures in the dominant culture and the adoption instead of a neoliberal model of minority tolerance and inclusion—which sometimes amounted to little more than a "politically correct" gesture of token inclusion for transgender people. Although some "LGBT" organizations genuinely addressed transgender concerns in addition to those of sexual orientation minorities, efforts at transgender inclusion often failed to grasp the ways in which transgender identity differed from sexual orientation and misconceptualized how they were alike.

Most transgender advocates used the word *transgender* as an adjective to describe a way of being a man or a woman, or as a way of resisting categorization by those labels. Like class or race or physical ability, *transgender* functioned for them as a descriptive term that cut across the sexual orientation categories, rather than as a noun describing a separate "species" of sexual identity. A transgender man could be gay or straight or bi, in other words, just as he could be black or poor or disabled. Many cisgender gays and lesbians, however, regarded the *T* precisely as a new species of sexual identity appended to their own. They considered trans people to be, first and foremost, trans people rather than members of the L, G, or B groups who also just happened to be trans. This construction of transgender identity as a noun rather than an adjective—as a kind of person rather than a descriptive quality attached to another category of personhood—had the unfortunate effect of reinforcing the idea that homosexuality and bisexuality were by definition "gender normative" and that anyone who deviated from the conventional definitions of "man" and "woman" automatically belonged in the transgender category. This way of thinking about transgender tended to reinforce the similarities between homosexual cultures and mainstream society based on shared concepts of gender and to perpetuate the marginalization of transgender people, within both the mainstream society and the LGBT movement.

One other related development in the early 1990s that deserves attention is the emergence of an intersex political movement. Cheryl Chase founded the Intersex Society of North America (ISNA) in 1993 with the single-minded goal of ending the practice of performing pediatric genital surgeries on babies born with ambiguous genitalia (clearly neither male nor female)—as had been done to Chase herself. Chase had been assigned male at birth, but a few years later doctors reversed their decision, told her parents to raise her as a girl, and performed surgery to reduce what they had formerly considered to be a very small penis to an "appropriate" size for what they now considered to be a too-big clitoris. Chase did not remember her early childhood gender reassignment, which is exactly what the medical professionals thought best in terms of helping intersex youth to develop a "normal" gender in their medically assigned sex. But rather than helping Chase feel normal, the nonconsensual genital surgeries, which severely compromised her sexual functioning later in life, left her feeling mutilated and freakish. When she discovered as an adult what had happened to her as a child, and that it had deliberately been kept secret from her, Chase felt as if her entire life had been built on a lie. Nothing had prepared her to accept either her intersex body or the surgeries that tried in vain to normalize it within the gender binary. After briefly contemplating suicide, Chase resolved instead that no other children should suffer what she herself had experienced. She moved from Japan, where she ran a computer technology company, to San Francisco, to learn what she could from the new queer and transgender activism that had erupted there.

The result was ISNA, which made tremendous progress in changing the way that the medical establishment pays attention to ambiguous genitalia, in providing peer support for intersex people and their families, and in educating the general public about intersexuality. Chase initially considered intersex politics to be related to queer and transgender politics not only because they all challenged heterosexist and gender-normative biases backed by medical authority, or because they called for the transformation of some of the same powerful social institutions, but also because the practice of normativizing genital surgery was such a visceral example of the idea that beliefs about gender actually produced the sex of the body, rather than the other way around. Bodies that did not originally fit the gender binary were literally cut to fit into it, and the process whereby the operation attempted to produce "normal" bodies as a result was rendered invisible, and its recipients silenced—just as the medical establishment had attempted to do with transsexuals. ISNA also offered a feminist perspective on intersex surgeries. The vast majority of children with ambiguous genitalia are eventually assigned as female, because surgeons find it far easier to remove "excess" tissue than to build up new body structures for genitals deemed insufficient for a normal male appearance. This fixation on penis size, coupled with a cultural devaluation of the feminine that already conceived of women as "lacking" what men have, conspires to inflict unnecessary surgeries on intersex children. As feminist sociologist Suzanne Kessler noted in her work on the biomedical ethics of intersex surgeries, ambiguous genitalia are rarely dangerous for a baby's health, but they are very dangerous for that baby's culture.

By 2006, ISNA had been largely successful in challenging the idea that genital surgeries performed on infants represented "best practices" in intersex care, and in reframing medical practice through the age-old wisdom that says "first do no harm," to advocate for a cautious wait-and-see approach that would create greater opportunities for the intersex person's consent to irrevocable and life-changing actions. That year, a "Consensus Statement on the Management of Intersex Disorders" was published in the journal *Pediatrics* that incorporated much of what ISNA had been proposing over the preceding decade. In 2007, to the outrage of many intersex activists, ISNA essentially abandoned its queer, trans, and feminist alliance politics to join with medical service providers in the new Accord Alliance, in which intersex advocates and medical experts would jointly work to implement the recommendations of the "Consensus Statement." Consequently, ISNA endorsed the use of the medical nomenclature "Disorders of Sex Development" (DSD), distanced itself from "intersex" as an overtly and counterproductively politicized identity term, declared "mission accomplished," and closed its doors in 2008. Its work is continued by the Alliance Accord, InterACT for Intersex Youth (formerly Advocates for Informed Choice), and the Organisation Internationale des Intersexués (OII), a decentralized global network of local, regional, and national intersex organizations. Although contemporary intersex and transgender activism have common roots in queer, trans, and feminist politics of the early 1990s, and still sometimes intersect and overlap with one another, they have trended in different directions.

Forging a National Transgender Movement

Transgender communities, organizations, and activist struggles grew in so many different directions during the 1990s, in so many different locations, that it's impossible to place all the developments into a single chronological narrative. Much of this proliferation can be attributed to the Internet. Although the Internet had been around for a long time by then, its use had been mostly confined to scientists and computer hobbyists, and its content was largely limited to email and electronic bulletin boards, until Netscape introduced Navigator, the first user-friendly web browser, in 1994. The Internet and World Wide Web became ubiquitous seemingly instantly thereafter, radically transforming communication, commerce, media, and culture in ways that are still evolving, and which are hard to grasp for those who have grown up afterward. But one immediate consequence was that many geographically dispersed and socially isolated individuals could now connect online with relative ease. Gradually, a far-flung network of new transgender groups and campaigns began to influence one another, forging a more coherent national perspective.

AEGIS (American Educational Gender Information Service) was founded by Dallas Denny in the Atlanta, Georgia, metropolitan area in 1990. The seemingly indefatigable Denny was one of the most influential trans activists of the decade, publishing *Chrysalis Quarterly,* establishing a significant archive of historical trans community materials, and pioneering the development of online resources for trans people. Denny played a leading role in organizing several important conferences and annual gatherings, perhaps most notably the first Southern Comfort transgender conference in Atlanta in 1991, a large-scale version of the same sorts of activities that have long characterized local transgender group meetings: guest speakers, workshops, discussions, entertainment, and socializing. Over the years, that event grew into one of the largest regular transgender gatherings in the country. It provided the setting for the award-winning 2001 documentary film *Southern Comfort,* which chronicled the final years in the life of trans man Robert Eads, a conference regular, who died of ovarian cancer after being unable to get health care because of his transgender status. Southern Comfort moved to Ft. Lauderdale, Florida, for its 2015 and 2016 conferences, after which it suspended operations. AEGIS morphed into GEA (Gender Education Association) around 1995, before gradually going dormant as more and more of its agenda to foster transgender depathologization and community empowerment seemed to have been met.

One of the first transgender-related events to break out into national prominence in the early days of the new transgender movement, even before the Internet took off, was the expulsion of Nancy Jean Burkholder, a trans woman, from the Michigan Womyn's Music Festival in 1991. The long-running festival, which combined outdoor camping with days and days of musical performances, and which advertised itself as a women-only event, had a tacit policy of not welcoming transgender women on the grounds that they were not "womyn-born-womyn"—that is, because trans women did not share the experience of being raised as girls, and had experienced early socialization as boys, they therefore could never really understand what it meant to be a woman under patriarchy or appreciate the need for women-only spaces. Burkholder, who claimed not to have known of the policy that excluded transgender women (but which still accommodated the participation of transgender men, implying that they were really cisgender women) was deeply troubled by her expulsion and began speaking out in queer and transgender publications. Her case quickly came to function as a litmus test for whether "queer" was indeed transgender inclusive and for which side of feminism had won the sex wars. In subsequent years, transgender activists and allies organized a "Camp Trans" near the music festival grounds to offer ongoing protest, educational outreach, dialogue, alternative community formations, and networking opportunities to combat feminist transphobia. The debates about transgender participation at the Michigan Womyn's Music Festival remained an important touchstone in continually evolving queer, transgender, and feminist political discussions for nearly a quarter century, until the festival finally folded in 2015, without ever formally lifting its "womyn-born-womyn" policy.

In 1992 in Houston, longtime transgender activist and attorney Phyllis Frye organized the first of six annual transgender law conferences, formally titled the International Conference on Transgender

Law and Employment Policy. The published proceedings of the conference did much to inspire a new burst of transgender legal activism and to connect activists at the national level. Frye was also instrumental in orchestrating a transgender contingent at the 1993 LGB March on Washington and in beginning to lobby federal legislators on transgender legal and policy issues—everything from health care coverage for transgender medical procedures to rules governing state-issued IDs to employment nondiscrimination protection to hate crimes legislation. Maryland's Jessica Xavier, who served on the local host committee for the 1993 march, also took an active role in transgender political lobbying in the early 1990s, founding both the Washington, DC, chapter of Transgender Nation and organizing another national transgender political lobbying group, It's Time America. Another trans activist from the nation's capital, Martine Rothblatt, drew parallels between race-based and transgender oppressions with her 1996 book, *The Apartheid of Sex*. Rothblatt, a highly successful telecommunications lawyer who founded Sirius satellite radio, went on to make a second fortune in pharmaceutical manufacturing, before turning her attention to life-extension and immortality research (and, in the process, becoming one of two known transgender billionaires).

In New York, activist Riki Wilchins cited lesbian and feminist history—specifically the Lavender Menace and Radicalesbians—when she launched the Transexual Menace in 1994, whose trademark image was a Goth-styled black T-shirt emblazoned with the group's name in blood-dripping red letters. Wilchins and the Menace garnered unprecedented media attention by sponsoring vigils outside of courthouses where cases involving antitransgender crimes were being tried, most notably the 1993 rape and murder of transmasculine teen Brandon Teena in Nebraska, and they became the subject of iconic gay liberation filmmaker Rosa Von Praunheim's 1996 documentary *Transexual Menace*. Wilchins, who did more than any other trans activist in the 1990s to shift the movement away from unfunded grassroots groups toward support by philanthropic foundations and corporate charity, went on to found the Gender Public Advocacy Coalition (GenderPAC), one of the better-staffed national organizations working on gender rights, to expand transgender lobbying efforts on Capitol Hill, and to serve as longtime executive director of TrueChild, an organization that helps donors and policymakers to "reconnect race, class, and gender through 'gender transformative' approaches that challenge rigid gender norms and inequalities." Wilchins wrote an acerbic primer on her version of the new transgender politics, *Read My Lips: Sexual Subversion and the End of Gender.*

In San Francisco, Kiki Whitlock and other transgender activists worked with the city's Human Rights Commission in 1993 and 1994 to produce a landmark report, principally written by FTM community leader Jamison Green, that documented human rights abuses against the transgender community at an unprecedented level of detail. That report became the basis for San Francisco's 1995 transgender antidiscrimination ordinance, one of several such local measures passed nationwide in the mid-1990s. Around the same time, in 1994, public health activists launched a program called "Tranny Tuesday" at the Tom Waddell Health Clinic, which pioneered a depathologized, harm-reduction, patient-centered approach to trans health. In the decade ahead, San Francisco built upon this foundation to begin offering its transgender citizens greater and greater legal protections against discrimination—and even offered transgender city employees health care benefits that covered the cost of their gender transitions more than a decade before such care became available nationally through the Affordable Care Act.

Along with political activism, transgender cultural production picked up pace in the early 1990s. Academic work reflecting the

REMEMBERING OUR DEAD

Transgender people as a group experience one of the highest rates of violence and murder in the United States. During the course of the 1990s and into the early twenty-first century, several high-profile homicides gave the transgender social justice movement a heightened sense of urgency.

One of the most notorious incidents took place outside Falls City, Nebraska, on December 31, 1993, during the first flush of the new wave of transgender activism, when John Lotter and Tom Nissen murdered an individual who had been assigned female at birth and who was just beginning to live as a young man who went by "Brandon" (among several other names). Brandon, who was christened Teena Brandon at birth, was originally from Omaha but had drifted to rural Falls City. There he began dating a young woman who claimed initially not to know that he was biologically female, and he was befriended by Lotter and Nissen. Upon the revelation of Brandon's anatomical sex, his supposed friends raped him; Brandon reported the rape to the county sheriff, who took no action. A few days later Nissen and Lotter tracked Brandon down at another friend's rented farmhouse, where early on the morning of New Year's Eve they shot and killed him along with two other young people staying in the house. The two killers were eventually convicted of homicide; Lotter received a death sentence (and is still on death row); Nissen was sentenced to life in prison without possibility of parole. Brandon gained posthumous celebrity as the subject of several mass media projects, including Aphrodite Jones's sensationalistic true crime paperback *All She Wanted,* the Guggenheim-commissioned web-based multimedia installation *Brandon,* the documentary film *The Brandon Teena Story,* and the feature film *Boys Don't Cry*.

Although it was the murder of a white transmasculine person that first catapulted deadly antitrans violence into the national spotlight, by far the most common targets of violence are trans women of color. Tyra Hunter, a twenty-five-year-old African American trans woman who had transitioned at age fourteen with her family's support, was on her way to work in Washington, DC, when the car she was riding

continues

REMEMBERING OUR DEAD *continued*

in was broadsided on August 7, 1995. As she lay seriously injured in the street, the first responders who initially offered medical care to her stopped when they discovered she had male genitalia; one remarked, "This bitch ain't no girl. . . . It's a nigger, he got a dick." After failing to receive life-saving assistance in a timely manner, Hunter died shortly thereafter in a hospital emergency room. Her family successfully sued the city for negligence and won a multimillion-dollar settlement. The murder of Rita Hester, an African American trans woman, in Boston in 1998 inspired Gwen Smith to found the Remembering Our Dead website that gave birth to Transgender Day of Remembrance (TDOR). Although TDOR has done much to call attention to the ongoing epidemic of antitrans violence, it is sometimes criticized as an event in which predominantly white trans people build community for themselves by memorializing black trans deaths.

In 2001, sixteen-year-old Fred Martinez, a Navajo (Diné) youth who self-represented to others as "gay," "two-spirit," and "Nadleeh" (a Diné term for a traditional nonbinary gender status), was murdered by schoolmates in Cortez, Colorado; the story is told in the 2009 documentary *Two Spirits*. In 2002, Gwen Araujo, a California teenager, was beaten and strangled to death by several male acquaintances, with some of whom she reportedly had been sexually active, after she was discovered to have male genitalia. Defense lawyers attempted to use the so-called panic defense, in which heterosexual defendants in antigay and antitransgender murder or assault cases claim their actions are justified because of the panic they experience when confronted with the possibility of committing an act they consider "homosexual." That argument was not successful in the Araujo case, which returned a guilty verdict; transgender legal activists took cold comfort in the tragedy of Araujo's death that the outcome of her case had the effect of weakening the panic defense nationwide. A Lifetime cable network movie about the story, *A Girl Like Me,* first aired on June 19, 2006, and a documentary feature *Trained in the Ways of Men* came out in 2010.

new transgender perspectives and political sensibilities began appearing in peer-reviewed professional journals, and many of the new breed of transgender scholars—a number of them struggling to break into the ranks of tenured professorships but finding in academe the same kinds of employment discrimination that transgender people faced everywhere—first met face to face at the 1994 Iowa Queer Studies Conference. The next year, historian of sexuality Vern Bullough organized the First International Conference on Cross-Dressing, Sex, and Gender at California State University, Northridge, which brought the new wave of transgender scholarship into face-to-face engagement with old-school researchers. Subsequent gatherings (which eventually started describing themselves as "transgender studies conferences") were held in Philadelphia, Oxford (UK), Perth (Australia), and other cities around the world. In 1998 the prestigious *Chronicle of Higher Education* published a feature article recognizing the emergence of transgender studies as a new interdisciplinary field. Transgender-related material was being integrated into college courses in a wide range of disciplines, and a steady stream of transgender scholarship was starting to roll off the press.

In the arts, playwright and actor Kate Bornstein prodded audiences from coast to coast to think about gender in new ways with her stage show *Hidden: A Gender* and her 1995 book, *Gender Outlaw: On Men, Women, and the Rest of Us*—both of which helped to define transgender style in the 1990s. Trans entertainer Justin Vivian Bond, a star (along with Kenny Mellman) of the Tony-nominated *Kiki and Herb* duet, got her first big break in Bornstein's play, while David Harrison, another playwright and actor who happened to be Bornstein's life partner at the time, chronicled female-to-male experience in his performance-festival-circuit crowd-pleaser, *FTM.* The first FTM Conference of the Americas was held in San Francisco in 1995 (ironically, at the San Francisco Women's Building, which makes meeting spaces available to a wide variety of progressive causes). Trans men soon received even more exposure through photographer Loren Cameron's portraiture work, collected in the 1996 volume *Body Alchemy,* which included an arresting self-portrait, *God's Will,* showing Cameron's own gym-sculpted and testosterone-enhanced physique, a remote camera-shutter release clutched in one hand, a syringe in the other, and the artist fully in control of both self-image and the image-making process. Another photographer, Mariette Pathy Allen, who had been documenting the male-to-female cross-dresser and transgender community since the early 1980s, and who has since gone on to document transgender youth and gender-variant practices in Asia, the Pacific Islands, and Cuba, also began to document the flourishing FTM scene in the mid-1990s.

Anohni (formerly Antony Hegarty) of the ensemble Antony and the Johnsons (named for transgender pioneer Marsha P. Johnson) infuses a transgender sensibility into the avant-garde group's musical performances. (PHOTO CREDIT: PIETER M. VAN HATTEM.)

Major stories on the new transgender scene started appearing in high-profile publications such as the *New Yorker,* the *New York Times,* and *Mother Jones.* Subcultural outlets for transgender culture erupted at the same time in a spate of new, low-budget, do-it-yourself zine publications, including Kansas City's *TransSisters: The Journal of Transsexual Feminism,* San Francisco's *TNT: The Transsexual News Telegraph,* and Toronto's *Gendertrash.* These publications continued a tradition of small-scale transgender community publishing that stretched back to Virginia Prince's first *Transvestia* magazine in 1952. Several of them, particularly *Gendertrash,* drew inspiration from the still-flourishing punk zine culture of the later 1970s and 1980s and formed part of the larger subcultural phenomenon sometimes called the "queer zine explosion," a remarkable outpouring of self-published, sometimes highly ephemeral, periodical publications about art, culture, and politics that constituted an important facet of the broader queer movement. The first half of the 1990s represented a high-water mark in the tradition of such publications, the numbers and frequency of which dropped off precipitously in the middle of the decade, in reverse proportion to the rise of the Internet, which almost overnight became a cheaper distribution outlet than even the cheapest paper-based, surface-mailed publications.

Mainstream media began paying heightened attention to transgender themes with the 1992 box-office smash *The Crying Game,* whose on-screen story, revolving around the gender ambiguity of the lead character, Dil, was echoed by off-screen speculations about the actual gender of the film's star, Jaye Davidson. Even more influential was Kimberly Peirce's 1999 *Boys Don't Cry,* which told the tragic story of Brandon Teena and won Hilary Swank a Best Actress Oscar for playing a transgender role. Although in recent years the film has been criticized for starring and being directed by cisgender women, and for not unambiguously representing Teena as a trans man with a completely unconflicted gender identity, the interpretation offered by Peirce grew from her personal involvement in the Transexual Menace vigils outside the Nebraska courthouse where Teena's murder trial transpired and her own sense of lesbian transmasculinity. As the philosopher Jacob Hale noted in an important early scholarly article on Brandon, one of the deepest tragedies of his story is that in being killed at such a young age, we really don't know what path his adult life would have taken. It feels just as important to acknowledge that his gender expression could have followed many different trajectories as it does to honor the way he was expressing his masculinity at the time of his death.

With the new millennium looming just a few years in the future, with the stock market racing to then-unheard-of heights in the speculative frenzy of the dot-com boom, and with technology transforming everyday life in unprecedented ways, transgender issues—which seemed to unhinge familiar reality by breaking the accustomed bonds between bodily sex and gendered appearance—came to be seen as harbingers of the strange new world beginning to take shape. This moment of premillennial fantasy was captured as it happened in experimental filmmaker Monika Treut's 1999 *Gendernauts,* which cast transgender people as bold adventurers setting out into the uncharted territory of humanity's technologically and biomedically enhanced future. But another film that year by two (not yet publicly out) transgender filmmakers—siblings Lana Wachowski and Lilly Wachowski's *The Matrix*—developed the implications of transgender perception into a full-blown aesthetic, one that became paradigmatic not only for transgender embodiment but for depicting the nature of representation and reality in the digital era.

Early Twenty-First-Century Transformations

The burst of transgender activism in the 1990s was framed, from beginning to end, by larger historical narratives. The Cold War, which had polarized geopolitics since World War II, had come to an end with the fall of the Berlin Wall in 1989 and the collapse of the Soviet Union in 1991, and many residents of the West were absolutely giddy with the prospect of what then-president George H. W. Bush called a "New World Order" to be dominated by the interests of the United States, the sole remaining superpower. The 1990s were a period when the growth of neoliberal forms of government accelerated and became more pervasive and entrenched all around the world. The flourishing of transgender movements for social change in these years has to be understood not just as part of a freedom struggle that was gaining strength but also as part of a broader shift in how societies and state powers managed and administered the lives of the people who constituted their collective body politic. Some concrete forms of greater freedom for some transgender people became possible precisely because the changes they needed and worked for also served other ends for other forms of power.

Early twenty-first-century transgender history in the United States continued many of the trends that characterized the 1990s. Trans men continued to gain in visibility, to the point that many younger people (especially those enrolled in traditionally women-only colleges) came to associate "transgender" more readily with transmasculinity than they did with trans women. A new crop of writing by trans men gained audiences larger than could have been anticipated a decade earlier, including such works as Jamison Green's *Becoming a Visible Man* and Max Wolf Valerio's *The Testosterone Files.* Rising-star performers such as Imani Henry, dancer Sean Dorsey of the Fresh Meat troupe, and hip-hop artist Katastrophe all began making names for themselves. Transgender mass media representation became both more frequent and less prejudicial, with cable shows such as *TransGenerations,* the feature film *TransAmerica,* and the stage and screen extravaganza *Hedwig and the Angry Inch* finding large and appreciative audiences. Musical performers such as Antony Hegarty, who has since come to identify as a trans woman and is now known as Anohni, pushed transgender style in unanticipated new artistic directions as lead singer of the performance ensemble Antony and the Johnsons (named in honor of transgender hero Marsha P. Johnson). A genderqueer denizen of New York nightclubs in the 1990s, Anohni's emotive vocal style and poignant lyrics expressed the power and pathos of living outside the gender binary. Their art—which broke out of the underground club scene thanks to the patronage of perennially cutting-edge artists Lou Reed and Laurie Anderson—linked transgender sensibilities to the cultural avant-garde in ways not seen since the 1960s. A spate of new authors in the transgender community include memoirists Jennifer Boylan, author of *She's Not There,* and Helen Boyd, author of *My Husband Betty* and *She's Not the Man I Married,* as well as transfeminist writer Julia Serano.

Gwen Smith's Remembering Our Dead website, first launched in 1999 as a sponsored project of AEGIS, put a spotlight on the chronic undercurrent of antitransgender violence that left one or two transgender people dead every month since records started being kept. An annual vigil Smith started in San Francisco in conjunction with the launch of the website became Transgender Day of Remembrance, which is now observed at hundreds of high school and college campuses and LGBT community centers throughout North America and Europe. It has become an annual opportunity to publicize the persistence of antitransgender prejudice and violence, particularly directed against trans women of color, in spite of decades of civil rights gains. At the outset of the 1990s, only three municipalities in the country offered any kind of legal protection for transgender people living and working in their jurisdictions, and only one state, Minnesota, offered protections at the state level, beginning in 1993. By the time the new century began, there were twenty-six localities with some form of transgender protections, and before the first decade of the twenty-first century came to a close there were more than a hundred, in addition to thirteen states and the District of Columbia. In 2007, a hate crimes bill, the first piece of federal legislation ever to address transgender concerns, passed both the Senate and House of Representatives. In 2008, Allen Andrade became the first person to receive enhanced punishment for an antitransgender hate crime, when he was sentenced for the first-degree murder of Angie Zapata, a trans woman he beat to death in Greeley, Colorado, after discovering she had been assigned male at birth.

A great deal of credit for early twenty-first-century legislative victories is due to a new wave of legal activist organizations, including the Sylvia Rivera Law Project in New York; the Transgender Law Center in San Francisco (which began as a project of the National Center for Lesbian Rights); the National Center for Transgender Equality (the lead transgender lobbying organization in Washington, DC); and the National Transgender Advocacy Coalition (NTAC), which draws its leadership from nonmetropolitan and noncoastal parts of the country. Two historically gay organizations, Lambda Legal and the National Gay and Lesbian Task Force (now known simply as The Task Force), have provided invaluable support for transgender legal campaigns undertaken by community leaders and allies such as Shannon Minter, Paisley Currah, Kylar Broadus, Cecilia Chung, Chris Daley, Monica Roberts, Autumn Sandeen, Marti Abernathey, Dean Spade, Pauline Park, Masen Davis, Kris Hayashi, and many others. In the international arena, GATE—Global Action for Trans* Equality—founded by Justus Eisfeld in the United States and Mauro Cabral in Argentina, helped keep transgender issues on the agenda at the United Nations and with the World Health Organization.

However much some aspects of early twenty-first-century transgender activism represented a steady continuation of longer-term trends, the terrorist attacks of September 11, 2001, represented a sharp inflection point for trans* politics. It brought about heightened border surveillance, increased attention to travel documents, and more stringent standards for obtaining state-issued identification, all of which made life more complicated for many transgender people. Depending on such variables as where one happened to be born or what levels of health care one might have been able to afford, some transgender people found it impossible to obtain tightly controlled identity documents (such as passports) that accurately reflected their current name or gender appearance—which made travel impossible in some circumstances and risky or dangerous in others. The restrictions on movement in the post-9/11 United States gave transgender people more in common with immigrants, refugees, and undocumented workers than they might have with the mainstream gay and lesbian movement. Pursuing transgender justice increasingly involved joining campaigns and struggles that might seem at first to have little to do with gender identity or expression—but everything to do with how the state polices those who differ from social norms and tries to solve the bureaucratic problems that arise from attempting to administer the lives of atypical members of its population.

A striking example of how transgender interests diverged from legal activism related to sexual orientation can be found in the debates about transgender inclusion in the federal Employment Non-Discrimination Act that took place in late 2007. First introduced for consideration by Congresswoman Bella Abzug in the 1970s, ENDA, as the bill is known, aimed to prohibit employment discrimination based on sexual orientation. The proposed legislation didn't make it out of committee for a full congressional debate until 1994, when the measure failed to pass by a single vote. At that time, the transgender movement did not have sufficient political clout to have gender identity or gender expression provisions added to the language of the bill—indeed, ENDA's primary lobbyist, the Human Rights Campaign (HRC), actively undermined transgender activists who were just then beginning to lobby Congress for transgender inclusion within the bill. But as the *T* became more and more integrated into the fabric of an LGBT community, major political organizations such as The Task Force, PFLAG (Parents, Families and Friends of Lesbians and Gays), and other groups began to advocate for transgender inclusion. Over the course of a decade, virtually every national and state organization representing LGBT interests came to support transgender inclusion in federal employment protection legislation. They argued that transgender people were in fact the most severely discriminated against of all the LGBT communities, and that, moreover, most discrimination against gay, lesbian, and bisexual people who were not transgender was rooted in prejudices about gender-normative appearances and behaviors—that is, it was the too-effeminate gay man, or the too-masculine woman, who were more vulnerable to employment discrimination than straight-looking, straight-acting gay men and lesbian women. A gradual consensus emerged among those most active in advancing the LGBT legislative agenda that adding employment protections for gender identity and expression was a necessary amendment to ENDA, one that would protect all US residents from being fired for failing to live up to a stereotype of masculine or feminine social roles but that would be especially beneficial for transgender people.

When Democrats took control of both houses of Congress after the midterm elections in 2006, ENDA was poised for passage for the first time since 1994. In the spring of 2007, even the HRC—long a holdout on a transgender-inclusive legislative strategy—finally got on board and lobbied in support of a version of ENDA that protected gender identity and expression as well as sexual orientation. All seemed to be going well until September 2007, when the bill's longtime sponsor, the openly gay Massachusetts congressman Barney Frank, decided, on the basis of an informal poll of his colleagues, that a sexual-orientation-only version of ENDA could pass, but that a transgender-inclusive version would fail. Rather than wait to gather additional support or conduct more extensive education and lobbying efforts, Frank took it upon himself to split ENDA into two separate bills—one for sexual orientation and the other for gender identity.

US CITIES AND COUNTIES WITH TRANSGENDER ANTI-DISCRIMINATION PROTECTIONS IN 2016

Alaska
Anchorage
Arizona
Phoenix
Tempe
Tucson
Arkansas
Fayetteville
Eureka Springs
California
Los Angeles
Oakland
Palm Springs
Sacramento
San Diego
San Francisco
Santa Cruz (County)
West Hollywood
Colorado
Boulder
Denver
District of Columbia
Washington
Florida
Atlantic Beach
Alachua (County)
Broward (County)
Gainesville
Gulfport
Key West
Lake Worth
Leon (County)
Miami Beach
Miami-Dade (County)
Monroe (County)
Palm Beach (County)
Pinellas (County)
Orlando
Tampa
Volusia (County)
West Palm Beach
Georgia
Atlanta
Idaho
Boise
Coeur d'Alene
Idaho Falls
Ketchum
Moscow
Pocatello
Sandpoint
Victor
Illinois
Aurora
Carbondale
Champaign
Chicago
Cook (County)
Decatur
DeKalb
Evanston
Peoria
Springfield
Indiana
Bloomington
Evansville
Indianapolis
Marion (County)
Monroe (County)
South Bend
Iowa
Ames
Cedar Rapids
Council Bluffs
Davenport

continues

Des Moines
Iowa City
Johnson (County)
Sioux
Waterloo
Kansas
Lawrence
Roeland Park
Kentucky
Covington
Danville
Frankfort
Jefferson (County)
Lexington
Lexington-Fayette (County)
Louisville
Morehead
Vicco
Louisiana
New Orleans
Shreveport
Maryland
Baltimore
Baltimore (County)
College Park
Howard (County)
Hyattsville
Montgomery (County)
Massachusetts
Boston
Cambridge
Northampton
Salem
Worcester
Michigan
Ann Arbor
Detroit
East Lansing
Ferndale
Grand Rapids
Huntington Woods
Kalamazoo
Lansing
Pleasant Ridge
Saugatuck
Sterling Heights
Traverse
Ypsilanti
Minnesota
Minneapolis
St. Paul
Missouri
Columbia
Clayton
Kansas City
Kirkwood
Olivette
St. Louis
St. Louis (County)
University City
Montana
Bozeman
Butte-Silver Bow
Helena
Missoula
Nebraska
Omaha
New York
Albany
Binghamton
Buffalo
Ithaca
New York
Rochester
Suffolk (County)
Syracuse
Tompkins (County)
Westchester (County)
North Carolina
Chapel Hill
Ohio
Athens
Bowling Green
Cincinnati
Cleveland
Columbus
Coshocton
Dayton
East Cleveland
Newark
Oxford
Summit (County)
Toledo
Yellow Springs
Oregon
Beaverton
Bend
Benton (County)
Corvallis
Eugene
Hillsboro
Lake Oswego
Lincoln City
Multnomah (County)
Portland
Salem
Pennsylvania
Abington Township
Allegheny (County)
Allentown
Bethlehem
Cheltenham Township
Doylestown
East Norriton
Easton
Erie (County)
Harrisburg
Hatboro
Haverford Township
Jenkintown Borough
Lansdowne Borough

continues

US CITIES AND COUNTIES WITH TRANSGENDER ANTI-DISCRIMINATION PROTECTIONS IN 2016 *continued*

Lower Merion Township
New Hope Borough
Newton Borough
Philadelphia
Pittsburgh
Pittston
Scranton
Reading
Springfield Township
State College Borough
Susquehanna Township
Swarthmore
Upper Merion Township
West Chester Borough
Whitemarsh Township
York
Rhode Island
Providence
South Carolina
Myrtle Beach
Texas
Austin
Dallas
Dallas (County)
Fort Worth
Plano
Utah
Alta
Grand (County)
Harrisville
Logan
Midvale
Moab
Murray City
Ogden
Salt Lake City
Salt Lake (County)
Springdale
Summit (County)
Taylorsville
West Valley City
Washington
Burien
King (County)
Seattle
Spokane
Tacoma
West Virginia
Charleston
Huntington
Wisconsin
Dane (County)
Madison
Milwaukee
Wyoming
Laramie

The reaction in the LGBT community was swift and unprecedented: more than three hundred national, state, and local organizations formed an ad hoc campaign, United ENDA, to demand that transgender-inclusive language be restored to the bill. LGBT activists across the country felt that more than a decade's worth of work to build an expansive movement had been betrayed at the last minute by the movement's congressional leadership. At the same time, many lesbian and gay people who had not felt entirely comfortable being linked to transgender issues since the mid-1990s gave voice to long-suppressed antitransgender attitudes they'd formerly considered too "politically incorrect" to express publicly and supported splitting ENDA into two bills. HRC, which had only recently come to support transgender-inclusive language in ENDA, lost what little credibility it had with the transgender community when it made an abrupt about-face and endorsed the sexual-orientation-only version of the bill. In the end, the trans-inclusive version of ENDA died in committee, while the sexual-orientation-only version passed the House of Representatives—a Pyrrhic victory, given that the Senate never considered it, and President Bush promised to veto any version of ENDA that made it to his desk.

As a result of the ENDA controversy, the trans-inclusive queer and LGBT movements that transgender people had worked to build since the early 1990s threatened to split apart. There were stark divisions between "homonormative" gay and lesbian people who seemed poised for mainstream acceptance and trans and gender-nonconforming people who were still targeted by discriminatory legislation and burdened by administrative practices that made their lives more precarious. At the same time, trans activists in the LGBT movement began foregrounding trans issues as the movement's most pressing concern, demanding accountability from their fellow social change agents and launching more independent and narrowly focused trans-activist projects. With the growing presence of positive transgender representation in mass media, and the increasing acceptance younger people seemed to exhibit toward transgender and gender-nonconforming identities and behaviors, the stage seemed set for dramatic breakthroughs or setbacks on transgender rights as the 2008 presidential campaign headed toward a historic electoral outcome and the nation plunged into the worst financial crisis since the Great Depression.

CHAPTER 6

THE TIPPING POINT?

THE CLOSER THE past approaches to the present, the easier it is for the welter of fleeting events to obscure the larger contours of the times we are living through. Already, though, it seems indisputable that the financial crisis of 2008 and the election that year of Barack Obama as president of the United States were major historical turning points that had, and continue to have, significant consequences for transgender social justice movements. The formal depathologization of transgender identity in 2013, when the *DSM-V* officially dropped the diagnostic category Gender Identity Disorder, was also a momentous milestone for trans people, as had been the election of the first two transsexual men ever to serve as president of the World Professional Association for Transgender Health (or WPATH, the successor organization to the Harry Benjamin International Gender Dysphoria Association): Stephen Whittle (2007–2009) and Jamison Green (2013–2015). Equally important for understanding the most recent developments in trans history are the explosion of mainstream media representations of trans issues actually produced by and inclusive of trans people, the dramatically higher percentage of trans and gender-nonconforming youth in the under-eighteen segment of the population, and deep but hard-to-define shifts—the cumulative consequence of decades of activism—in how our culture understands gender and is coming to accept transgender phenomena as part of everyday reality.

When a 2014 *Time* magazine cover story featuring a glamorous full-length photo of the trans actor Laverne Cox asked "Is America at a Transgender Tipping Point?" the answer at that moment seemed an obvious "yes." Something had clearly changed. But the election of Donald Trump as president in November 2016, which promises to undo many of the concrete gains of recent years, forcefully demonstrated that this "tipping point" is more like the fulcrum of a teeter-totter, tipping backward as well as forward, than like a summit where, after a long upward climb, progress toward legal and social equality starts rolling effortlessly downhill. Still, however much damage Trumpism's rise does to trans lives in the near term, it will be extremely difficult to turn back the tide of gender change that has already swept through society in profound and probably irreversible ways.

Statistical Portraits and Trans Generations

According to a 2013 poll, more than 90 percent of people living in the United States now report having heard the term *transgender,* and three-quarters of them know more or less what the word means. This is a dramatically different cultural climate than existed a generation ago. As a consequence of the immense amount of mass media coverage given to trans issues during Caitlyn Jenner's highly orchestrated coming out and transition process in 2015, the overall number of people who claimed actually to know a trans person doubled between 2014 and 2016, from 8 percent to 16 percent. These numbers were drastically higher for Millennials, more than a quarter of whom know or work with a trans person, than they were for people over forty-five, only 9 percent of whom do. But however

CELEBRITY TRANS CULTURE

The second decade of the twenty-first century saw an explosion of highly visible transgender presence in the mass media. Caitlyn Jenner—the former Olympic athlete, Kardashian clan member, and reality television star—finally came out after years of tabloid speculation, in a series of high-profile media events in 2015, including a ratings-grabbing interview with Diane Sawyer on the broadcast news show *20/20,* a cover story in *Vanity Fair* that featured photographs by acclaimed photographer Annie Leibovitz, and a short-lived, much-maligned reality TV show, *I Am Cait*. Jenner might have had a higher profile, but actors like Laverne Cox and writers like Janet Mock had more staying power and more substantive things to say, as did the transgender sisters Lana Wachowski and Lilly Wachowski. Their Netflix original series *Sense8* offered one of the most narratively complex, visually arresting, and aesthetically challenging works in contemporary mainstream media. The sci-fi thriller revolved around eight individuals from around the world, all born at the same moment, who suddenly begin to share the same sensory experiences; trans actor Jamie Clayton plays transsexual lesbian Nomi Marks, one of the "sensates." The most critically acclaimed and commercially successful trans-centered show was Amazon's *Transparent,* based loosely on show-runner Jill Soloway's experience as the adult child of a late-transitioning transgender parent and produced by transgender culture makers Rhys Ernst and Zackary Drucker.

Sense8. (Photo credit: Netflix 2015.)

Zackary Drucker and Rhys Ernst, co-producers of *Transparent*. (Photo credit: JUCU, 2014.)

much familiarity has risen, there remains a great deal of ignorance about actual trans lives. Until fairly recently, even calculating the number of trans and gender-nonconforming people in the United States involved a fair bit of speculation. Two surveys, one in 2011 and the other in 2016, provide the first statistical portraits of trans life in the contemporary United States, and other studies are now beginning to offer a clearer sense of how many trans and gender-nonconforming youth there are.

Researchers at the UCLA School of Law's Williams Institute, which conducts policy-oriented population-based studies pertaining to sexual orientation and gender identity, conservatively estimate that slightly more than one-half of 1 percent of the adult US population is transgender, roughly 1.5 million people. This is a conservative estimate because it is based on data that make it possible to determine when a person assigned one sex at birth now lives in the gender not typically associated with that sex; that is, it assumes a gender binary and reflects only the number of people who have made clear and unambiguous gender transitions. Accounting for the number of gender-nonconforming people would certainly increase the percentage of adults who fall outside normative gender expectations, but such individuals are harder to count. There are fewer national-level data on trans and gender-nonconforming youth, but based on the best available state and local studies, a conservative estimate as of 2016 is that roughly 1.7 percent of contemporary youth identify as trans or gender-nonconforming, that is, more than three times the figures for adults.

Over the past decade there has been a seismic shift in the level of attention paid to trans childhood and youth issues. Stephanie Brill and Rachel Pepper, two parents of trans-identified kids, provided one of the earliest resources with their 2008 book, *The Transgender Child: A Handbook for Families and Professionals.* The LGBTQ educational policy advocacy group GLSEN issued an important report in 2009, *Harsh Realities: The Experience of Transgender Youth in Our Nation's Schools*. The subsequent years have witnessed a huge upsurge in summer camps for trans and gender-nonconforming young people and support groups for their parents, nonprofit organizations devoted to trans youth advocacy (such as Gender Spectrum and the Trans Youth Equality Foundation), use of "hormone blockers" to delay the onset of irreversible physical changes at puberty for trans and gender-questioning youth, gender-affirming private schools, and new medical programs designed to assess and assist early-transitioning children. Clinical psychologist

Transgender celebrity Laverne Cox and sex-worker-rights activist Monica Jones at an ACLU-sponsored event in Phoenix, Arizona, fall 2014, in support of Jones's case challenging her arrest on charges of "manifesting an intent to prostitute." They are holding copies of the first issue of TSQ: Transgender Studies Quarterly *(Duke University Press, 2014), which featured on its cover an image of trans political prisoner Chelsea Manning.* (Photo credit: Susan Stryker 2014.)

Diane Ehrensaft's 2016 book, *The Gender Creative Child: Pathways for Nurturing and Supporting Children Who Live Outside Gender Boxes,* provides one of the latest and most comprehensive resources.

Media representation of trans and gender-nonconforming youth has expanded considerably since the breakthrough 1997 film *Ma Vie En Rose* to include works as wide-ranging as the independent feature films *Gun Hill Road, Boy Meets Girl,* and *Tomboy* and as accessible as the reality TV show *I Am Jazz,* starring trans youth celebrity Jazz Jennings. Even more significant than commercially produced media is the explosion in user-generated content on online platforms like YouTube, which contains millions of trans-related videos, including "how to transition" tutorials, video blogs and diaries, and visual documentation of the gender exploration and transition process, most of them oriented toward young people. In 2014, a suicide note posted on Tumblr by trans teen Leelah Alcorn, shortly before she took her own life, sparked an international conversation about teen suicide, bullying, parental rejection, and the use of "conversion therapy" to try to change a young person's trans feelings or identity. Literary representation of trans youth has increased in similar proportions to visual media. The current wave started in 2004 with Julie Ann Peters's *Luna,* the first trans youth title published by a major commercial publisher, and has grown to include more than fifty commercially produced books for young readers of every age, including *George,* Alex Gino's 2015 book about a trans girl who comes out by auditioning for the lead role in her fourth-grade class's production of *Charlotte's Web,* published by the venerable Scholastic Press. The Girl Scouts have welcomed trans and gender-nonconforming girls since 2015, but the Boy Scouts have been less accommodating of trans and nonbinary boys; in December 2016, a New Jersey Cub Scouts troop kicked out eight-year-old Joe Maldonado for being assigned female at birth (a decision that the organization reversed in early 2017).

Remembering Trans Young People, Omer Yavin, 2015. Group portrait of five trans youth who committed suicide in 2015: Leelah Alcorn (November 15, 1997–December 28, 2015), Ash Haffner (December 28, 1998–February 26, 2015), Melonie Rose (August 7, 1995–November 11, 2015), Zander Mahaffey (2000–February 15, 2015), and Taylor Alesana (1999–April 2, 2015). (PHOTO CREDIT: PUBLIC DOMAIN IMAGE, HTTPS://COMMONS.WIKIMEDIA.ORG/WIKI/FILE%3AREMEMBERING_TRANS_YOUNG_PEOPLE_2015.JPG.)

The increasing prevalence of gender variance in younger generations is already transforming culture at large. It touches on everything from a rising preference for non-gender-specific pronouns, to youth fashion trends that defy the gender binary, to the number of gender options available on Facebook profiles, to needing to rethink admissions policies at same-sex educational institutions and designing new bureaucratic forms that accommodate nonbinary options (as Oregon did in 2016, after a state court ruled that "nonbinary" was a legal gender). As children are allowed to express transgender feelings or gender-nonconforming behaviors at increasingly earlier ages, and as parents and other caring adults become increasingly accepting of those feelings and behaviors, what it means to be "transgender" in the future will be something drastically different from what it has meant in the past or what it means in the present.

The first large survey of the adult transgender population in the United States, *Injustice at Every Turn: A Report of the National Transgender Discrimination Survey,* was published in 2011, based on 6,456 respondents surveyed in 2008–2009. An even larger follow-up study based on 27,715 respondents was published in 2016 as the *Report on the 2015 National Transgender Survey.* Although the second survey showed some measurable improvements in the quality of life for trans and nonbinary people over the preceding five years, continuities in the pattern and prevalence of discrimination were far more pronounced. Nearly 40 percent of those surveyed in 2015 who were out to their families experienced rejection, which resulted in significantly higher rates of homelessness, interruptions in schooling, psychological distress, and suicide attempts compared to those surveyed who enjoyed familial support. Thirty-nine percent of all respondents had attempted suicide at some point in their life—down 2 percent from 2011, but still nearly ten times the rate of attempted suicide in the general population. Half had been physically or sexually assaulted at some point in their life.

Only 10 percent of respondents had changed their name and gender on *all* of their identity documents, whereas more than two-thirds had changed *none* of their documents, primarily because of the cost of updating them; a third of those with incongruent documentation experienced some form of harassment or discrimination as a result. More than half reported some problem in getting medical care, either because they were denied treatment, couldn't afford it, or avoided treatment over fear of being outed as trans or discriminated against. The prevalence of living with HIV infection is five times higher among trans people than in the population at large;

the poverty rate is four times higher, and the unemployment rate, three times as great. Most trans people have had a negative interaction with the police, and most said they would avoid interacting with police if possible, even if they had been the victim of a crime. A majority of transgender people have experienced some form of discrimination in schools, housing, workplaces, government offices, social services, stores, restaurants, and other businesses. More than half have avoided using a public toilet out of fear of violence or harassment. Perhaps because they can so clearly see that society needs to change even more than it already has, trans people tend to be more politically active and socially engaged than is typical. Although informal and noninstitutional forms of political activism are harder to gauge, three-quarters of adult trans citizens are registered to vote compared to 65 percent in the general population, and more than half actually vote regularly, compared to only about 40 percent nationally. Fifty percent of the survey respondents identified as Democrats, 48 percent as Independents, and only 2 percent as Republicans.

Leaderless Revolts, Critical Resistance, and Trans Countercultures

Since the early 1970s—when neoliberal privatization and austerity policies started to become the new norm, and the large government spending programs that had pulled the United States out of the Great Depression, made it possible to win World War II, allowed it to build a booming consumer-oriented postwar economy, and funded an ambitious War on Poverty collapsed—real earning power and wages for most people in the United States have been static or declining when adjusted for inflation. During the accelerated globalization of the neoliberal economy in the 1990s, income inequality began trending sharply upward. When the speculative subprime mortgage bubble burst and credit markets suddenly froze in 2008, the world confronted the gravest economic crisis since the 1930s. The so-called Great Recession wiped out lifetime savings, sparked a wave of home foreclosures, produced acute and widespread short-term misery, resulted in greater unemployment and deeper debt, and led to income disparities unlike anything in living memory for most people. By the middle of the second decade of the twenty-first century, a third the US population—nearly 110 million people—was living in poverty or was classified as "low income," while the top one-tenth of 1 percent of the population—about 325,000 individuals—earned 20 percent of all income. For transgender people, who, because of discrimination, still must clear additional hurdles to gain jobs, find housing, pursue education, and access health care, this economic climate has been especially brutal.

The global financial crisis of late 2008 ignited a years-long wave of "leaderless revolts" around the world, ranging from mass protests in tiny Iceland that toppled the government for mismanaging the economy to antiausterity movements that sprang up all across Europe, especially in southern European countries like Greece; the so-called Arab Spring uprisings across Northern Africa and the Middle East that culminated in the Egyptian revolution and the Syrian Civil War; and the short-lived, diffuse, and decentralized phenomenon known as Occupy, which established impromptu protest encampments in cities from Tokyo to Sydney to London but which started in North America as Occupy Wall Street and had its epicenter in New York City's Zuccotti Park. Trans participation in these leaderless revolts was especially visible in Europe and North America, particularly so among the *Indignados* movement in Spain and in cities with strong anarchist traditions and communities, like Oakland, California, and Bologna, Italy. Anarchist movements, oriented against state-based power and taking more local and DIY approaches to change making, have offered congenial homes for radical transgender activism that focuses on analyzing the micropolitics of day-to-day living for trans and gender-nonconforming people and on cultivating the revolutionary potentials they grasp as they come to understand better, through participation in counter-dominant ways of existing, what freedom and equality can actually feel like. It was a twenty-six-year-old trans anarchist named Justine Tunney who had the foresight to register the domain name OccupyWallStreet.org and who, along with other members of a Philadelphia anarchist collective that jokingly called itself Trans World Order, ran the servers that allowed the far-flung global movement to communicate and disseminate information.

The anarchist-flavored Anonymous, a loose-knit international online network known for its "hacktivist" attacks on entities it deems dangerous to liberty, has long used as its symbol the Guy Fawkes mask, popularized as a symbol of popular insurrection by the film *V for Vendetta,* produced by the transgender filmmakers Lana Wachowski and Lilly Wachowski. But another Internet activist group, WikiLeaks, has a much more concrete connection to a trans woman who wanted to change the world. In 2010, Chelsea Manning was a smart, computer-savvy, working-class twenty-three-year-old US Army soldier assigned to an intelligence unit in Iraq. She was still living publicly as a man but struggling with lifelong gender dysphoria, the effects of fetal alcohol syndrome, and the psychological difficulties of a tumultuous upbringing. She had thought that joining the hypermasculine military might "make a man" of her as well as provide a stable living situation and eventually help fund a college education, but enlisting only intensified her distress and made her the butt of ceaseless bullying over being perceived as effeminate and gay.

Manning's position in the military was quite precarious, not only because her emotional challenges created behavior and discipline problems that threatened to result in her discharge but also because her apparent gayness made her vulnerable under the "Don't Ask, Don't Tell" policy then still in place, which allowed gay people to serve in the military as long as they weren't out, and because military policy explicitly excluded service by transgender people. Her emotional troubles aside, Manning, already a person with strong political opinions, was simultaneously undergoing a deepening of her political consciousness, as she became more and more aware—and more and more critical—of exactly what the US-led wars in Afghanistan and Iraq entailed, not just on the battlefield but also in terms of covert operations, drone strikes that killed civilians, spying on allies, and engaging in domestic surveillance. It's neither possible nor necessary to separate Manning's increasingly acute emotional distress, her reaction to personal experiences of transphobic and homophobic discrimination in a hostile military environment, and her conscientious opposition to US actions on the world stage: all played their part in what happened next.

Starting February 3, 2010, Manning transmitted hundreds of thousands of classified and sensitive documents, videos, and diplomatic cables about US military and governmental operations to WikiLeaks, which, with the help of several major international newspapers (the *New York Times,* the *Guardian* in the United Kingdom, and *Der Spiegel* in Germany) made them public over the course of several months. The disclosure of US government secrets was absolutely unprecedented in terms of scope, scale, and significance, and it contributed to the global geopolitical upheavals already underway as a result of the financial crisis—some of the leaked cables that exposed government corruption in Tunisia are credited with kicking off the Arab Spring protests there. Manning's professed goal in leaking the material was "revealing the true nature of 21st century asymmetric warfare," because "without information, you cannot make informed decisions as a public." Manning genuinely believed that the leaked documents would lead people to question not only the current US wars but all future wars.

The United States government saw things differently. Upon her arrest in May 2010, the military kept Manning caged in total isolation for several weeks at a detention facility in Kuwait, and then in solitary confinement in a six-foot-by-eight-foot cell at a Marine base in Quantico, Virginia, for the next nine months, in conditions that a United Nations special rapporteur said met the definition of torture. Manning was charged, convicted, and court-martialed in 2013 after pleading guilty to violating the Espionage Act and other crimes, and sentenced to thirty-five years in military prison. After her sentencing, Manning publicly disclosed her transgender status, and it was then that her ordeal became even more dire. Manning was incarcerated in a men's facility, and although she was allowed to start low doses of estrogen, she was unable to access gender counseling or surgery, was not allowed to change her name on official documents or to grow out her hair, and was subjected to what she and many of her supporters considered to be cruel and arbitrary punishments, such as having privileges revoked and her time for eligibility for parole extended for having transgender-related reading material in her cell—material the prison itself had allowed to reach her through the mail. The most outrageous charge against her was for "medicine misuse" because the use-by date on her tube of toothpaste had expired. She twice tried to commit suicide, and for doing so was placed in solitary confinement for extended periods of time. More than a hundred thousand people petitioned the government asking that Manning be granted parole or clemency, given that whistle-blowers in comparable cases typically have served around three years; that none of the material she released, though confidential and sensitive, was classified as "top secret"; and that there was no documented harm to any US personnel as a result of the disclosures. ACLU staff attorney Chase Strangio (who also happens to be trans) shepherded Manning's case through the appeals process and worked to keep Manning in the public's awareness until January 17, 2017, when Barack Obama, in one of his last acts as president of the United States, commuted Manning's sentence to time served and ordered her to be released on May 17, 2017.

Manning's was undoubtedly the most high-profile transgender incarceration case, but the difficulties she encountered are far from unique. Sixteen percent of all transgender people have been incarcerated, including more than 20 percent of trans women and almost half of all black trans people. By comparison, about 5 percent of the total US population has been incarcerated, including an unconscionable third of all black men. One significant factor contributing to the high rate of trans incarceration is the criminalization of sex work, which many otherwise unemployable trans people find necessary for their survival, coupled with the prejudicial assumption on the part of many law enforcement officers that trans people in public are likely to be engaging in prostitution. In 2013, Monica Jones, a black trans woman in Phoenix who sometimes worked in the sex industry, was arrested by an undercover cop in a sting operation at a time when she was not working, not long after she spoke at a protest rally opposing a new law that criminalized "manifesting" an intent to prostitute—that is, a law that allowed the police to make "pre-crime" arrests of individuals they thought *might* engage in prostitution. The ACLU took Jones's case as well, and she has gone on to become a powerful activist voice, speaking at the United Nations on the need to decriminalize sex work.

Incarceration is a huge, increasingly privatized industry in the United States, which has the highest rate of incarceration in the world: the country accounts for only four and a half percent of the global population but nearly a quarter of all incarcerated people worldwide. The growth of the prison-industrial complex falls hard on trans people, whose multiple social vulnerabilities make them three times more likely to wind up incarcerated than a cisgender person. The plight of trans people in custody is truly horrific, resulting in large part from the sex-segregated nature of jails and prisons and the policy of incarcerating people based on their genital status rather than their appearance or identity. In practice, this results either in the segregation of trans prisoners who have not had genital surgeries (often in solitary confinement, itself a form of "cruel and unusual punishment") or else in their placement in a general prison population whose gender is different from their own, where they can be at extreme risk of violence from other prisoners and staff. Nearly a third of all trans prisoners have experienced physical or sexual assault while incarcerated, and more than a third who were taking hormones at the time of their incarceration were denied them while incarcerated.

Trans incarceration issues—and trans participation in the radical prison abolition movement—have gained increasing recognition in recent years with the publication of the anthology *Captive Genders: Trans Embodiment and the Prison Industrial Complex,* the documentary films *Cruel and Unusual* and *Criminal Queers,* attention to the CeCe McDonald case (in which a black trans woman in Minnesota went to jail for accidentally killing a male attacker in self-defense), and Laverne Cox's role as a trans woman serving time in a women's prison in the entertaining but utterly unrealistic Netflix original series *Orange Is the New Black.* The nonprofit TGI Justice Project works on behalf of currently and formerly incarcerated trans and gender-nonconforming people and has long been led by formerly incarcerated trans women of color, including veteran activists Miss Major Griffin-Gracy (subject of the film *Major!*) and Janetta Johnson.

One of the most significant grassroots political developments of the past decade has been the emergence of Black Lives Matter

(BLM). Founded by Alicia Garza, Patrisse Cullors, and Opal Tometi in the aftermath of the vigilante killing of unarmed black teen Trayvon Martin in 2012, but gaining greater traction after the fatal police shooting of Michael Brown in Ferguson, Missouri, in 2014 and the dozens of other questionable deaths of black people in encounters with the police that have transpired since, the movement has called needed attention to the specifically antiblack nature of much of the violence that structures contemporary life. Although BLM is a national chapter-based organization, it, like the Occupy movement before it, became a viral social phenomenon whose influence far exceeds those who formally participate in it. It has succeeded in mobilizing resistance, articulating a platform to reduce police violence, and launching a newly urgent conversation on race—a conversation that takes seriously feminist questions of intersectionality, including the intersections of transness and race. This has been especially important at a time when the deliberate killing of black trans women has reached an all-time high, with twenty-four known murders in 2016. As noted on the official BLM website, the movement's vision goes beyond the familiar black politics of "keeping straight cis Black men in the front of the movement." They state:

> Black Lives Matter affirms the lives of Black queer and trans folks, disabled folks, Black undocumented folks, folks with records, women and all Black lives along the gender spectrum. It centers those that have been marginalized within Black liberation movements.

Perhaps the highest-profile illustration of the cultural centrality of this vital attention to black lives and resistance to racism, along with its intersection with trans issues, can be found in the immense popularity the entertainer Beyoncé Knowles enjoyed in 2016 with her "Formation" music video, performed as part of a Black Panther

Party–themed halftime performance at the fiftieth Super Bowl and incorporated into her *Lemonade* album and concert tour. The song, video, and concerts all featured vocal samples of Big Freedia, the gender-nonconforming star of the outrageously sexy "bounce" hip-hop scene, which lent a subtly powerful trans sensibility to Beyoncé's performances.

As Big Freedia's successful musical career demonstrates, not all forms of trans resistance have to be somberly militant to be influential. When trans and gender-nonconforming lives are lived joyously and unapologetically in plain sight or their hard truths and dangers are spoken out loud, when the knowledge that comes from living those lives is channeled into music and dance, written about and written from, played with and fantasized over, when their beauty and weirdness, their sharp edges and dark recesses are creatively explored and collectively experienced, that is equally as important as heavy political activism. Sometimes, the best places to engage in these sorts of practices are in semipublic subcultural scenes that revolve around particular interests or artistic genres or alternative cultural practices such as communal living spaces, polyamorous communities, nightclubs, cosplay conventions, furry lifestyles, kink and fetish practices, consensual sadomasochism, drag king competitions, trans beauty pageants, performance art, science fiction, fan fiction, fantasy fiction, graphic novels, commix, and goth, punk, electronica, hip-hop, or neo-folk music subcultures—all of which can become sites not only for pleasure and social connection in the present but also playful experimental workshops for the transformation of existing realities into desired futures.

Such spaces of possibility are as vulnerable and contested as they are necessary and life-sustaining. The Pulse nightclub in Orlando, Florida, became the target of the deadliest terrorist act in the United States since 9/11 when a homophobic gunman opened fire on patrons attending Latin Night at the gay club on June 12, 2016, killing forty-nine and wounding fifty-three, including members of trans and drag communities of color. The December 2, 2016, Ghost Ship warehouse fire in Oakland, California, claimed the lives of thirty-six people who were attending an underground concert there, making it the deadliest structure fire in California since the great San Francisco earthquake and fire of 1906. Fatalities ran so high because the warehouse, which was not licensed for residential or performance use, had makeshift staircases made of stacked wooden pallets, no smoke detectors or fire alarms, and no clearly marked exits. And yet, without such dangerous and criminalized spaces, artists nurtured by and hungry for the Bay Area's fabled cultural openness would not be able to remain in the now exorbitantly expensive region, where gentrification had pushed rents for one-bedroom apartments above $3,000 a month by 2015. Among those who lost their lives in the fire were three trans women—Cash Askew (of the band Them Are Us Too), Feral Pines, and Em Bohlka—all actively making the kind of culture they wanted to live in.

Trans Cultural Production and Mass Media Representation

As long as trans and nonbinary people remain a distinct and politically marginalized minority, there will likely always be spaces geared more toward trans community, identity, and audiences than toward mainstream society. In recent years, the annual Gender Odyssey conference in Seattle (established in 2001) and the Philadelphia Trans Health Conference (established in 2002) have grown into major community venues. *Original Plumbing,* a fashion-forward transmasculine-oriented print and online publication steeped in the hipster styles of Brooklyn and San Francisco's Mission District, was launched in 2009 by Amos Mac and Rocco Kayiatos. That same year Luis Venegas launched *Candy,* an annual limited-edition high-concept transfeminine-focused publication advertised as "The First Transversal Style Magazine," whose first issue featured cross-dressed actor James Franco on its cover. Tom Léger founded Topside Press in 2010, which has published a remarkable burst of new fiction by trans authors, including Imogen Binnie's *Nevada* (2013), Ryka Aoki's *He Mele a Hilo* (2014), and the anthology *The Collection: Short Fiction from the Transgender Vanguard.* In 2012 Trystan Cotten founded the Transgress Press collective, a transcentric feminist and queer publisher that allows authors to retain copyright and donates profits to social justice organizations. Both presses, along with Jay Sennett's Homofactus Press, have helped emerging transgender writers flourish as never before. Poetry has become a particularly exciting form of creative expression, with TC Tolbert and Trace Peterson's massive 2013 anthology *Troubling the Line: Trans and Genderqueer Poetry and Poetics* and breakout work by poets such as Samuel Ace (who as Linda Smukler had published *Normal Sex* in 1994), Trish Salah (*Desiring in Arabic* and *Lyric Sexology Vol. 1*), Joy Ladin (*Transmigration*), and Eli Clare (*The Marrow's Telling*). Conceptual artist Chris Vargas adds a layer of tongue-in-cheek metacommentary to the tremendous outpouring of trans cultural work in his ingenious Museum of Transgender Hirstory and Art, a virtual museum that both celebrates and dissects trans culture.

One of the first indications that transgender issues were headed toward higher visibility in mass media and celebrity culture was the public gender transition between 2004 and 2006 of Alexis Arquette, who hailed from a prominent acting family and who had a long career as a drag entertainer as well as a screen actor, followed by the even more highly publicized transition of Chaz Bono, the only child of superstar Cher and her late former husband Sonny Bono, between 2009 and 2011. Stephen Ira, the trans son of Hollywood icons Warren Beatty and Annette Bening, kept a lower profile but still made a name for himself in the 2010s as an outspoken trans advocate on social media. FTM Thomas Beatie made headlines for a few years as the "pregnant man," after conceiving, carrying, and giving birth to his children posttransition. Transgender models began gracing the catwalks and the covers of fashion magazines as never before, most notably Andreja Pejic, who successfully modeled both men's and women's fashion before transitioning full-time to womanhood in 2013. It became routine to see trans actors and contestants showing up on daytime soap operas and reality television shows like *America's Next Top Model* or *Survivor,* while *RuPaul's Drag Race* has been a constant presence on the Logo network since 2009. A growing number of younger celebrities like Miley Cyrus and Jaden Smith publicly embraced gender-fluid and nonbinary styles and identities. Caitlyn Jenner's spectacular level of publicity in spring 2015 dwarfed previous attention to trans issues in the media, but it was simply the most notable instance of a long-developing trend toward greater mass media presence.

Increasingly, trans people play a decisive role in how transgender issues are represented on-screen, and more and more trans people are finding mainstream success in film and television. Laverne Cox broke fresh ground as the first trans person to play a recurring trans character in a mass-marketed scripted series. Jill Soloway's multiple-award-winning show *Transparent,* on Amazon, chronicles the trials and tribulations of a Jewish family in Los Angeles, the Pfeffermans, and their former *paterfamilias,* the late-transitioning Maura. The show has been remarkable for the degree to which it has practiced "transfirmative action." Although it stars primarily cisgender actors, it is coproduced by Rhys Ernst and Zackary Drucker, two prolific trans culture makers whose photographic work has been featured in the Whitney Biennial; the writing staff includes trans vocal artist Our Lady J, and many episodes are directed by Silas Howard, former guitarist of the lesbian punk band Tribe 8 and codirector, with Harry Dodge, of the underground trans cinema cult classic

By Hook or By Crook. Trans actors Alexandra Billings and Trace Lysette also have recurring roles.

Independent feature films also provided new opportunities for trans talent in Hollywood. *Tangerine,* an edgy low-budget movie about two trans sex workers on the prowl for a cheating boyfriend, won trans actor Mya Taylor an Independent Spirit Award for Best Supporting Actress in 2015. Sydney Freeland, a Navajo filmmaker and trans woman, won raves at Sundance for her debut feature *Drunktown's Finest* and similar acclaim (plus an Emmy nomination) for her web series with Jen Richards, *Her Story,* about the lives of trans women in contemporary Los Angeles. In spite of advances in having trans people play trans characters on-screen, stereotypical transgender-themed material made by cis people with cis people for cis people continues to be popular and successful, as witnessed by Academy Award wins for such films as *The Dallas Buyers Club* and *The Danish Girl.*

Print media witnessed a similar outpouring of high-profile work by and about trans people. Accomplished memoirist and frequent media spokesperson on trans issues Jennifer Finney Boylan published *Stuck in the Middle with You* in 2013, her tale of "parenting in three genders." Janet Mock, a former editor at *People* magazine, won acclaim for her best-selling 2014 autobiography *Redefining Realness,* which told a Cinderella story of growing up on the surprisingly mean streets of Honolulu as a mixed-race trans woman before finding love and success in New York City. In 2015, the *New York Times* launched an ongoing series of in-depth special features and reports called "Transgender Today" that chronicle the rapid evolution of trans in contemporary society. In 2016, the National Book Award–winning feminist journalist Susan Faludi published *In the Darkroom,* her memoir of reconnecting with her estranged former father, who became Stefanie after abandoning the family and returning to her native Hungary in the 1990s.

TRANS ACADEMIA

Transgender studies attained an unprecedented level of institutional support and legitimation in the first decades of the twenty-first century, furthering the long-term project of centering trans voices in the production of knowledge about trans-related topics and trans lives. Several important field-shaping anthologies appeared, notably the two-volume *Transgender Studies Reader, Transfeminist Perspectives in and Beyond Transgender and Gender Studies, Trans Studies: The Challenge to Hetero/Homo-Normativities,* and *Debates in Transgender, Queer, and Feminist Theory,* as well as dozens of scholarly monographs and hundreds of peer-reviewed articles. In 2011 the University of Victoria in British Columbia opened its Transgender Archive, based on important collections of historical records amassed over many years by sociologist Aaron Devor. The University of Arizona announced a faculty cluster hire in trans studies in 2013, with the intention to offer the first trans studies graduate minor in the world. In 2014, the prestigious Duke University Press began publishing *TSQ: Transgender Studies Quarterly,* the first peer-reviewed interdisciplinary journal for the field (the *International Journal of Transgenderism,* which has been around since the 1990s and which was once the house organ for the World Professional Association for Transgender Health, is more narrowly focused on psychomedical and empirical social-scientific scholarship). In 2015, K. J. Rawson launched a new online resource, the Digital Transgender Archive, funded in part through a grant from the American Council of Learned Societies. And in 2016, Devor was appointed to the world's first endowed chair in transgender studies, funded by a $2 million gift from billionaire trans philanthropist Jennifer Pritzker, heir to the Hyatt Hotels fortune. Numerous colleges and universities across the country started listing expertise in transgender issues as a desired specialization in new faculty hiring, offering postdoctoral fellowships for emerging scholars in the field, and holding numerous symposia, colloquia, and small conferences devoted to various aspects of trans studies—all reflections of how important it suddenly seemed to study and understand the remarkable upsurge of trans presence in society. Trans topics are now widely taught in college and university curricula and routinely represented in most major

continues

humanities and social sciences journals and professional meetings. A trans studies conference at the University of Arizona in 2016 drew more than 450 interdisciplinary scholars from around the world and announced the hope of establishing an International Transgender Studies Association.

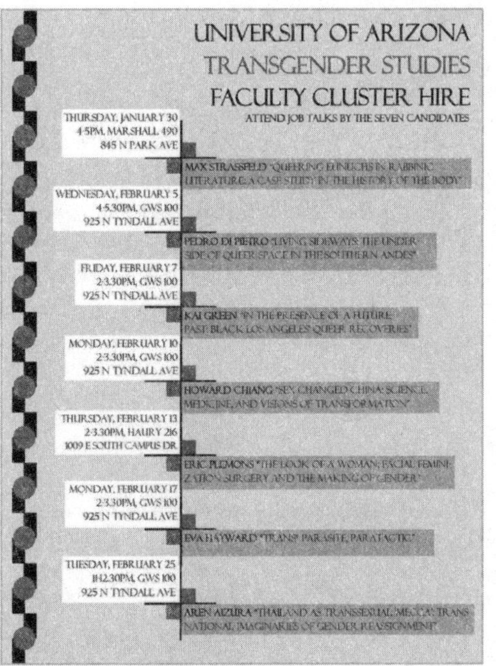

University of Arizona, Transgender Studies Faculty Cluster Hire, 2014. (Poster credit: Megan Coe, 2014.)

Transgender professors Trish Salah and mícha cárdenas, and Carle Brioso and Kai Green, attending the 2016 Trans Studies Conference.* (Photos by Samuel Ace, 2016.)

The Digital Transgender Archive was established in 2015 by K. J. Rawson, a trans studies professor at College of the Holy Cross, with support from the American Council of Learned Societies. It contains many digitized copies of rare transgender materials from archives throughout North America. (Logo used with permission. https://www.digitaltransgenderarchive.net.)

Mainstreaming Trans Politics

While trans and gender-nonconforming subcultural scenes and spaces proliferated to an uncatalogable extent in the early twenty-first century, and transgender cultural production found vast new mass audiences, the fight for trans rights also moved strongly into the mainstream. This increased level of familiarity and acceptance was reflected in the truly unprecedented advances in civil rights for trans people during the Obama administration, as a result of changing social attitudes and perspectives finally being reflected within the highest reaches of government. Campaigning in Florida during the 2012 presidential election, Vice President Joe Biden said he considered ending antitransgender discrimination to be "the civil rights issue of our time."

The United States is on track to be a majority-minority nation with no one ethnic or racial group accounting for more than half the population by the 2050s. Already, more than 40 percent of the Millennial generation born after 1980 is nonwhite, and immigration to the United States is highest from non-white-majority countries in Latin America and Asia. These demographic shifts undoubtedly contributed to the election in 2008 of Barack Obama as the first culturally black mixed-race president of the United States, just as the global financial crisis was at its worst. Obama's election in the midst of the economic meltdown sharpened the already stark polarizations between US Americans who thought that "their" country was slipping away from them versus those who felt energized by trying to find their niche in a polyglot, multicultural society. During his presidency, many dichotomies became more deeply entrenched: those between rural and urban ways of life, between those who profit from the globalized neoliberal economy and those who are marginalized within it, those who welcome immigration and those who oppose it, those who think the police systematically target racial minorities and those who don't, those who consider climate change to be the greatest threat facing humanity and those who consider it a hoax, those who advocate for expanding opportunities and civil rights for women and minorities and those who think such efforts have already gone too far, and those who push the envelope of possibilities for living in radically new ways and those who want to "return" to vanishing ways of life.

The divergence in worldviews about the manifold challenges we now face and how best to solve them has become truly profound. This results in part from the channelization of news and information within a fragmented social media landscape filled with many varieties of bias, including blatant propaganda and deliberate falsehood, that allows everyone to surround themselves in bubbles of like-minded people. But the result is that it feels we are all living in separate realities, each struggling to ground itself in the same territory, the same state, the same social and economic structures as the others. Over the course of the Obama administration, transgender identity became a curiously important bellwether in this virtual civil war.

Throughout most of his presidency, because of the intransigence of congressional Republicans, Obama relied on executive orders to advance his agenda, including support for transgender rights. The federal government amended the requirements for changing name and gender on identity documents, including passports; it forbid discrimination against LGBT people in federal employment and contracts involving federal funds; lifted the ban on trans people serving openly in the military; and allowed the Veterans Administration to provide medical and psychological services to transgender veterans. Obama appointed trans people to government positions, including Amanda Simpson as a deputy assistant secretary of the Department of Defense, and hired others, such as Raffi Freedman-Gurspan, who became an outreach and recruitment director for the White House personnel office in 2015. Another symbolically important action that year was to establish a gender-neutral toilet in the White House.

On Obama's watch, the National Park Service issued the massive *LGBTQ America,* a twelve-hundred-page study of places of historical significance to LGBTQ communities in the United States, which included a chapter on transgender history. The Stonewall Inn became the first National Historic Site to be landmarked because of its significance to LGBTQ history. In San Francisco, a group of antigentrification activists used the report to argue that the Tenderloin neighborhood and its legacy businesses (such as gay bars) merited preservation through the establishment of a Compton's Cafeteria National Transgender Historic District. President Obama actually mentioned the riot at Compton's Cafeteria in his official 2016 Pride Month remarks, praising "people who aren't afraid to ruffle feathers in the name of justice and equality," and asserting "that's always been our story—not just in Selma or Seneca Falls, but in Compton's Café and the Stonewall Inn." In spite of his remarkable embrace of trans rights, Obama nevertheless faced criticism from some trans activists for his actions on other matters that also affect trans people, such as immigration. At a White

House reception in 2015, Jennicet Gutiérrez, an undocumented trans-Latina activist with the Los Angeles–based La Familia Trans Queer Liberation group, stirred controversy when she interrupted President Obama's remarks to protest his administration's deportation policies and their impact on trans immigrants and detainees.

One of the most significant accomplishments of the Obama years was the passage of the Patient Protection and Affordable Care Act (ACA), better known as Obamacare, in 2010. It was the signature achievement of the Obama administration's first two years, accomplished during the small window of opportunity when the Democratic Party controlled not only the presidency but both the Senate and House of Representatives, before the 2010 midterm elections resulted in a Republican-majority House that persistently obstructed Obama's agenda. Nevertheless, because of the inclusion of a civil rights provision in the historic health care bill, it became clearly illegal to discriminate in the provision of health care, and thus legally necessary to cover medical transition costs for trans people seeking those services. Although implementation of the ACA proved politically contentious and many states dragged their feet on covering transition-related care, trans legal advocates won an impressive string of victories challenging the exclusion of health care benefits for trans people seeking to medically transition.

These efforts were bolstered by one of most significant legal rulings ever on trans rights, *Macy v. Holder,* in 2012. Ever since *Price Waterhouse v. Hopkins* in 1989, trans people had been able to contest discrimination based on sex stereotyping, but they still were not covered against discrimination based simply on being trans, and they still were deemed not covered by Title VII of the Civil Rights Act, which forbids sex-based discrimination. Passage of a gender-inclusive Employment Non-Discrimination Act would have put the matter to rest, but after the debacle of 2007, ENDA was never reintroduced. Although the Obama administration was supportive of ENDA, it prioritized its health care agenda and passage of the ACA, after which it had spent most of its political capital and no longer enjoyed the support of Congress. The *Schroer v. Billings* case in 2008 took matters a step further. It ruled that, in rescinding a job offer to Diane Schroer after she informed her prospective supervisor that she was in the process of gender transition, her would-be employer, the National Archives, discriminated against her not only on the basis of sex stereotyping (claiming she looked like a man) but also because she was a particular kind of person—namely, a person who was changing sex. But in *Macy v. Holder,* the Equal Employment Opportunity Commission (EEOC) ruled that Mia Macy, who, like Schroer, had a job offer rescinded once she notified the prospective employer of her intent to transition, was discriminated against specifically for being transgender and that this constituted illegal sex discrimination under Title VII.

This landmark ruling—an administrative agency's interpretation of existing law rather than the passage of a new law—opened the door to further federal actions. It cemented the coverage of trans health care provision under the ACA and gave the green light to new cases related to toilet and locker room access at public schools that received federal funding. The most significant such case involved Gavin Grimm, a young trans person in Virginia seeking to settle once and for all the question of appropriate public toilet access for trans people under both Title VII and Title IX of the Civil Rights Act. The Supreme Court agreed in October 2016 to hear his case.

In this new legal context, long-standing structural tensions between state and national powers within the federal system of governance started playing themselves out in relation to trans issues, just as they had in other health care matters, such as access to abortion and contraception, and other struggles over federal, state, and local educational policies, such as charter schools and government vouchers for tuition at religious schools. By 2016, several conservative-majority states had filed lawsuits against the federal government seeking to block the new rulings on health care and public toilet access for trans people, most notably in North Carolina, where passage of House Bill 2, which revoked existing LGBT civil rights protections at the municipal level and mandated that trans people use public toilets that matched their birth-assigned sex rather than their identity and appearance. The HB2 controversy resulted in a boycott and numerous cancelations of planned business investments, conferences, concerts, and sporting events, including the 2017 NCAA men's basketball playoffs. It also spurred a federal civil rights lawsuit to compel the state to comply with the EEOC interpretation of existing antidiscrimination law. In publicly announcing her intent to sue North Carolina to compel the state to acknowledge the civil rights of trans people, US Attorney General Loretta Lynch, the first black woman to hold that job, deliberately evoked the history of the African American civil rights struggles of the 1960s and directly addressed the transgender community, saying:

> Some of you have lived freely for decades. Others of you are still wondering how you can possibly live the lives you were born to lead. But no matter how isolated or scared you may feel today, the Department of Justice and the entire Obama Administration wants you to know that we see you; we stand with you; and we will do everything we can to protect you going forward. Please know that history is on your side.

The movement of transgender civil rights into the mainstream played out at every level of society as increasing numbers of trans people moved into institutional politics throughout the United States. Diego Sanchez became the first openly transgender person to work as a congressional staffer when he served in Massachusetts congressman Barney Frank's office between 2008 and 2012 and helped organize historic hearings on transgender discrimination. Those hearings featured testimony by attorney Kylar Broadus, founder of the Trans People of Color Coalition, who became the first trans person ever to testify on Capitol Hill. Twenty-eight openly trans people served as delegates to the Democratic Party's presidential nominating convention in 2016, including Barbra Casbar Siperstein, a member of the Democratic National Committee, and Sarah McBride, who became the first trans person to speak from the convention stage on national television. Only a handful of people known to be trans have ever been elected to public office in the United States, many of them during the Obama years. In addition to the outed Althea Garrison, who held a seat in the Massachusetts legislature 1992–1994, Michelle Bruce held a city council seat for one term in Riverdale, Georgia, starting in 2003 before she, too, was outed and subsequently not reelected; Jessica Orsini, who campaigned as an openly trans woman and practicing pagan, was elected to three terms as alderwoman in Centralia, Missouri, starting in 2006. Kim Coco Iwamoto was elected in 2006 to Hawaii's State Board of Education and subsequently was appointed by the governor to the Hawaii Civil Rights Commission, 2012–2016. Stu Rasmussen became mayor of Silverton, Oregon, in 2008. Victoria Kolakowski was elected as a judge in Alameda County, California, in 2010 and reelected in 2015; Stacie Laughton was elected to the New Hampshire House of Representatives in 2012.

The advancement of lesbian and gay rights during the Obama years significantly altered the relationship between trans communities and the broader LGBTQ coalition, which had been strained ever since trans interests had been thrown under the bus in the failed effort to pass ENDA. With the 2011 repeal of the

Clinton-era Don't Ask, Don't Tell (DADT) policy that disallowed the open service of lesbian women and gay men in the military, and particularly after the right to same-sex marriage was secured by the *Windsor* (2013) and *Obergefell* (2015) Supreme Court decisions, transgender emerged as a "cutting-edge" civil rights issue for LGBT organizations. Mainstream advocacy groups like the Human Rights Campaign that had previously marginalized trans concerns suddenly developed a keen interest in the topic, and the Palm Center, a think tank affiliated with University of California, Santa Barbara, that had been instrumental in the overturn of DADT, shifted attention to trans military policy—work enabled by a 2013 grant of more than a million dollars from army veteran, military history enthusiast, and trans philanthropist Jennifer Pritzker. At the same time, a host of new trans-focused community-based advocacy and activist groups sprouted in cities and states across the country and became more insistent on addressing concerns specific to trans needs, while established groups such as the National Center for Transgender Equality, the Transgender Law Center, and Global Action for Trans* Equality dramatically expanded their operations. Funding levels for trans NGOs worldwide reached new (but still inadequate) heights, thanks in large part to the international coordination of philanthropic giving through the Trans Funders Working Group, a part of the Funders for LGBTQ Issues nonprofit organization. As of 2014, global private funding for trans-related activism, advocacy, and support totaled roughly $12 million annually.

The rapprochement between trans activism and the liberal gay and lesbian movement, as well as the emergence of more robust independent trans politics, was part of the more general mainstreaming of trans issues. By 2016, it seemed that transgender lives were on the cusp of full legal equality and that the biggest challenge facing the more progressive and radical elements within the transgender community was the quest to ensure that the recent gains were available to all trans people, not just those most privileged by race, class, and ability.

Backlash, Survival, and Resistance

It would be remarkable if all the historic changes in how society understands and accepts trans and gender-nonconforming people failed to produce a backlash among people hostile to those changes. One dimension of that pushback came from quarters of the feminist movement that had long been hostile to trans people. In 2013, several well-known feminist activists and academics published *Forbidden Discourse: The Silencing of Feminist Criticism of "Gender,"* an open letter that articulated what has come to be known as "gender-critical" feminism—that is, that the very concept of gender is a depoliticized substitution for the concept of sexism, nothing more than an ideological smokescreen masking the persistence of male supremacy and the oppression of women by men. They argued that "transgender" was the nonsensical offspring of this politically pernicious embrace of the gender concept, and they contested what they considered to be the silencing of their views by a powerful "transgender lobby." These and similar ideas were further elaborated in Sheila Jeffreys's 2014 book *Gender Hurts: A Feminist Analysis of the Politics of Transgenderism,* which did little more than dress up Janice Raymond's thirty-five-year-old transphobic rhetoric from *Transsexual Empire* in twenty-first-century drag, arguing that "gender ideology" had been promulgated by misguided trans women who displaced their own unhappiness onto others in ways that were harmful to cisgender women and girls. In an effort to distance themselves from such transphobic sentiments, some cisgender radical feminists started using the acronym TERF (trans-exclusionary radical feminist), coined in 2008 by feminist blogger

TigTog as a neutrally descriptive term for feminists like Jeffreys, which was quickly embraced by many transfeminists as a useful shorthand for describing a sadly persistent set of beliefs among a small minority of feminists. The term is typically rejected as insulting and defamatory by the people to whom it refers, though the intent in coining and using the term was simply to point out that some feminists include trans issues and trans people within feminism, and some don't.

A far more consequential backlash took place on November 3, 2015, when the voters repealed HERO, the Houston Equal Rights Ordinance. Passed by an 11–6 vote of the Houston City Council in 2014, HERO was a sweeping piece of legislation that banned discrimination based on age, race, color, ethnicity, national origin, genetic profile, disability, family or marital status, pregnancy, religion, military service, sex, sexual orientation, and gender identity. It applied not only to municipal employment and contracts but also to housing, private employers, and the provision of public accommodation in such businesses as restaurants and hotels. Opponents of HERO—upset over the inclusion of sexual orientation and gender identity protections and inflamed by what they considered to be the overreach of "liberal elites" foisting their values on ordinary people who did not share them—successfully petitioned to place a referendum on the November 2015 ballot seeking to repeal it. That measure, known as Proposition 1, asked voters to vote "yes" to keep HERO in place or to vote "no" to repeal it.

Campaign for Houston, the organization founded specifically to combat Proposition 1, focused with laser-like precision solely on the supposed danger that transgender women, whom they vilified as deranged male sex predators in drag, would pose to the safety of women and girls in public restrooms. They reductively characterized the wide-ranging HERO as a "bathroom ordinance" and plastered signs with the slogan "No Men in Women's Bathrooms"

TOILET TROUBLE

Transgender access to public toilets and locker rooms, particularly in K–12 schools receiving federal funds, became a heated battleground for trans rights starting in November 2015, when voters in Houston, Texas, unexpectedly repealed the HERO, the Houston Equal Rights Ordinance, after a fierce campaign that stirred up unwarranted fear about sexual predators using HERO's transgender protections to molest women and girls in sex-segregated public toilets. The transgender toilet issue went on to figure in a similar rollback of civil rights protections in North Carolina in early 2016 and became an issue in the Republican presidential primary elections. It was a contentious enough topic that it wound up on the cover of *Time* magazine (May 30, 2016). After the election of Donald Trump, a

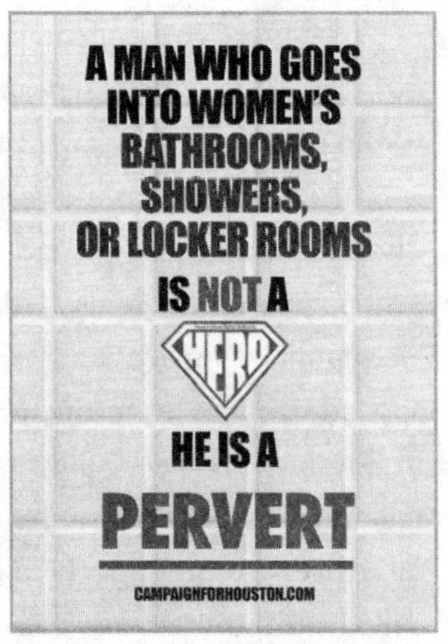

Campaign for Houston Twitter Advertisement, 2015. (Image in public domain.)

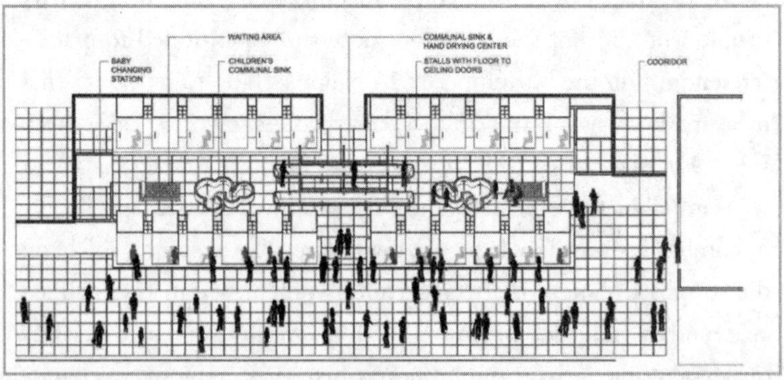

Stalled! Project, all-gender-inclusive public toilet prototype, Joel Sanders Architects, 2016.

continues

All-gender restroom sign. (Unattributed, 2016.)

dozen or more states introduced legislation similar to that in Houston and North Carolina, and a lawsuit on behalf of Virginia transgender teenager Gavin Grimm, seeking to protect his access to his school's boys' bathroom, headed to the Supreme Court in March 2017. But why not just design bathrooms in a different way? That's the question that New York architect Joel Sanders asked when he launched *Stalled!*, a project to use innovative design to solve problems of social justice. By changing how bathrooms are laid out, it's possible to create safety and privacy without relying on sex segregation. And it doesn't have to cost a lot of money. Mable's Smokehouse, a BBQ joint in Williamsburg, Brooklyn, redesigned its restrooms in a way that has several single-stall toilets arranged around a communal—and highly visible—washing up area next to the bar.

Gender-inclusive public toilet area, Mable's Smokehouse, Williamsburg, Brooklyn, New York. (Photo credit: Susan Stryker, 2016.)

all across the city. A television ad aired frequently at the height of the campaign that showed a man lurking in a toilet stall to corner an unsuspecting little girl, while ominously declaring "Any man, at any time, could enter a women's restroom, simply by claiming to be a woman that day—even registered sex offenders." To the consternation of many left-leaning citizens, Proposition 1 overwhelmingly failed, 39 percent to 61 percent, and the far-reaching ordinance was revoked. In voting to repeal HERO, a majority of Houstonians expressed their willingness not merely to deny the expansion of civil rights but actually to strip away existing rights from some of their fellow citizens. It was an early expression of the reactionary populism already boiling to the surface of public life that would propel Donald Trump to the White House a year later.

Trans issues were the topic of frequent debate during the Republican presidential primary contests and were raised most persistently by failed candidates Mike Huckabee and Ted Cruz. Eventual nominee Donald Trump personally took a more disinterested stance, publicly announcing that he could care less which toilet the Republican transgender celebrity Caitlyn Jenner used when she paid a visit to Trump Tower. Trump's conservative evangelical vice-presidential running mate Mike Pence, however, supported a number of harsh anti-LGBT measures during his years as governor of Indiana.

With Trump's unexpected victory in the 2016 presidential election, the movement for transgender rights experienced a setback of such proportions that it threatens to utterly wipe out the remarkable gains of the preceding eight years. Trump nominated, and Congress approved, staunch opponents of trans rights to important cabinet positions, including Jeff Sessions as attorney general and Betsy DeVos as secretary of education. Sessions's views on minority rights are so reactionary he was denied a federal judgeship over them in the 1980s; DeVos, heir to the Amway fortune, has been a champion of government vouchers for private religious education, while her family's private foundation has been a leading funder of "bathroom bill" and "religious freedom" legislation, and a past contributor to a group that supports conversion therapy for LGBT youth.

One of the first acts of the Justice Department under Sessions was to drop an appeal to overturn a ruling by a federal judge in Texas that temporarily stayed the implementation of the Obama administration's "guidance" to interpret Title IX protections against sex discrimination as inclusive of gender identity, before going on a few weeks later to issue a new federal guidance that rescinded the previous one issued by the Obama administration and that asserted instead that the interpretation of Title IX was a state, not federal, matter. Sessions dropped Attorney General Loretta Lynch's lawsuit against North Carolina's HB2 in April 2017. The Supreme Court changed course, too, sending the Gavin Grimm case back to the lower courts. In doing so, it likely pushed a definitive victory for transgender civil rights back by a generation. A proposed executive order in the early days of the Trump administration that would have allowed religiously motivated discrimination against LGBT people was quietly tabled as a result of opposition from first daughter Ivanka and her husband, Jared Kushner, but the ultimate fate of transgender health care under Trump, as attempts to systematically dismantle the Affordable Care Act continue after an early failure to "repeal and replace" it, remains to be seen.

If there is a lesson to be learned from US transgender history at the dispiriting moment in which these words are being written, it is that trans people have a long record of survival in a world that is often hostile to us. Most of that time we have survived while being criminalized and psychopathologized, with no civil rights, misrepresented by others in public discourse while our own voices have largely been silenced and our living presence in the world rendered invisible, and subjected to forms of violence both acute and diffuse, personal and systemic. Although it stings to have one's being-in-the-world undermined, and one's worth belittled, we can take solace in what those who came before us accomplished with far fewer resources. Our elders and ancestors got us here. It is up to us, who live now, to take their torch and run our own leg of the race before we pass it on to those who will surely come after us. It has been inspiring to see so many forms of grassroots activism spring up in trans communities, in alliance with many other communities, in resistance to the US government's sudden rightward lurch, and to what that shift likely means for trans people and other minorities—everything from stockpiling hormones that may no longer be available through the health care system so that they can be distributed in the years ahead, to setting up legal clinics helping people rush through name and gender change paperwork while they still can, to calling the offices of elected officials to register disagreement and opposition to specific policies or proposals, to seeking weapons and martial arts training for self-defense. As "alt-right," white-supremacist, and right-wing populist provocateurs like Milo Yiannopoulos, David Duke, and Ann Coulter—emboldened by the Trump victory and the presence of reactionary Breitbart News mastermind Steve Bannon in the White House as Trump's chief strategist—increasingly target transgender people in deliberately inflammatory public statements made under the guise of "free speech," trans resistance has escalated in response, including highly visible participation in disruptive "antifa" (antifascist) and "black bloc" anarchist counteractions. Notably, trans activists and allies repeatedly vandalized and obstructed the path of the so-called Free Speech Bus, sponsored by a Far Right religious organization, that attempted to tour the United States to promote the idea that it's impossible to actually be transgender, and that transgender people don't really exist.

One of the first large-scale public protests of the Trump administration's priorities was the January 21, 2017, Women's March on Washington, held the day after Trump's inauguration. By some estimates, it was the largest single-day protest in US history, with at least half a million people attending in Washington, DC, and roughly three million more at nearly seven hundred sister marches in every state of the union and every continent on earth—including Antarctica. The marches were notable not only for their sheer size and for the forceful repudiation they offered to a wide range of Trump policy goals, ranging from immigration to Muslim registries to environmental issues to reproductive choice, but for the evidence they offered of how trans issues had become fully integrated into a progressive political agenda. The march's official "Guiding Vision and Definition of Principles" statement named trans pioneers Sylvia Rivera, Marsha P. Johnson, and Miss Major Griffin-Gracy among "the legions of revolutionary leaders who paved the way for us to march." March organizers described themselves as "a women-led movement bringing together people of all genders," who refused to cede "the power to control our bodies" and asserted the right to "be free from gender norms, expectations and stereotypes." They explicitly acknowledged their "obligation to uplift, expand and protect the rights of our gay, lesbian, bi, queer, trans or gender non-conforming brothers, sisters and siblings," including "access to non-judgmental, comprehensive healthcare with no exceptions or limitations; access to name and gender changes on identity documents; full antidiscrimination protections; access to education, employment, housing and benefits; and an end to police and state violence."

High-profile speakers at the Washington, DC, rally who explicitly addressed trans issues included actress Ashley Judd, who offered a raucous spoken-word performance about "nasty women," and revolutionary feminist icon Angela Davis, who denounced the prison-industrial complex for, among other things, its treatment of incarcerated trans people, as she spelled out the interlocking violences enacted through colonialism, racism, and capitalist labor exploitation. Janet Mock offered a passionate defense of sex workers; singer and actress Janelle Monae's call-and-response performance named individual trans women killed in recent years, and the Transgender Law Center's Raquel Willis offered a powerful personal statement about her life as a southern black trans woman. Though the march was far from being the most radical form of resistance, did not adequately address trans men's stake in feminism, and adopted as its unofficial emblem knitted pink "pussy hats," which some marchers felt recentered white, cisgender, and biological-essentialist notions of womanhood and feminism, its vision nevertheless offered a powerful testament to intersectional feminist principles and boldly announced a mass determination to stand up to disconcerting political developments. The multitudes who turned out in support of a feminist mass protest that put its trans-inclusive and trans-affirmative politics up front attested to just how far trans issues had moved from the margins toward the center of cultural awareness.

"Making history" is an action that we take today, in the present moment, that links our understanding of the past to the future we strive to build. In his essay "The Uses and Abuses of History for the Present," the philosopher Friedrich Nietzsche noted that rich and powerful people have little use for history other than as a raw material to build a monument to their own greatness, whereas most people look to the past merely with a sense of nostalgia, hoping to find there something familiar and comforting to salve the alienations of present day. "Only those who are crushed by a present circumstance," Nietzsche said, "and who are determined at all cost to throw off their oppression," have any need for a critical relationship to the history that has produced them. This little book, written as an approachable introductory text on transgender history in the United States, will have achieved its modest goal if it helps its readers to develop just such a critical historical consciousness. As the Reverend Martin Luther King Jr. famously said, paraphrasing

The January 21, 2017, Women's March on Washington, DC, was a massive public protest against the Trump administration that had been inaugurated the day before. It drew more than half a million people to the nation's capital and millions more to sister marches throughout the United States and around the world. The marches were explicitly transgender inclusive and affirming, and the rally at the national march featured a number of prominent trans women speakers. (Photo credit: Ted Eytan from Washington, DC [January 21, 2017, Women's March Washington, DC, USA 00095] [CC BY-SA 2.0; http://creativecommons.org/licenses/by-sa/2.0], via Wikimedia Commons.)

the nineteenth-century abolitionist Theodore Parker, "the arc of the moral universe is long"; like him, we must have faith that it "bends toward justice." But like him, as well, we can do more than cross our fingers and hope for the best if we ourselves work together to bend our little corner of the universe in that direction.

ACKNOWLEDGMENTS

Thanks to Brooke Warner at Seal Press for asking me to write this book in the first place; to Denise Silva for guiding it through the initial stages and for compiling the Further Reading and Resources; to Jennie Goode for (her) grace under (my) pressure in seeing the original manuscript across the finish line; and to Stephanie Knapp, Christina Palaia, Elisa Rivlen, and Michael Clark at Perseus for their work on the second edition. Thanks as well for the 2008 edition to my research assistant in Vancouver, Sarah Sparks, and to Denali Dalton Toevs for giving up part of our Thanksgiving vacation to help me wrap up a few final details; Saoirse Lorenzon picked up where Denali left off in providing research assistance for the 2017 second edition. I'd like to collectively thank many colleagues, too numerous to name individually, for many years of conversation and shared research collaboration on transgender history. Special shout-out to the dozens of Facebook friends who participated in crowdsourcing topics for the new edition's Chapter 6, and to my agent Jane von Mehren. As always, my deepest love and appreciation to Mimi Klausner for making her life with me.

READER'S GUIDE

QUESTIONS FOR DISCUSSION

How did this book change your perspective on transgender history?

What do you consider the most important development in the past fifty years for transgender rights? Why?

Name or describe three transgender people you've seen portrayed in the media. How were these individuals depicted? What social values or ideas do you think these depictions reflect? Has media representation of trans issues changed over time—and if so, how? What difference does it make if trans people represent themselves in mass media versus being represented by others?

What issues do you think the transgender movement most urgently needs to work on in your location?

What does it mean when an employer agrees to not discriminate against workers or customers on the basis of their gender identity? What sort of actions, policies, or changes do you think this nondiscrimination would involve?

Consider the different approaches that people in the transgender movement have used to effect civic change (street activism, uprisings, marches, letter writing, lobbying, the formation of nonprofit organizations, et cetera). What do you see as the successes and failings of each approach? Do you think any one approach has been more effective than the rest? Explain your answers.

How has attention to transgender issues changed feminism? How do you think third and fourth wave feminism differ from second wave feminism regarding its approach to transgender issues? Is there a need to distinguish transfeminism from feminism more generally?

How does being trans intersect with other forms of social oppression such as those related to race, ethnicity, religion, language, or disability? How is oppression related to being trans like, and unlike, these other structural oppressions?

TOPICS FOR RESEARCH

Pick one of the following topics and research how the situation in your location has evolved in past decades.

History

Questions to consider: How have the newspapers published around where you live covered trans issues throughout history? Talk with a librarian about how to access searchable online databases of historic newspapers—it can be pretty easy. You might have to be creative about how you search for information about the transgender past, because the word *transgender* wasn't widely used before the 1990s. You can search for words and phrases like "man disguised as woman," "woman disguised as man," "revealed to be a man," "revealed to be a woman," "true sex discovered," and other similar expressions. There's a huge amount of history yet to be recovered and written about.

Human Rights

Questions to consider: What sort of legal rights do transgender individuals have in your area? If your state has antidiscrimination laws protecting transgender people, what protections do they afford? How did these laws come about? What groups or individual activists have worked on the issue in your state? Did transgender people and cisgender people work together on transgender rights issues in your state?

Employment

Questions to consider: In your area, are transgender people legally protected from workplace discrimination? If not, what groups or individuals are working to institute these workplace protections? Have there been any individual or class-action lawsuits in your state to address discrimination? Which employers in your state have policies that prohibit discrimination based on gender identity?

Access to Health Services

Questions to consider: What local health services exist that address transgender people's health needs? When were they established? If you cannot find any such organizations in your state, where is the nearest transgender-friendly health service you can find? How much would it cost to travel there from your city? How have trans people where you live been affected by changes in how health care is provided at the national level?

Identity

Questions to consider: Are transgender individuals in your state allowed to change their sex on legal documents, such as driver's licenses? If so, when was this right instituted? If not, what groups are working to change the law? What concrete differences does this right make in the lives of transgender people?

FURTHER READING AND RESOURCES

BOOKS: NONFICTION

Atkins, Dawn, ed. *Looking Queer: Body Image and Identity in Lesbian, Bisexual, Gay, and Transgender Communities.* New York: Haworth, 1998.

Bailey, J. Michael. *The Man Who Would Be Queen: The Science of Gender-Bending and Transsexualism.* Washington, DC: Joseph Henry, 2003.

Beam, Cris. *Transparent: Love, Family, and Living the T with Transgender Teens.* New York: Harcourt, 2007.

Beemyn, Genny, and Sue Rankin. *The Lives of Transgender People.* New York: Columbia University Press, 2011.

Bender-Baird, Kyla. *Transgender Employment Experiences: Gendered Perceptions and the Law.* Albany: State University of New York Press, 2011.

Benjamin, Harry. *The Transsexual Phenomenon.* New York: Julian, 1966.

binaohan, b. *Decolonizing Trans/Gender 101.* Toronto: Biyuti Publishing, 2014.

Blackwood, Evelyn, and Saskia Wieringa, eds. *Female Desires: Same-Sex Relations and Transgender Practices Across Cultures.* New York: Columbia University Press, 1999.

Bloom, Amy. *Normal: Transsexual CEOs, Crossdressing Cops, and Hermaphrodites with Attitude.* New York: Random House, 2002.

Bolin, Anne. *In Search of Eve: Transsexual Rites of Passage.* South Hadley, MA: Bergin and Garvey, 1987.

Bornstein, Kate. *Gender Outlaw: On Men, Women, and the Rest of Us.* New York: Routledge, 1994.

Bullough, Bonnie, ed. *Gender Blending.* Amherst, MA: Prometheus, 1997.

Bullough, Vern, and Bonnie Bullough. *Cross Dressing, Sex, and Gender.* Philadelphia: University of Pennsylvania, 1993.

Butler, Judith. *Bodies That Matter: On the Discursive Limits of "Sex."* New York: Routledge, 1993.

———. *Gender Trouble: Feminism and the Subversion of Identity.* New York: Routledge, 1990.

———. *Undoing Gender.* New York: Routledge, 2004.

Califia, Patrick. *Sex Changes: The Politics of Transgenderism.* San Francisco: Cleis, 2003.

Cameron, Loren. *Body Alchemy: Transsexual Portraits.* San Francisco: Cleis, 1996.

Cromwell, Jason. *Transmen and FTMs: Identities, Bodies, Genders, and Sexualities.* Urbana: University of Illinois, 1999.

Currah, Paisley, Richard M. Juang, and Shannon Price Minter, eds. *Transgender Rights.* Minneapolis: University of Minnesota, 2006.

Denny, Dallas, ed. *Current Concepts in Transgender Identity.* New York: Routledge, 1997.

Devor, Holly. *FTM: Female-to-Male Transsexuals in Society.* Bloomington: Indiana University, 1997.

———. *Gender Blending: Confronting the Limits of Duality.* Bloomington: Indiana University, 1989.

Diamond, Morty, ed. *From the Inside Out: Radical Gender Transformation, FTM and Beyond.* San Francisco: Manic D, 2004.

Docter, Richard. *Transvestites and Transsexuals: Toward a Theory of Cross-Gender Behavior.* New York: Plenum, 1988.

Ekins, Richard. *Male Femaling: A Grounded Theory Approach to Cross-Dressing and Sex-Changing.* New York: Routledge, 1997.

Ekins, Richard, and Dave King. *The Transgender Phenomenon.* London: Sage, 2006.

Elliot, Patricia. *Debates in Transgender, Queer, and Feminist Theory.* Farnham, Surrey, England: Ashgate, 2010.

Epstein, Julia, and Kristina Straub, eds. *Body Guards: The Cultural Politics of Gender Ambiguity.* New York: Routledge, 1991.

Fausto-Sterling, Anne. *Sexing the Body: Gender Politics and the Construction of Sexuality.* New York: Perseus, 1999.

Feinberg, Leslie. *Transgender Warriors: Making History from Joan of Arc to Dennis Rodman.* Boston: Beacon Press, 1996.

———. *Trans Liberation: Beyond Pink or Blue.* Boston: Beacon Press, 1998.

Feinbloom, Deborah Heller. *Transvestites and Transsexuals.* New York: A Delta Book, 1976.

Foucault, Michel. *Herculine Barbin: Being the Recently Discovered Memoirs of a Nineteenth-Century Hermaphrodite.* New York: Pantheon, 1980.

———. *The History of Sexuality: An Introduction.* New York: Vintage, 1990. First published 1978.

Friedman, Mack. *Strapped for Cash: A History of American Hustler Culture.* Los Angeles: Alyson, 2003.

Green, Richard, and John Money, eds. *Transsexualism and Sex Reassignment.* Baltimore: Johns Hopkins University, 1969.

Grosz, Elizabeth. *Space, Time, and Perversion: Essays on the Politics of Bodies.* New York: Routledge, 1995.

———. *Volatile Bodies: Toward a Corporeal Feminism.* Bloomington: Indiana University, 1994.

Grosz, Elizabeth, and Elspeth Probyn, eds. *Sexy Bodies: The Strange Carnalities of Feminism.* New York: Routledge, 1995.

Halberstam, Judith. *Female Masculinity.* Durham, NC: Duke University, 1998.

———. *In a Queer Time and Place: Transgender Bodies, Subcultural Lives.* New York: New York University Press, 2005.

Halberstam, Judith, and Ira Livingston, eds. *Posthuman Bodies.* Bloomington: Indiana University, 1995.

Hausman, Bernice L. *Changing Sex: Transsexualism, Technology, and the Idea of Gender.* Durham, NC: Duke University, 1995.

Haynes, Felicity, and Tarquam McKenna, eds. *Unseen Genders: Beyond the Binaries.* New York: Peter Lang, 2001.

Irvine, Janice. *Disorders of Desire: Sex and Gender in Modern American Sexology.* Philadelphia: Temple University, 1990.

Jacobs, Sue-Ellen, Wesley Thomas, and Sabine Lang, eds. *Two-Spirit People: Native American Gender Identity, Sexuality, and Spirituality.* Urbana: University of Illinois, 1997.

Johnson, Mark. *Beauty and Power: Transgendering and Cultural Transformation in the Southern Philippines.* Oxford: Berg, 1997.

Kane-Demaios, J. Ari, and Vern L. Bullough, eds. *Crossing Sexual Boundaries: Transgender Journeys, Uncharted Paths.* Amherst, MA: Prometheus, 2005.

Kessler, Suzanne J. *Lessons from the Intersexed.* Piscataway, NJ: Rutgers University, 1998.

King, Dave. *The Transvestite and the Transsexual: Public Categories and Private Identities.* Aldershot: Avebury, 1993.

Kotula, Dean. *The Phallus Palace: Female to Male Transsexuals.* Boston: Alyson, 2002.

Kroker, Arthur, and Marilouise Kroker. *The Last Sex: Feminism and Outlaw Bodies.* New York: St. Martin's, 1993.

Kugle, Scott Alan. *Living Out Islam: Voices of Gay, Lesbian, and Transgender Muslims.* New York: New York University Press, 2013.

Kuklin, Susan. *Beyond Magenta: Transgender Teens Speak Out.* Somerville, MA: Candlewick Press, 2014.

Lang, Sabine. *Men as Women, Women as Men: Changing Gender in Native American Cultures.* Austin: University of Texas, 1998.

Laqueur, Thomas. *Making Sex: Body and Gender from the Greeks to Freud.* Cambridge, MA: Harvard University Press, 1990.

Lothstein, Leslie Martin. *Female-to-Male Transsexualism: Historical, Clinical, and Theoretical Issues.* New York: Routledge and Kegan Paul, 1983.

MacKenzie, Gordene Olga. *Transgender Nation.* Bowling Green, OH: Bowling Green University, 1994.

Mattilda, a.k.a. Matt Bernstein Sycamore, ed. *Nobody Passes: Rejecting the Rules of Gender and Conformity.* Berkeley, CA: Seal Press, 2006.

Meyerowitz, Joanne. *How Sex Changed: A History of Transsexuality in the United States.* Cambridge, MA: Harvard University Press, 2002.

More, Kate, and Stephen Whittle, eds. *Reclaiming Genders: Transsexual Grammars at the Fin de Siècle.* London: Cassell, 1999.

Namaste, Vivian K. *Invisible Lives: The Erasure of Transsexual and Transgendered People.* Chicago: University of Chicago, 2000.

———. *Sex Change, Social Change: Reflections on Identity, Institutions, and Imperialism.* Toronto: Women's Press, 2005.

Nanda, Serena. *Gender Diversity: Crosscultural Variations.* Long Grove, IL: Waveland, 1999.

———. *Neither Man Nor Woman: The Hijras of India.* Belmont, CA: Wadsworth, 1990.

Nestle, Joan, Clare Howell, and Riki Wilchins, eds. *Genderqueer: Voices from Beyond the Sexual Binary.* Boston: Alyson, 2002.

Preciado, Paul B. *Testo Junkie: Sex, Drugs, and Biopolitics in the Pharmacopornographic Era.* New York: The Feminist Press, 2013.

Ramet, Sandra P., ed. *Gender Reversals and Gender Cultures: Anthropological and Historical Perspectives.* New York: Routledge, 1996.

Rothblatt, Martine. *The Apartheid of Sex: A Manifesto on the Freedom of Gender.* New York: Crown, 1995.

Rudacille, Deborah. *The Riddle of Gender: Science, Activism, and Transgender Rights.* New York: Pantheon, 2005.

Salamon, Gayle. *Assuming a Body: Transgender and Rhetorics of Materiality.* New York: Columbia University Press, 2010.

Serano, Julia. *Whipping Girl: A Transsexual Woman on Sexism and the Scapegoating of Femininity.* Berkeley, CA: Seal Press, 2007.

Sharpe, Andrew. *Transgender Jurisprudence: Dysphoric Bodies of Law.* London: Cavendish, 2002.

Straayer, Chris. *Deviant Eyes, Deviant Bodies: Sexual Re-Orientation in Film and Video.* New York: Columbia University Press, 1996.

Stryker, Susan, ed. *The Transgender Issue. GLQ: A Journal of Lesbian and Gay Studies* 4, no. 2 (1998).

Stryker, Susan, and Aren Aizura, eds. *The Transgender Studies Reader 2.* New York: Routledge, 2013.

Stryker, Susan, and Stephen Whittle, eds. *The Transgender Studies Reader.* New York: Routledge, 2006.

Teich, Nicholas M., and Jamison Green. *Transgender 101: A Simple Guide to a Complex Issue.* New York: Columbia University Press, 2012.

Terry, Jennifer, and Jacqueline Urla, eds. *Deviant Bodies.* Bloomington: Indiana University Press, 1995.

Tully, Bryan. *Accounting for Transsexualism and Transhomosexuality.* London: Whiting and Birch, 1992.

Whittle, Stephen. *Respect and Equality: Transsexual and Transgender Rights.* New York: Routledge, 2002.

———. *The Transgender Debate: The Crisis Surrounding Gender Identities.* South Street, 2000.

Wilchins, Riki. *Read My Lips: Sexual Subversion and the End of Gender.* Ann Arbor, MI: Firebrand, 1997.

BOOKS: BIOGRAPHY, AUTOBIOGRAPHY, AND FICTION

Ames, Jonathan, ed. *Sexual Metamorphosis: An Anthology of Transsexual Memoirs.* New York: Vintage, 2005.

Andrews, Arin. *Some Assembly Required: The Not-So-Secret Life of a Transgender Teen.* New York: Simon & Schuster, 2014.

Blumenstein, Rosalyne. *Branded T.* Bloomington, IN: First Books Library, 2003.

Boyd, Helen. *My Husband Betty: Love, Sex, and Life with a Crossdresser.* New York: Thunder's Mouth, 2003.

———. *She's Not the Man I Married: My Life with a Transgender Husband.* Berkeley, CA: Seal Press, 2007.

Boylan, Jennifer Finney. *She's Not There: A Life in Two Genders.* New York: Broadway, 2003.

DeLine, Elliott. *Refuse.* N.L.: Create Space, 2011.

Feinberg, Leslie. *Stone Butch Blues.* Ann Arbor, MI: Firebrand, 1993.

Green, Jamison. *Becoming a Visible Man.* Nashville, TN: Vanderbilt University, 2004.

Hodgkinson, Liz. *Michael Née Laura: The Story of the World's First Female to Male Transsexual.* London: Columbus, 1989.

Howey, Noelle. *Dress Codes: Of Three Girlhoods—My Mother's, My Father's, and Mine.* New York: Picador, 2002.

Jorgensen, Christine. *Christine Jorgensen: A Personal Autobiography.* 2nd ed. San Francisco: Cleis, 2000.

Kailey, Matt. *Just Add Hormones: An Insider's Guide to the Transsexual Experience.* Boston: Beacon Press, 2005.

Khosla, Dhillon. *Both Sides Now: One Man's Journey through Womanhood.* New York: Tarcher, 2006.

McCloskey, Deirdre N. *Crossing: A Memoir.* Chicago: University of Chicago Press, 1999.

Middlebrook, Diane Wood. *Suits Me: The Double Life of Billy Tipton.* Boston: Houghton Mifflin, 1998.

Nettick, Geri. *Mirrors: Portrait of a Lesbian Transsexual.* New York: Rhinoceros, 1996.

Rees, Mark Nicholas Alban. *Dear Sir or Madam: The Autobiography of a Female-to-Male Transsexual.* London: Cassell, 1996.

Roscoe, Will. *The Zuni Man-Woman.* Albuquerque: University of New Mexico, 1991.

Rose, Donna. *Wrapped in Blue: A Journey of Discovery.* Round Rock, TX: Living Legacy, 2003.

Scholinski, Daphne. *The Last Time I Wore a Dress.* New York: Riverhead, 1997.

Sullivan, Louis G. *From Female to Male: The Life of Jack B. Garland.* Boston: Alyson,1990.

Valerio, Max Wolf. *The Testosterone Files: My Hormonal and Social Transformation from Female to Male.* Berkeley, CA: Seal, 2006.

Zander, Erica. *TransActions.* Stockholm: Periskop, 2003.

DOCUMENTARIES/FEATURE FILMS

Adventures in the Gender Trade. Directed by Kate Bornstein. New York: Filmmakers Library, 1993.

The Adventures of Priscilla, Queen of the Desert. Directed by Stephan Elliott. New York: PolyGram Video, 1994.

All About My Father (Alt Om Min Far). Directed by Eva Benestad. Norway: Oro Film, 2001.

All About My Mother (Todo sobre mi madre). Directed by Pedro Almodóvar. El Deseo S.A., 1999.

Almost Myself. Directed by Tom Murray. T. Joe Murray Videos, 2006.

The Badge. Directed by Robby Henson. Emma/Furla Films, 2002.

Beautiful Boxer. Directed by Ekachai Uekrongtham. GMM Pictures, 2003.

Boys Don't Cry. Directed by Kimberly Peirce. Beverly Hills, CA: Twentieth Century Fox Home Entertainment, 1999.

The Brandon Teena Story. Directed by Susan Muska. New York: Bless Bess Productions, 1998.

The Cockettes. Directed by Billy Weber and David Weissman. Grandelusion, 2002.

Cruel and Unusual. Directed by Janet Baus, Dan Hunt, and Reid Williams. Reid Productions, 2007. Distributed by Frameline.

The Crying Game. Directed by Neil Jordan. British Screen Productions, 1992.

Different for Girls. Directed by Richard Spence. Fox Lorber, 1997.

Female Misbehavior. Directed by Monika Treut. Germany: Hyena Films, 1992.

Flawless. Directed by Joel Schumacher. Tribeca Productions, 1999.

Gendernauts. Directed by Monika Treut. USA/Germany, 1999.

Hedwig and the Angry Inch. Directed by John Cameron Mitchell. New Line Home Entertainment, 2001.

The Iron Ladies (Satree-lex). Directed by Yongyoot Thongkongtoon. Santa Monica, CA: Strand Releasing Home Video, 2002.

Junk Box Warrior. Directed by Preeti Mistry. USA: Frameline Distribution, 2002.

Law of Desire (La ley del deseo). Directed by Pedro Almodóvar. New York: Cinevista Video, 1987.

M. Butterfly. Directed by David Cronenberg. Burbank, CA: Warner Home Video. 1993.

Multiple Genders: Mind and Body in Conflict. Produced by Anna Laura Malago. Princeton, NJ: Films for the Humanities and Sciences, 1998.

My Life in Pink (Ma vie en rose). Directed by Alain Berliner. Sony Pictures Classica/La Sept Cinema, 1997.

Normal. Directed by Jane Anderson. Avenue Pictures, 2003.

Orlando. Directed by Sally Potter. Adventure Pictures, 1994.

Paper Dolls (Bubot Niyar). Directed by Tomer Heymann. Strand Releasing, 2005.

Princesa. Directed by Henrique Goldman. Bac Films, 2001.

Screaming Queens: The Riot at Compton's Cafeteria. Directed by Susan Stryker and Victor Silverman. KQED/Independent Television Productions, 2005.

En Soap. Directed by Pernille Fischer Christensen. Netherlands: Garage Film AB, 2006.

Southern Comfort. Directed by Kate Davis. HBO Theatrical Documentary. New York: Q-Ball Productions, 2001.

Transamerica. Directed by Duncan Tucker. Belladonna Productions, 2005.

TransGeneration. Directed by Jeremy Simmons. Logo Entertainment, 2005.

Transsexual Menace. Directed by Rosa Von Praunheim. USA/Germany: Video Data Bank, 1996.

Venus Boyz. Directed by Gabriel Baur. USA/Switzerland: Clock Wise Productions, 2002.

We've Been Around. Directed by Rhys Ernst. USA/Nonesuch Productions, 2016.

Wild Side. Directed by Sébastien Lifshitz. Maïa Films, 2004.

WEBSITES

American Civil Liberties Union: www.aclu.org
Camp Trans: www.wevebeenaround.com/camp-trans/
Campus Pride: www.campuspride.net
Compton's Cafeteria Riot Commemoration: www.comptonscafeteriariot.org
FIERCE!: www.fiercenyc.org
GenderTalk: www.gendertalk.com
GLBT Historical Society: www.glbthistory.org
International Foundation for Gender Education/Transgender Tapestry: www.ifge.org
National Center for Transgender Equality: www.nctequality.org
NOVA: Sex Unknown: www.pbs.org/wgbh/nova/gender
Recommendations for Enhancing College Environments for Transsexual and Transgender Students: http://ai.eecs.umich.edu/people/conway/TS/College.html
Renaissance Transgender Association: www.ren.org
Susan's Place: Transgender Resources: www.susans.org
Sylvia Rivera Law Project: www.srlp.org
Trans-Academics.org: www.trans-academics.org
TransAdvocate: www.transadvocate.com
Transgender Aging Network: www.forge-forward.org/tan
Transgender American Veterans Association: www.tavausa.org
Transgender Day of Remembrance: www.dayofsilence.org
Transgender Law and Policy Institute: www.transgenderlaw.org
Transgender Law Center: www.transgenderlawcenter.org
TransGriot: http://transgriot.blogspot.com

SOURCES

CHAPTER 1

Third Wave Feminism: Stacy Gillis, Gillian Howe, and Rebecca Munford, eds., *Third Wave Feminism: A Critical Exploration,* rev. 2nd ed. (London: Palgrave, 2007); Daisy Hernández and Bushra Rehman, eds., *Colonize This! Young Women of Color on Today's Feminism* (New York: Seal Press, 2002).

Intersectional Feminism: Kimberle Crenshaw, "Mapping the Margins: Intersectionality, Identity Politics, and Violence Against Women," *Stanford Law Review* 43, no. 6 (1991): 1241–1299; Gloria Anzaldúa and Cherrie Moraga, eds., *This Bridge Called My Back: Writings by Radical Women of Color* (New York: Kitchen Table, Women of Color Press, 1983); Chela Sandoval, *Methodology of the Oppressed* (Minneapolis: University of Minnesota Press, 2000).

Transfeminism: Term coined by Emi Koyama on http://eminism.org/; *Transgender Studies Quarterly* 3, nos. 1–2 (2016); Julia Serano, *Whipping Girl* (Berkeley, CA: Seal Press, 2016); Krista Scott-Dixon, *Trans/forming Feminisms: Trans/Feminist Voices Speak Out* (Toronto: Sumach Press, 2006).

Social Movements: Minority rights have long been a factor in US politics: see Alexis de Tocqueville, *Democracy in America* (New York:

Penguin Classics, 2003; orig. pub. 1835, 1840); for a discussion of sexual minority movement formation, see Barry D. Adam, *The Rise of a Gay and Lesbian Movement,* rev. ed. (Woodbridge, CT: Twayne, 1997).

A Biological Basis?: Joan Roughgarden, *Evolution's Rainbow: Diversity, Gender, and Sexuality in Nature and People* (Berkeley: University of California Press, 2004), 241–244; Deborah Rudacille, "Fear of a Pink Planet," in *The Riddle of Gender: Science, Activism, and Transgender Rights* (New York: Pantheon, 2005), 240–276. Christine Johnson revised and expanded her paper "Endocrine Disrupting Chemicals and Transsexualism," cited by Rudacille. The revised document is "Transsexualism: An Unacknowledged Endpoint of Developmental Endocrine Disruption?" (master's thesis, Environmental Studies, Evergreen State College, Olympia, WA, 2004), http://www.antijen.org/transadvocate/TS_EDCs.pdf.

Glossary of Terms/Gender Identity Disorder: The "Transgender" article on Wikipedia (http://en.wikipedia.org/wiki/Transgender) is well documented; for more recent terms, see also the glossary of terms on TransWhat? at https://transwhat.org/glossary/; on disorders of sexual development, which remain controversial in the intersex community, see DSD Guidelines at http://dsdguidelines.org; on some of the pitfalls of cross-cultural comparisons of gender variance, see Evan Towle and Lynn Morgan, "Romancing the Transgender Native: Rethinking the Use of the 'Third Gender' Concept," in *The Transgender Studies Reader,* edited by Susan Stryker and Stephen Whittle (New York: Routledge, 2006), 666–684; the official diagnostic criteria for Gender Dysphoria can be found in *Diagnostic and Statistical Manual of Mental Disorders,* 5th ed. (Washington, DC: American Psychiatric Association, 2015).

Asterisk: Avery Thompson, "Asterisk," *Transgender Studies Quarterly* 1, nos. 1–2 (2014).

Cisgender: A. Finn Enke, "The Education of Little Cis," in *Transgender Studies Reader 2,* edited by Susan Stryker and Aren Aizura (New York: Routledge, 2013).

Habitus: Pierre Bourdieu, *Outline of a Theory of Practice* (Cambridge: Cambridge University Press, 1977).

Identity: Harold Noonan and Ben Curtis, "Identity," in *Stanford Encyclopedia of Philosophy,* edited by Edward N. Zalta, December 15, 2004, updated April 25, 2014, https://plato.stanford.edu/entries/identity/.

Identity Politics: Cressida Heyes, "Identity Politics," in *Stanford Encyclopedia of Philosophy,* edited by Edward N. Zalta, July 16, 2002, updated March 23, 2016, https://plato.stanford.edu/entries/identity-politics/.

Transvestism: Magnus Hirschfeld, *The Transvestites: The Erotic Drive for Disguise* (Buffalo, NY: Prometheus, 1991; orig. pub. 1910).

Psychopathia Transexualis: D. O. Caldwell, "Psychopathia Transexualis," *Sexology* 16 (1949): 274–280, http://web.archive.org/web/20070610124058/http://www.symposion.com/ijt/cauldwell/cauldwell_02.htm.

Transgender: David Valentine, *Imagining Transgender: An Ethnography of a Category* (Durham, NC: Duke University, 2007).

Subcultural Terms: Philip Herbst, *Wimmin, Wimps and Wallflowers: An Encyclopaedic Dictionary of Gender and Sexual Orientation Bias in the United States* (Boston: Intercultural, 2001); Guy Strait, *The Lavender Lexicon: A Dictionary of Gay Words and Phrases* (San Francisco: Strait and Associates, 1964); Marlon M. Bailey, *Butch Queen Up in Pumps: Gender, Performance, and Ballroom Culture in Detroit* (Ann Arbor: University of Michigan Press, 2013).

Why Transgender Is Such a Hot Topic Now: Susan Stryker, "(De) Subjugated Knowledges: An Introduction to Transgender Studies," in *The Transgender Studies Reader,* edited by Susan Stryker and Stephen Whittle (New York: Routledge, 2006), 1–17.

Religion and Transgender: Virginia Ramey Mollenkott, *Omnigender: A Trans-religious Approach* (Cleveland, OH: The Pilgrim Press, 2001; revised and expanded, 2007); *The Transformation* (directed by Carlos Aparicio and Susan Aikin, Frameline Distribution, 1995) offers a fascinating portrait of a male-to-female transgender person's participation in an evangelical Christian community. Max Strassfeld, "Translating the Human: The *Androginos* in Tosefta Bikurim," *Transgender Studies Quarterly* 3, nos. 3–4 (2016): 587–604; Ertug Altinay, "Islam and Islamophobia," *Transgender Studies Quarterly* 1, nos. 1–2 (2014).

Transgender and Postmodern Representation: Susan Stryker, "Christine Jorgensen's Atom Bomb: Mapping Postmodernity through the Emergence of Transsexuality," in *Playing Dolly: Technocultural Formations, Fictions, and Fantasies of Assisted Reproduction,* edited by E. Ann Kaplan and Susan Squier (New Brunswick, NJ: Rutgers University, 1999), 157–171.

Biotechnology and the Posthuman Future: Katherine Hayles, *How We Became Posthuman: Virtual Bodies in Cybernetics, Literature, and Informatics* (Chicago: University of Chicago Press, 1999); Judith Halberstam and Ira Livingston, eds., *Posthuman Bodies* (Bloomington: Indiana University Press, 1995); Marquard Smith and Joanne Morra, *The Prosthetic Impulse: From a Posthuman Present to a Biocultural Future* (Cambridge, MA: MIT, 2007).

CHAPTER 2

Early Gender-Variant History: Rudolph Dekker and Lotte C. Van der Pol, *The Tradition of Transvestitism in Early Modern Europe* (New York: St. Martin's, 1989); Leslie Feinberg, *Transgender Warriors: Making History from Joan of Arc to Dennis Rodman* (Boston: Beacon Press, 1996); Kathleen M. Brown, *Good Wives, Nasty Wenches, and Anxious Patriarchs: Gender, Race, and Power in Colonial Virginia* (Chapel Hill: University of North Carolina Press, 2002); Elizabeth Reis, *Bodies in Doubt: An American History of Intersex* (Baltimore: Johns Hopkins University Press, 2012); Bambi L. Lobdell, *A Strange Sort of Being: The Transgender Life of Lucy Ann/Joseph Israel Lobdell* (Jefferson, NC: McFarland, 2012); *Early American Studies* (Philadelphia: University of Pennsylvania Press, Fall 2014).

Regulating Public Gender: William Eskridge, *Gaylaw: Challenging the Apartheid of the Closet* (Cambridge, MA: Harvard University Press, 1997); Clare Sears, "A Dress Not Belonging to His or Her Sex: Cross-Dressing Law in San Francisco, 1860–1900" (PhD diss., Sociology Department, University of California, Santa Cruz, 2005).

Outlawing Cross-Dressing: The quoted statute appeared in the *Revised Orders of the City and County of San Francisco,* 1863; cited in William Eskridge, *Gaylaw: Challenging the Apartheid of the Closet* (Cambridge, MA: Harvard University Press, 1997); table compiled by Clare Sears in "A Dress Not Belonging to His or Her Sex: Cross-Dressing Law in San Francisco, 1860–1900" (PhD diss., Sociology Department, University of California, Santa Cruz, 2005), based on data from Eskridge's *Gaylaw.*
Capitalism and Gay Identity: John D'Emilo, "Capitalism and Gay Identity," in *Powers of Desire: The Politics of Sexuality,* edited by Ann Snitow, Christine Stancell, and Sharon Thompson (New York: Monthly Review, 1983), 100–113.
Transmasculine People: Dr. Mary Edwards Walker, http://www.biography.com/people/mary-walker-9522110; Murray Hall, http://www.smithsonianmag.com/history/the-mystery-of-murray-hall-35612997/; Jack Bee Garland, http://www.lavendermagazine.com/uncategorized/jack-bee-garland-aka-babe-bean/; Alan Hart, https://oregonencyclopedia.org/articles/hart_alan_1890_1962_/#.WTmfQsbauUk, Wilmer Broadnax, http://transguys.com/profiles/wilmer-little-axe-broadnax; Pauli Murray, http://www.biography.com/people/pauli-murray-214111.
Modernity and Womanhood: Joanne Meyerowitz, *Women Adrift: Women Wage Earners in Chicago, 1880–1930* (Chicago: University of Chicago Press, 1988).
First Wave Feminism: Mary Wollstonecraft, *Vindication of the Rights of Woman* (New York: Bartleby.com, 1999); Sojourner Truth, *Ain't I a Woman?* (speech delivered 1851, Women's Convention, Akron, Ohio), text available at http://www.feminist.com/resources/artspeech/genwom/sojour.htm.
Bloomerism: Dexter C. Bloomer, *Life and Writings of Amelia Bloomer* (New York: Schocken, 1975; orig. pub. 1895).
Social Power of Medicine: Georges Canguilhem, *The Normal and Pathological,* translated by Carolyn R. Fawcett and Robert S. Cohen (New York: Zone, 1991); Michel Foucault, *The Birth of the Clinic,* translated by Sheridan Smith (New York, Vintage, 1994; orig. pub. 1963).

Early Surgical Request: Bryan Tully, *Accounting for Transsexualism and Transhomosexuality* (London: Whiting and Birch, 1992).

Ulrichs and Kertbeny: Karl Heinrich Ulrichs, *The Riddle of "Man-Manly" Love,* translated by Michael Lombardi-Nash (Buffalo: Prometheus, 1994); Hubert Kennedy, *Karl Heinrich Ulrichs: Pioneer of the Modern Gay Movement* (San Francisco: Peremptory, 2002).

Sexology: Richard von Krafft-Ebing, *Psychopathia Sexualis* (New York: Arcade, 1998; orig. pub. 1886); Jay Prosser, "Transsexuals and the Transsexologists: Inversion and the Emergence of Transsexual Subjectivity," in *Sexology in Culture: Labelling Bodies and Desires,* edited by Lucy Bland and Laura Doan (Oxford: Polity, 1998), 116–132; for information on Hirschfeld and other notable sexologists, see Erwin Haeberle's Archive of Sexology website at Humboldt University (Berlin), https://www.ub.hu-berlin.de/en/literature-search/historical-collections/historical-and-special-collections-of-the-library/overview-of-the-historical-and-special-collections-of-the-library/haeberle-hirschfeld-archive-of-sexology/haeberle-hirschfeld-archive-of-sexology?set_language=en; on Ellis, see http://en.wikipedia.org/wiki/Havelock_Ellis.

Hitler on Hirschfeld: Leslie Katz, "Life of Gay German Jewish Sexologist Honored," *Jewish News of Northern California,* June 6, 1997, http://www.jweekly.com/1997/06/06/life-of-gay-german-jewish-sexologist-honored-in-s-f/.

The Cercle Hermaphroditos: Earl Lind, *Autobiography of an Androgyne* (New York: Medico-Legal Journal, 1918), 151; see also Earl Lind, *The Female Impersonators* (New York: Medico-Legal Journal, 1922).

UCSF Research: Karl Bowman, "California Sex Deviates Research Act, Progress Report, 1951" (typescript, Don Lucas Collection, San Francisco: GLBT Historical Society, 1951), 1–25; Karl Bowman, *My Years in Psychiatry, 1915–1968: An Interview with Karl M. Bowman, M.D., San Francisco, February 27 and 28, 1968* (Sacramento, CA: California Department of Mental Hygiene, 1969).

Louise Lawrence: Manuscript Journal, Louise Lawrence Collection, Kinsey Institute, Indiana University, Bloomington; Joanne Meyerowitz, "Sex Research at the Borders of Gender: Transvestites, Transsexuals, and Alfred Kinsey," *Bulletin of the History of Medicine* 75, no. 1 (2001): 72–90.

Mayhem: Robert Veit Sherwin, "Legal Aspects of Male Transsexualism," in *Transsexualism and Sex Reassignment,* edited by Richard Green and John Money (Baltimore: Johns Hopkins University Press, 1969), 417–430.

Prince: "Virginia Prince: Pioneers of Transgendering," special issue, *International Journal of Transgenderism* 8, no. 4 (2006).

Christine Jorgensen: Christine Jorgensen, *A Personal Autobiography,* 2nd ed. (San Francisco: Cleis, 2000).

Jorgensen Correspondents: Christine Jorgensen Collection, Correspondence Files, Royal Danish Library and Archives, Copenhagen.

Popular Reception of Jorgensen: David Serlin, "Christine Jorgensen and the Cold War Closet," in *Replaceable You: Engineering the Body in Cold War America* (Chicago: University of Chicago Press, 2004), 159–190.

Virginia Prince Arrest: Richard Docter, *From Man to Woman: The Transgender Journey of Virginia Prince* (Los Angeles: Docter, 2004), 109–110.

Postal Crime: Charles Smith, "The Homosexual Federal Offender: A Study of 100 Cases," *Journal of Criminal Law, Criminology, and Police Science* 44, no. 5 (Jan.–Feb. 1954): 582–591, quote 586.

Literature and Obscenity Cases: Jackie Hatton, "The Pornographic Empire of H. Lynn Womack: Gay Political Discourse and Popular Culture, 1955–1970," *Thresholds: Viewing Culture* 7 (Spring 1993): 9–33; Sanford Aday Collection, Special Collections, California State University Library, Fresno.

Kinsey Reports: Alfred C. Kinsey, Wardell B. Pomeroy, and Clyde E. Martin, *Sexual Behavior in the Human Male* (Philadelphia: W. B. Saunders, 1948); Alfred C. Kinsey et al., *Sexual Behavior in the Human Female* (Philadelphia: W. B. Saunders, 1953).

Early Cross-Dresser Organizations: Darrell Raynor, *A Year Among the Girls* (New York: L. Stuart, 1966); Robert Hill, "A Social History of Heterosexual Transvestism in Cold War America" (PhD diss., American Studies, University of Michigan, 2007).

Drag Balls: Miss Major interview conducted by Susan Stryker, January 29, 1998, on deposit at the GLBT Historical Society, San Francisco, CA.

CHAPTER 3

Cooper Do-Nut Incident: Lillian Faderman and Stuart Timmons, *Gay L.A.: A History of Sexual Outlaws, Power Politics, and Lipstick Lesbians* (New York: Basic, 2006), 1–2.
John Rechy: *City of Night* (New York: Grove, 1963), 96–97, 105.
Dewey's Incident: Marc Stein, *City of Sisterly and Brotherly Loves: Lesbian and Gay Philadelphia, 1945–1972* (Chicago: University of Chicago, 2000), 246–247.
Compton's Cafeteria Incident: Raymond Broshears, "History of Christopher Street West—SF," *Gay Pride: The Official Voice of the Christopher Street West Parade '72 Committee of San Francisco, California,* June 25, 1972, 8; *Screaming Queens: The Riot at Compton's Cafeteria* (directed by Susan Stryker and Victor Silverman; Frameline Distribution, 2005); Elizabeth Armstrong and Suzanna Crage, "Movements and Memory: The Making of the Stonewall Myth," *American Sociological Review* 71, no. 5 (2006): 724–751.
Tenderloin: Neil L. Shumsky and Larry M. Springer, "San Francisco's Zone of Prostitution, 1880–1934," *Journal of Historical Geography* 7, no. 1 (1981): 71–89; Clark Taylor et al. *Final Report: The Tenderloin Ethnographic Research Project* (San Francisco: Hospitality House, 1977).
War-Related Prostitution Crackdowns: Allan Berube, *Coming Out Under Fire: The History of Gay Men and Women in World War II* (New York: Free Press, 2000); Xavier Maine, *The Intersexes: A History of Similisexualism as a Problem of Social Life* (New York: Arno Reprints, 1975; orig. pub. 1908), 212–226.
Midcentury Urban Transformations: Chester Hartman, *City for Sale: The Transformation of San Francisco* (Berkeley: University of California Press, 2002); Nan Alamilla Boyd, *Wide Open Town: A History of Queer San Francisco to 1965* (Berkeley: University of California Press, 2003); Gayle Rubin, "The Valley of the Kings: Leathermen in San Francisco, 1960–1990" (PhD diss., Anthropology, University of Michigan, 1994).
Glide Memorial United Methodist Church: Glide website, http://www.glide.org.

Anti-poverty Campaign: Ed Hansen Papers, GLBT Historical Society, San Francisco; Don Lucas Papers, GLBT Historical Society, San Francisco.

Alinsky: Saul Alinsky, *Reveille for Radicals* (New York: Vintage, 1989; orig. pub. 1946).

Homophile Activism: John D'Emilio, *Sexual Politics, Sexual Communities: The Making of a Homosexual Minority in the United States, 1940–1970* (Chicago: University of Chicago Press, 1983); Martin Meeker, *Contacts Desired: Gay and Lesbian Communications and Community, 1940s–1970s* (Chicago: University of Chicago Press, 2006).

Harry Benjamin: Harry Benjamin, *The Transsexual Phenomenon* (New York: Julian, 1966), http://www.agnodice.ch/IMG/pdf/Harry_Benjamin_-_The_Transsexual_Phenomenon.pdf.

New Transgender Networks: Members of the Gay and Lesbian Historical Society, "MTF Transgender Activism in San Francisco's Tenderloin: Commentary and Interview with Elliot Blackstone," *GLQ: A Journal of Lesbian and Gay Studies* 4, no. 2 (1998): 349–372; Edward Sagarin, "Transvestites and Transsexuals: Boys Will Be Girls," in *Odd Man In: Societies of Deviants in America* (Chicago: Quadrangle, 1969), 111–141; "Ms. Leslie: A Transexual Counselor," *Drag* 3, no. 10 (1973): 34–35.

Reed Erickson: Aaron Devor and Nicholas Matte, "ONE Inc. and Reed Erickson: The Uneasy Collaboration of Gay and Trans Activism, 1964–2003," *GLQ: A Journal of Gay and Lesbian Studies* 10, no. 2 (2004): 179–209.

Mario Martino: Mario Martino, with Harriet, *Emergence: A Transsexual Autobiography: The First Complete Female-to-Male Story* (New York: Crown, 1977).

Stonewall: David Carter, *Stonewall: The Riots That Sparked the Gay Revolution* (New York: St. Martin's, 2004); Martin Duberman, *Stonewall* (New York: Penguin, 1993).

Radical Transsexual: Suzy Cooke interview conducted by Susan Stryker, January 10, 1998, on deposit at the GLBT Historical Society, San Francisco.

Sylvia Rivera: "Leslie Feinberg Interviews Sylvia Rivera," http://www.workers.org/ww/1998/sylvia0702.php.
STAR: Stephan Cohen, *The Gay Liberation Youth Movement in New York: An Army of Lovers Cannot Fail* (New York: Routledge, 2007).
Gay Militancy: Donn Teal, *The Gay Militants* (New York: Stein and Day, 1971).
Angela K. Douglas: Angela K. Douglas, *Triple Jeopardy* (Sneeds, FL: Angela K. Douglas, 1982), copy on deposit at GLBT Historical Society, San Francisco.

CHAPTER 4

Cockettes: Pam Tent, *Midnight at the Palace: My Life as a Fabulous Cockette* (Los Angeles: Alyson, 2004); *The Cockettes* (directed by David Weissman and Bill Weber; Strand Releasing, 2002).
Sylvester: Joshua Gamson, *The Fabulous Sylvester: The Legend, the Music, the Seventies in San Francisco* (New York: Picador, 2006).
Black Feminist Organizations: See "Statement of Purpose" (National Black Feminist Organization, 1973); see "Combahee River Collective Statement" (Combahee River Collective, 1974); Miriam Schneir, ed., *Feminism in Our Time: The Essential Writings, World War II to the Present* (New York: Vintage Books, 1994).
Christopher Street Liberation Day Speech: See archival footage of speech by Sylvia Rivera at https://www.youtube.com/watch?v=0lD75vnGc-E.
NTCU Bust: Members of the Gay and Lesbian Historical Society, "MTF Transgender Activism in San Francisco's Tenderloin: Commentary and Interview with Elliot Blackstone," *GLQ: A Journal of Lesbian and Gay Studies* 4, no. 2 (1998): 349–372.
Sex Change Clinics: Joanne Meyerowitz, *How Sex Changed: A History of Transsexuality in the United States* (Cambridge, MA: Harvard University Press, 2002), 212–226.
Trans Liberation Newsletter: Article reprinted in *Gay Sunshine* 5 (January 1971): 3.

Gay Gender Style/Clone Look: Crawford Barton, *Beautiful Men* (Los Angeles: Liberation, 1976); the Castro website, http://thecastro.net/scenes/scene05.html.

Depathologization of Homosexuality: *Changing Our Minds: The Story of Dr. Evelyn Hooker* (directed by Richard Schmiechen; Frameline Distribution, 1992); Ronald Bayer, *Homosexuality and American Psychiatry* (Princeton, NJ: Princeton University Press, 1987).

Feminine Mystique: Betty Friedan, *The Feminine Mystique* (New York: W. W. Norton, 2001; orig. pub. 1963).

Second Sex: Simone de Beauvoir, *The Second Sex* (New York: Vintage, 1989; orig. pub. in French, 1949).

Radical Feminism: Alice Echols, *Daring to Be Bad: Radical Feminism in America, 1967–1975* (Minneapolis: University of Minnesota, 1990).

Radicalesbians: Karla Jay, *Tales of the Lavender Menace* (New York: Basic Books, 1999); "The Woman-Identified Woman," in *For Lesbians Only: A Separatist Anthology,* edited by Sarah Lucia Hoagland and Julia Penelope (London: Onlywomen, 1988), 17–22.

Gay Pride 1972: James Finefrock, "A Parade by 1000 S.F. Gays," *San Francisco Examiner,* June 26, 1972; on Raymond Broshears, see "Ray Who? A Crusader," *Gay Focus,* January 15, 1982, 1–4.

Beth Elliott: Geri Nettick, as told to Beth Elliott, *Mirrors: Portrait of a Lesbian Transsexual* (New York: Masquerade, 1996).

Daughters of Bilitis History: Marcia Gallo, *Different Daughters: A History of Daughters of Bilitis and the Rise of the Lesbian Rights Movement* (Berkeley, CA: Seal Press, 2006).

West Coast Lesbian Feminist Conference, 1973: *The Lesbian Tide* (Apr.–May, 1973), special issue on the West Coast Lesbian Feminist Conference.

Robin Morgan at WCLFC: "Lesbianism and Feminism: Synonyms or Contradictions?" in *Going Too Far: The Personal Chronicle of a Feminist,* edited by Robin Morgan (New York: Random House, 1977), 170–189.

Olivia/Stone Boycott: Sandy Stone (interviewed by Davina Gabriel), "Interview with the Transsexual Vampire: Sandy Stone's Dark Gift," *TransSisters: The Journal of Transsexual Feminism* 8 (1995): 14–33.

Mary Daly: Mary Daly, *Gyn/Ecology: The Metaethics of Radical Feminism* (Boston: Beacon Press, 1978).

Janice Raymond: Janice Raymond, *The Transsexual Empire: The Making of the She-Male* (Boston: Beacon Press, 1979; reissued with new introduction, 1994).

Raymond, Policy Implications: Janice Raymond, "Paper Prepared for the National Center for Health Care Technology on the Social and Ethical Aspects of Transsexual Surgery, June, 1980" (manuscript in National Transgender Library and Archives, Special Collections, University of Michigan Library, Ann Arbor).

Second Wave Feminism: Candy Coleman, "Broken Chains: Sisters All?" *Gay Crusader,* June–July 1973, 3; Deborah Feinbloom, "Lesbian/Feminist Orientation among Male-to-Female Transsexuals," *Journal of Homosexuality* 2, no. 1 (1976): 59–71; Shulamith Firestone, *The Dialectic of Sex: A Case for Feminist Revolution* (New York: Morrow, 1970), 11; C. Tami Weyant, letter to the editor, *Sister,* August–September 1977, 3.

Transphobic Screed: Debbie Mikuteit, letter to the editor, *Coming Up!* (San Francisco), February 1986, 3–4.

GID/Standards of Care: World Professional Organization for Transgender Health (formerly Harry Benjamin International Gender Dysphoria Association), *Standards of Care,* 6th rev. ed. (2001), text available at http://www.wpath.org/site_page.cfm?pk_association_webpage_menu=1351&pk_association_webpage=4655.

Antipornography Feminism and the State: *US Attorney General's Commission on Pornography: Final Report, July 1986* (Washington, DC: US Department of Justice, 1986), commonly referred to as the Meese Report, text available at www.porn-report.com.

Shift from Depathologizing Homosexuality to Pathologizing Gender Variance: Janice Irvine, "Boys Will Be Girls," in *Disorders of Desire: Sex and Gender in Modern American Sexology* (Philadelphia: Temple University Press, 1990), 229–278.

Transgender HIV: Kristen Clements-Nolle et al., "HIV Prevalence, Risk Behaviors, Health Care Use, and Mental Health Status of Transgender

Persons: Implications for Public Health Intervention," *American Journal of Public Health* 91, no. 6 (2001): 915–921.

Lesbian/Butch/FTM Border Wars: Henry Rubin, "Border Wars: Lesbian and Transsexual Identities," in *Self-Made Men: Identity and Embodiment among Transsexual Men* (Nashville, TN: Vanderbilt University Press, 2003), 77–92.

FTM Community: Joanne Meyerowitz, *How Sex Changed: A History of Transsexuality in the United States* (Cambridge, MA: Harvard University Press, 2002), 226–241; Jamison Green, *Becoming a Visible Man* (Nashville, TN: Vanderbilt University Press, 2004); Max Wolf Valerio, *The Testosterone Files: My Hormonal and Social Transformation from Female to Male* (Berkeley, CA: Seal Press, 2006); *What Sex Am I?* (directed by Lee Grant; HBO Films, 1985).

Lou Sullivan: Brice Smith, *Yours in Liberation: The Queer Life of Trans Pioneer Lou Sullivan* (Oakland, CA: Transgress Press, 2017); Susan Stryker, "Portrait of a Transfag Drag Hag as a Young Man: The Activist Career of Louis G. Sullivan," in *Reclaiming Gender: Transsexual Grammars at the Fin de Siècle,* edited by Kate More and Stephen Whittle (London: Cassells, 1999), 62–82.

Lou Sullivan Journals and Articles: Louis Graydon Sullivan Collection, GLBT Historical Society, San Francisco, on deposit at San Francisco History Center, San Francisco Public Library (Main Branch).

CHAPTER 5

Legislative History: Katrina C. Rose, "The Proof Is in the History: The Louisiana Constitution Recognizes Transsexual Marriages and Louisiana Sex Discrimination Law Covers Transsexuals—So Why Isn't Everyone Celebrating?" *Deakin Law Review* 9, no. 2 (2004): 399–460.

Transsexual Rights Committee: See https://www.aclu.org/other/aclu-history-advocacy-behalf-transgender-people.

Ari Kane and Fantasia Fair: http://www.cowart.com/outreach/ari.html, http://fantasiafair.org.

International Foundation for Gender Education (IFGE): See http://www.ifge.org.

Dallas Denny: http://dallasdenny.com; "Five Questions with Dallas Denny," En|Gender (blog), October 5, 2005, http://www.myhusbandbetty.com/?p=427.

Transgender Etymology: Robert Hill, "A Social History of Heterosexual Transvestism in Cold War America" (PhD diss., American Studies, University of Michigan, 2007).

Holly Boswell: Holly Boswell, "The Transgender Alternative," *Chrysalis Quarterly* 1, no. 2 (Winter 1991–1992): 29–31.

Feinberg: Leslie Feinberg, *Transgender Liberation: A Movement Whose Time Has Come* (New York: World View Forum, 1992); *Stone Butch Blues* (Ithaca, NY: Firebrand, 1993).

Sandy Stone: Sandy Stone, "The 'Empire' Strikes Back: A Posttranssexual Manifesto," in *Body Guards: The Cultural Politics of Gender Ambiguity,* edited by Julia Epstein and Kristina Straub (New York: Routledge, 1991), 280–304.

Feminist Hybridity: Cherrie Moraga and Gloria Anzaldúa, eds., *This Bridge Called My Back: Writings by Radical Women of Color* (New York: Kitchen Table, 1983); Gloria Anzaldúa, *Borderlands/La Frontera: The New Mestiza* (San Francisco: Aunt Lute/Spinsters, 1987).

Gender/Embodiment/Technology: Donna Haraway, "A Cyborg Manifesto: Science, Technology, and Socialist Feminism in the Late Twentieth Century," in *The Cybercultures Reader,* edited by David Bell and Barbara Kennedy (New York: Routledge 1999), 291–324.

Wired Interview: Susan Stryker, "Sex and Death among the Cyborgs," *Wired,* May 1996, 134–136.

Queer Gender and Feminism: Teresa de Lauretis, "The Technology of Gender," in *Technologies of Gender: Essays on Theory, Film, and Fiction* (Bloomington: Indiana University Press, 1987), 1–31.

Michel Foucault: *The History of Sexuality Volume 1: An Introduction* (New York: Vintage, 1990; orig. pub. 1978).

Barnard Conference: Carole S. Vance, *Pleasure and Danger: Exploring Female Sexuality* (Boston: Routledge and Kegan Paul, 1984).

Gayle Rubin: "Thinking Sex: Notes for a Radical Theory of the Politics of Sexuality," in *Pleasure and Danger,* edited by Carole Vance (Boston: Routledge and Kegan Paul, 1984).

Judith Butler: *Gender Trouble: Feminism and the Subversion of Identity* (New York: Routledge, 1990); *Bodies That Matter: On the Discursive Limits of "Sex"* (New York: Routledge, 1993).

AIDS Activism and Trans Community: "Transgender and HIV: Assessment, Risk, Care," special issue, *International Journal of Transgenderism* 3, nos. 1–2 (January–June 1999); Juana Rodriquez, *Queer Latinidad: Identity Practices, Discursive Spaces* (New York: New York University Press, 2003).

ACT UP: See oral history project at ACT UP at http://www.actuporal history.org/index1.html; Debra Gould, *Moving Politics* (Chicago: University of Chicago Press, 2009).

AIDS and Queer: David Halperin, *Saint=Foucault* (Oxford: Oxford University Press, 1997); Cindy Patton, "The Heterosexual AIDS Panic: A Queer Paradigm," *Gay Community News,* 1985.

Transgender Nation: Anne Ogborn interview by Susan Stryker (July 5, 1998), audiotape in author's possession; Susan Stryker, "Transgender History, Homonormativity, and Disciplinarity," *Radical History Review* 100 (2007): 144–157.

March on Washington: Phyllis Randolph Frye, "Facing Discrimination, Organizing for Freedom: The Transgender Community," in *Creating Change: Sexuality, Public Policy, and Civil Rights,* edited by John D'Emilio, William Turner, and Urvashi Vaid (New York: St. Martin's Press, 2000), 451–468.

ISNA: Cheryl Chase, "Hermaphrodites with Attitude: Mapping the Emergence of Intersex Political Activism," *GLQ: Journal of Gay and Lesbian Studies* 4, no. 2 (1998): 189–211.

Intersex "Dangerous" to Society: Suzanne Kessler, *Lessons from the Intersexed* (New Brunswick, NJ: Rutgers University Press, 1998).

Michigan Womyn's Music Festival: See http://www.michfest.com; Emi Koyama, "Whose Feminism Is It Anyway: The Unspoken Racism of the Trans Inclusion Debate," in *The Transgender Studies Reader,* edited by Susan Stryker and Stephen Whittle (New York: Routledge, 2006),

698–705; "Roundtable: A Fest in Distress," Michigan/Trans Controversy Archive, http://eminism.org/michigan/documents.html.

Southern Comfort: Film, *Southern Comfort* (directed by Kate Davis; Q-Ball Productions, 2002).

International Conference on Transgender Law and Employment Policy (ICTLEP): See History of the International Conference on Transgender Law and Employment Policy, Inc., http://www.transgender legal.com/ictlephis1.htm.

Martine Rothblatt: *The Apartheid of Sex: A Manifesto on the Freedom of Gender* (New York: Crown, 1995); Lisa Miller, "The Trans-Everything CEO," *New York* magazine, September 7, 2014, http://nymag.com/news /features/martine-rothblatt-transgender-ceo/.

Riki Anne Wilchins/Transexual Menace/GenderPAC: Riki Anne Wilchins, *Read My Lips: Sexual Subversion and the End of Gender* (Ithaca, NY: Firebrand, 1997); *Transexual Menace* (directed by Rosa Von Praunheim; Praunheim Filmproduktion, 1996).

San Francisco Human Rights Commission Report: Jamison Green, *Investigation into Discrimination against Transgendered People: A Report of the San Francisco Human Rights Commission* (San Francisco: Human Rights Commission, 1994).

Remembering Our Dead: The Remembering Our Dead project has been subsumed by Transgender Day of Remembrance, https://tdor .info/about-2/; to visit the archived Remembering Our Dead website, see https://web.archive.org/web/20120409032158/http://www.remember ingourdead.org/day/what.html.

Trans Academics: Robin Wilson, "Transgender Scholars Defy Tradition, Seek to Be Heard," *Chronicle of Higher Education,* February 6, 1998, A10+; see online at http://www.chronicle.com/article/Transgendered -Scholars-Defy/100747.

Body Alchemy: Loren Cameron, *Body Alchemy: Transsexual Portraits* (San Francisco: Cleis, 1996); Cameron's early work is now part of Cornell University's Human Sexuality collection; see http://rmc.library.cornell .edu/EAD/htmldocs/RMM07677.html.

Mariette Pathy Allen: *Transformations: Crossdressers and Those Who Love Them* (New York: Dutton, 1989); *The Gender Frontier* (Heidelberg, Germany: Kehrer Verlag, 2003).

Mid-1990s Media Coverage: Richard Levine, "Crossing the Line: Are Transsexuals at the Forefront of a Revolution, or Just Reinforcing Old Stereotypes About Men and Women?" *Mother Jones* 19, no. 3 (May–June 1994): 43+; Amy Bloom, "The Body Lies," *New Yorker,* July 18, 1994, 38+; Carey Goldberg, "Shunning 'He' and 'She,' They Fight for Respect," *New York Times,* September 8, 1996.

Zines: Queer Zine Archive Project, see www.qzap.org.

Jamison Green: Jamison Green, *Becoming a Visible Man* (Nashville, TN: Vanderbilt University, 2004); see http://www.jamisongreen.com.

Max Wolf Valerio: Max Wolf Valerio, *The Testosterone Files: My Hormonal and Social Transformation from Female to Male* (Berkeley, CA: Seal Press, 2006).

Jennifer Boylan: Jennifer Finney Boylan, *She's Not There: A Life in Two Genders* (New York: Broadway, 2003).

Helen Boyd: Helen Boyd, *My Husband Betty: Love, Sex, and Life with a Crossdresser* (New York: Thunder's Mouth, 2003); *She's Not the Man I Married: My Life with a Transgender Husband* (Berkeley, CA: Seal Press, 2007); see http://www.myhusbandbetty.com.

Nobody Passes: Matt Bernstein Sycamore, aka Mattilda, *Nobody Passes: Rejecting the Rules of Gender and Conformity* (Berkeley, CA: Seal Press, 2007).

Transgender Legal Activism in the 1990s: Excellent resources at the Transgender Law and Policy Institute, http://www.transgenderlaw.org.

Transgender Rights: Paisley Currah and Shannon Minter, *Transgender Equality: A Handbook for Activists and Policymakers* (Washington, DC: National Gay and Lesbian Task Force, 2000), 17; see: http://thetaskforce.org/downloads/reports/reports/TransgenderEquality.pdf.

Wachowski Sisters: Cael Keegan, *Lana and Lilly Wachowski: Imaging Transgender* (Champaign: University of Illinois Press, forthcoming).

Tyra Hunter: Jin Haritaworn and C. Riley, "Trans Necropolitics," in *Transgender Studies Reader 2,* edited by Susan Stryker and Aren Z. Aizura (New York: Routledge, 2013).

Fred Martinez: *Two Spirits* (directed by Lydia Nibley, 2009).

Employment Non-Discrimination Act (ENDA): Isaac West, *Transforming Citizenships: Transgender Articulations of the Law* (New York: New York University Press, 2013).

CHAPTER 6

WPATH: World Professional Association for Transgender Health, http://www.wpath.org/.

Transgender Tipping Point: Katy Steinmetz, "The Transgender Tipping Point," *Time*, May 29, 2014, http://time.com/135480/transgender-tipping-point/.

Transgender Awareness Poll: Zeke Stokes, "New Poll: Number of Americans Who Report Knowing a Transgender Person Doubles," *GLAAD*, September 17, 2015, https://www.glaad.org/blog/new-poll-number-americans-who-report-knowing-transgender-person-doubles.

Trans Life in Contemporary United States: Jaime Grant, Lisa Mottet, Justin Tanis, Jack Harrison, Jody Herman, and Mara Keisling, *Injustice at Every Turn: A Report of the National Transgender Discrimination Survey* (Washington, DC: National Center for Transgender Equality and National Equality and National Gay and Lesbian Task Force, 2011); Sandy James, Jody Herman, Susan Rankin, Mara Keisling, Lisa Mottet, and Ma'ayan Anafi, *The Report of the 2015 U.S. Transgender Survey* (Washington, DC: National Center for Transgender Equality, 2016).

Transgender Children: Stephanie Brill and Rachel Pepper, *The Transgender Child: A Handbook for Families and Professionals* (San Francisco: Cleis Press, 2008); Diane Ehrensaft, *The Gender Creative Child: Pathways for Nurturing and Supporting Children Who Live Outside Gender Boxes* (New York: The Experiment, 2016).

Experience of Transgender Youth in Schools: Emily Greytak, Joseph Kosciw, and Elizabeth Diaz, *Harsh Realities: The Experiences of Transgender Youth in Our Nation's Schools* (New York: GLSEN, 2009).

Media Representations of Trans and Gender-Nonconforming Youth: *Ma Vie en Rose* (directed by Alain Berliner; Belgium, 1997); *Gun Hill Road* (directed by Rashaad Green; USA, 2011); *Boy Meets Girl* (directed by Eric Schaeffer; USA, 2014); *Tomboy* (directed by Céline Sciamma; France, 2011); *I Am Jazz* (TLC reality series, 2 seasons; United States, 2015–2017).

User-Generated Trans-Related Content Online: Tobias Raun, *Out Online: Trans Self-Representation and Community Building on YouTube* (London: Routledge, Taylor & Francis Group, 2016).

Leelah Alcorn: Ed Pilkington, "Ohio Transgender Teen's Suicide Note: 'Fix Society. Please,'" *Guardian,* January 5, 2015, https://www.theguardian.com/world/2015/jan/05/sp-leelah-alcorn-transgender-teen-suicide-conversion-therapy.

Trans Youth Literature: Alexandra Alter, "Transgender Children's Books Fill a Void and Break a Taboo," *New York Times,* June 6, 2015, https://www.nytimes.com/2015/06/07/business/media/transgender-childrens-books-fill-a-void-and-break-a-taboo.html?_r=0.

Girl Scouts and Boy Scouts: Dani Heffernan, "Girl Scouts of Colorado Released Statement Welcoming Transgender Youth," GLAAD, October 26, 2011, https://www.glaad.org/blog/girl-scouts-colorado-released-statement-welcoming-transgender-youth; Editorial Board, "Welcoming Transgender Boy Scouts," *New York Times*, February 2, 2017, https://www.nytimes.com/2017/02/02/opinion/welcoming-transgender-boy-scouts.html.

Nonbinary in Oregon: Corinne Segal, "Oregon Court Rules That 'Nonbinary' Is a Legal Gender," PBS, June 11, 2016, http://www.pbs.org/newshour/rundown/oregon-court-rules-that-nonbinary-is-a-legal-gender/.

Great Recession and Income Inequality: Paul Wiseman, "Richest 1 Percent Earn Biggest Share Since '20s," Associated Press, 2011.

Leaderless Revolts: Manuel Castells, *Networks of Outrage and Hope: Social Movements in the Internet Age* (Cambridge: Polity, 2012).

Trans-anarchism: Mattathias Schwartz, "Pre-Occupied—The Origins and Future of Occupy Wall Street," *New Yorker,* November 28, 2011, http://www.newyorker.com/magazine/2011/11/28/pre-occupied.

Chelsea Manning: Charlie Savage, "Chelsea Manning to Be Released Early as Obama Commutes Sentence," *New York Times,* January 17, 2017; Matthew Shaer, "The Long, Lonely Road of Chelsea Manning," *New York Times Magazine,* June 12, 2017.

Incarceration Rates: Roy Walmsley, "World Prison Population List (tenth edition)" (London: International Centre for Prison Studies, 2013); Sandy James, Jody Herman, Susan Rankin, Mara Keisling, Lisa Mottet, and Ma'ayan Anafi, *The Report of the 2015 U.S. Transgender Survey* (Washington, DC: National Center for Transgender Equality, 2016).

Monica Jones: Alessandra Soler, "Case against Monica Jones Dismissed!" ACLU of Arizona, February 23, 2015, https://www.acluaz.org/en/press-releases/case-against-monica-jones-dismissed.

Trans Incarceration Issues: Eric Stanley, Nat Smith, and CeCe McDonald, *Captive Genders: Trans Embodiment and the Prison Industrial Complex* (Oakland, CA: AK Press, 2015); Merlin Dervisevic, *Cruel and Unusual* (directed by Janet Baus, Dan Hunt, and Reid Williams, 2006); Eric Stanley and Chris Vargas, *Criminal Queers* (2015); Jenji Kohan, *Orange Is the New Black* (New York, 2013); TGI Justice Project at http://www.tgijp.org/; Annalise Ophelian, *Major!* (United States, Floating Ophelia Productions, 2015).

Black Lives Matter: Black Lives Matter at http://blacklivesmatter.com/.

Beyoncé's *Formation:* Beyoncé Knowles, *Formation* (New York: Parkwood Entertainment, Columbia Records, 2016).

Big Freedia: Big Freedia, *Big Freedia: God Save the Queen Diva* (New York: Gallery Books, 2015); Big Freedia, *Big Freedia: Queen of Bounce* (United States, World of Wonder, 2013).

Ghost Ship Warehouse Fire: "Oakland Fire: Dozens Feared Dead in Club Night Blaze," BBC News, December 4, 2016, http://www.bbc.com/news/world-us-canada-38195612; Los Angeles Times Staff, "Victims of the Oakland Warehouse Fire: Who They Were," *Los Angeles Times,* December 9, 2016, http://www.latimes.com/local/california/la-me-oakland-fire-victims-2016-htmlstory.html.

Conferences, Magazines, Presses for Trans and Nonbinary People: Gender Odyssey Conference (Seattle) at http://www.genderodyssey.org;

Philadelphia Trans Health Conference at https://www.mazzonicenter.org/trans-health/about-the-conference; Amos Mac and Rocco Kayiatos, *Original Plumbing* (New York, 2009); Luis Venegas, *Candy* (Spain, Luis Venegas, 2009); Topside Press at http://topsidepress.com ; Imogen Binnie, *Nevada* (New York: Topside Press, 2013); Ryka Aoki, *He Mele A Hilo (A Hilo Song)* (New York: Topside Press, 2014); Tom Léger and Riley MacLeod, *The Collection: Short Fiction from the Transgender Vanguard* (New York: Topside Press, 2012); Transgress Press at http://www.transgresspress.org; Homofactus Press at http://homofactuspress.com; TC Tolbert and Trace Peterson, *Troubling the Line: Trans and Genderqueer Poetry and Poetics* (Callicoon, NY: Nightboat Books, 2013); Samuel Ace, *Normal Sex* (Ithaca, NY: Firebrand Books, 1994); Trish Salah, *Wanting in Arabic* (Toronto: TSAR Publications, 2013); Trish Salah, *Lyric Sexology, Vol. 1* (New York: Small Press Distribution, 2014); Joy Ladin, *Transmigration: Poems* (Riverdale, NY: Sheep Meadow Press, 2009); Eli Clare, *The Marrow's Telling: Words in Motion* (Ypsilanti, MI: Homofactus Press, 2007); Chris Vargas's Museum of Trans Hirstory and Art at http://www.sfmotha.org.

Trans Studies: Susan Stryker and Stephen Whittle, eds., *Transgender Studies Reader,* Vol. 1 (New York: Routledge, 2006); Susan Stryker and Aren Aizura, eds., *The Transgender Studies Reader 2* (New York: Routledge, 2013); Anne Enke, *Transfeminist Perspectives In and Beyond Transgender and Gender Studies* (Philadelphia: Temple University Press, 2012); Yolanda Martínez-San Miguel and Sarah Tobias, *Trans Studies: The Challenge to Hetero/Homo Normativities* (New Brunswick, NJ: Rutgers University Press, 2016); Patricia Elliot, *Debates in Transgender, Queer, and Feminist Theory: Contested Sites* (London: Routledge, 2016); the University of Victoria's Transgender Archives at http://www.uvic.ca/transgenderarchives/; the University of Arizona Gender & Women's Studies Department, "Transgender Studies Faculty Cluster Hire Underway!" University of Arizona, College of Social and Behavioral Sciences, 2013, https://gws.arizona.edu/news/transgender-studies-faculty-cluster-hire-underway; *TSQ: Transgender Studies Quarterly* at http://tsq.dukejournals.org; *International Journal of Transgenderism* at http://www

.tandfonline.com/action/journalInformation?show=aimsScope&journalCode=wijt20&; Digital Transgender Archive at https://www.digitaltransgenderarchive.net; Cleis Abeni, "Trans Billionaire Funds World's First Endowed Chair in Trans Studies," *Advocate,* January 22, 2016, http://www.advocate.com/transgender/2016/1/22/trans-billionaire-funds-worlds-first-endowed-chair-trans-studies; University of Arizona College of Social and Behavioral Sciences, "UA to Host Inaugural Transgender Studies Conference," UA News, August 31, 2016, https://uanews.arizona.edu/story/ua-host-inaugural-transgender-studies-conference.

Thomas Beatie: Guy Trebay, "He's Pregnant. You're Speechless," *New York Times,* June 22, 2008, http://www.nytimes.com/2008/06/22/fashion/22pregnant.html.

Trans Models: Ruth La Ferla, "In Fashion, Gender Lines Are Blurring," *New York Times,* August 19, 2015, https://www.nytimes.com/2015/08/20/fashion/in-fashion-gender-lines-are-blurring.html.

Trans People on Reality TV Shows: *America's Next Top Model* (The CW, VH1, UPN, 2003); *RuPaul's Drag Race* (Logo TV, 2009).

Caitlyn Jenner: Ravi Somaiya, "Caitlyn Jenner, Formerly Bruce, Introduces Herself in Vanity Fair," *New York Times,* June 1, 2015, https://www.nytimes.com/2015/06/02/business/media/jenner-reveals-new-name-in-vanity-fair-article.html.

Trans People on Mainstream TV: *Orange Is the New Black* (Netflix, 2013); *Transparent* (Amazon, 2014); *Sense8* (Netflix, 2015).

Trans People in Feature Films: *Tangerine* (2015); *Drunktown's Finest* (2014); *Her Story* (2015); *The Dallas Buyer's Club* (2013); *The Danish Girl* (2015).

Trans People in Print Media: Jennifer Finney Boylan, *Stuck in the Middle with You: A Memoir of Parenting in Three Genders* (New York: Broadway Books, 2014); Janet Mock, *Redefining Realness: My Path to Womanhood, Identity, Love & So Much More* (New York: Simon & Schuster, 2015); Various authors, "Transgender Today," *New York Times,* July 25, 2015, https://www.nytimes.com/interactive/2015/07/23/opinion/transgender-today-article-collection.html; Susan Faludi, *In the Darkroom* (New York: Metropolitan Books/Henry Holt, 2016).

Joe Biden Quote: Julie Bolcer, "Biden Calls Transgender Discrimination 'Civil Rights Issue of Our Time,'" *Advocate,* October 30, 2012, http://www.advocate.com/politics/transgender/2012/10/31/biden-calls-transgender-discrimination-civil-rights-issue-our-time.

Minority-Majority Nation: Noor Wazwaz, "It's Official: The U.S. Is Becoming a Minority-Majority Nation," *US News & World Report,* July 6, 2015, https://www.usnews.com/news/articles/2015/07/06/its-official-the-us-is-becoming-a-minority-majority-nation.

***Macy v. Holder* and *Schroer v. Billings*:** Joanna L. Grossman, "The EEOC Rules That Transgender Discrimination Is Sex Discrimination: The Reasoning Behind That Decision," *Justia: Verdict,* May 1, 2012, https://verdict.justia.com/2012/05/01/the-eeoc-rules-that-transgender-discrimination-is-sex-discrimination.

NC HB2: J. Bryan Lowder, "North Carolina's Anti-LGBT Law Encourages Dangerous Gender Surveillance," *Slate,* May 25, 2016, http://www.slate.com/blogs/outward/2016/03/25/north_carolina_s_hb2_encourages_gender_policing_on_trans_folks_and_everyone.html.

Loretta E. Lynch Remarks: Loretta E. Lynch, "North Carolina House Bill 2 Complaint Remarks," Washington, DC, 2016.

Gavin Grimm: Gavin Grimm, "I'm Transgender and Can't Use the Student Bathroom. The Supreme Court Could Change That," *Washington Post,* October 27, 2016, https://www.washingtonpost.com/opinions/im-transgender-and-cant-use-the-student-bathroom-the-supreme-court-could-change-that/2016/10/27/19d1a3ae-9bc1-11e6-a0ed-ab0774c1eaa5_story.html?utm_term=.77b619f13be5.

National Parks Report: Read at https://www.nps.gov/subjects/lgbtqheritage/upload/lgbtqtheme-places.pdf.

Stonewall Inn National Historic Site: Eli Rosenberg, "Stonewall Inn Named National Monument, a First for the Gay Rights Movement," *New York Times,* June 24, 2016, https://www.nytimes.com/2016/06/25/nyregion/stonewall-inn-named-national-monument-a-first-for-gay-rights-movement.html.

Compton's Cafeteria National Transgender Historic District: Caleb Pershan, "SF to Designate Nation's First Transgender Historic District in the Tenderloin," *sfist,* January 31, 2017, http://sfist.com/2017/01/31/transgender_tenderloin_district_com.php.

LGBT Pride Remarks: President Barack Obama, remarks at LGBT Pride Reception, June 9, 2016, https://www.humanrights.gov/dyn/06/president-obama-remarks-at-lgbt-pride-reception/.

Jennicet Gutiérrez: Liam Stack, "Activist Removed After Heckling Obama at LGBT Event," *New York Times,* June 24, 2015, https://www.nytimes.com/2015/06/25/us/politics/activist-removed-after-heckling-obama-at-lgbt-event.html.

Trans Political Events: Jordy Yager, "I Was Not a Pretty Girl, and I Felt Like a Man," *The Hill,* March 10, 2009, http://thehill.com/capital-living/24154-i-was-not-a-pretty-girl-and-i-felt-like-i-was-a-man; Katie Halper, "Kylar Broadus: First Transgender Person to Testify Before the Senate," Feministing, June 12, 2012, http://feministing.com/2012/06/12/kylar-broadus-first-transgender-person-to-testify-before-the-senate/; Reena Flores, "Meet the Transgender Delegates at the Democratic Convention," CBS News, July 28, 2016, http://www.cbsnews.com/news/transgender-delegates-democratic-convention/.

Trans Politicians: Neal Broverman, "Meet America's (Shockingly Small) Pool of Trans Elected Officials," *Advocate,* November 14, 2012, http://www.advocate.com/politics/transgender/2012/11/14/meet-shockingly-small-pool-trans-elected-officials; Ed Mazza, "Texas Mayor Jess Herbst Comes Out as Transgender," *Huffington Post,* February 1, 2017, http://www.huffingtonpost.com/entry/jess-herbst-texas-transgender-mayor_us_58914f6fe4b0522c7d3e0153.

Marriage Equality: Steve Sanders, "Windsor and Obergefell: Marriage Equality as Equal Dignity," American Constitutional Society, June 30, 2016, http://www.hrc.org/blog/windsor-and-obergefell-marriage-equality-as-equal-dignity.

Palm Center: Parker Marie Molloy, "Study Urges U.S. Military to Reconsider Ban on Transgender Personnel," *Advocate,* March 13, 2014, http://www.advocate.com/politics/transgender/2014/03/13/study-urges-us-military-reconsider-ban-transgender-personnel.

Trans-focused Advocacy Groups: National Center for Transgender Equality, http://www.transequality.org/; Transgender Law Center, https://transgenderlawcenter.org/; Global Action for Trans Equality, https://transactivists.org/.

Transgender Funding: Kristina Wertz and Naa Hammond, *TRANSformational Impact: US Foundation Funding for Trans Communities* (New York: Funders for LGBT Issues, 2015); for more info, see https://www.lgbtfunders.org/initiatives/trans-funding-working-group/.

Feminist Resistance to Gender Concept: FireInMyBelly, "Forbidden Discourse: The Silencing of Feminist Criticism of 'Gender,'" https://feministuk.wordpress.com/2013/08/19/forbidden-discourse-the-silencing-of-feminist-criticism-of-gender; Sheila Jeffreys, *Gender Hurts: A Feminist Analysis of the Politics of Transgenderism* (New York: Routledge, 2014).

Origin of TERF: Cristan Williams, "TERF: What It Means and Where It Came From," The Transadvocate, May 14, 2014.

No on Prop 1: See political ad at https://www.youtube.com/watch?v=D7thOvSvC4E; Mimi Swartz, "The Equal Rights Fight over Houston's Bathrooms," *New York Times,* October 27, 2015, https://www.nytimes.com/2015/10/28/opinion/the-equal-rights-fight-over-houstons-bathrooms.html.

Trans Legislation in 2016: See research by Williams Institute at http://williamsinstitute.law.ucla.edu/category/research/.

Republican Presidential Candidates on Trans Issues: See overview at https://ballotpedia.org/2016_presidential_candidates_on_LGBTQ_rights.

Women's March on Washington: Women's March on Washington, "Guiding Vision and Definition of Principles," 2017, https://static1.squarespace.com/static/584086c7be6594762f5ec56e/t/587ffb31d2b857e5d49dcd4f/1484782386354/WMW+Guiding+Vision+%26+Definition+of+Principles.pdf; Tim Wallace and Alicia Parlapiano, "Crowd Scientists Say Women's March on Washington Had 3 Times as Many People as Trump's Inauguration," *New York Times,* January 22, 2017.

Making History: Friedrich Nietzsche, "On the Use and Abuse of History for Life," *Untimely Meditations,* 1876, http://la.utexas.edu/users/hcleaver/330T/350kPEENietzscheAbuseTableAll.pdf.

INDEX

ABOUT THE AUTHOR

Susan Stryker earned her PhD in United States History at the University of California, Berkeley, in 1992, and has helped shape the public conversation on transgender issues for more than twenty-five years. She was a founding member of the activist group Transgender Nation in the early 1990s; co-wrote, -produced, and -directed the Emmy-winning documentary film *Screaming Queens: The Riot at Compton's Cafeteria* (2005); co-edited the *Transgender Studies Reader* volumes 1 and 2 (2006 and 2013); and co-edits the academic journal *TSQ: Transgender Studies Quarterly* (2014–). She was executive director of the GLBT Historical Society in San Francisco (1999–2003) and director of the Institute for LGBT Studies at the University of Arizona (2011–2016), where she is currently associate professor of Gender and Women's Studies.